THE COURSE OF THE
SOUTH TO SECESSION

THE COURSE
OF THE
SOUTH TO SECESSION

An Interpretation by

ULRICH BONNELL PHILLIPS

Edited by
E. MERTON COULTER

American Century Series
HILL AND WANG • NEW YORK

Copyright, 1939, by the American Historical Association
All rights reserved
Standard Book Number: 8090-0070-9
Library of Congress catalog card number: 64-24835

FIRST AMERICAN CENTURY SERIES EDITION SEPTEMBER 1964

This book is reprinted in its present edition
by permission of the American Historical Association,
which prepared the original edition.

Manufactured in the United States of America
34567890

FOREWORD

Professor Ulrich B. Phillips, in the course of his distinguished career, was a prominent figure in the American Historical Association and influential in its counsels. When the Association decided to seek endowment, he was earnest in his coöperation with his friend, former Senator Albert J. Beveridge, who was in the forefront of the campaign. It was appropriate, therefore, that he be made chairman of a committee to administer the substantial gift in memory of Senator Beveridge presented to the Association by his friends. From 1929 until his untimely death in 1934, Professor Phillips served in this capacity and carried forward the plans for the use of this fund which he himself had largely formulated. His enthusiasm was not dampened by illness, and in the last months of his life he did not spare himself, but gave many hours to editorial supervision of the committee's publications. The American Historical Association publishes this volume with deep appreciation of Professor Phillips' fruitful labors.

THE BEVERIDGE MEMORIAL FUND COMMITTEE

INTRODUCTION

It is generally agreed that no one had a more thorough knowledge and a keener appreciation of the ante-bellum South than Ulrich Bonnell Phillips. Born in the plantation region of Georgia and graduated at the University of Georgia, he early acquired historical interests which he pursued to the end of his life. He had a viewpoint enriched by inheritance and early training in the South and broadened by long residence in the North. Apart from his instructorship at the University of Georgia immediately after his graduation and three years of teaching at Tulane University, he spent his professional life in the North and West, at the University of Wisconsin, the University of Michigan, where he did most of his work, at the University of California, and at Yale University, where in 1934 he died.[1]

Professor Phillips' development in his historical writing was a normal process, both as to locale and as to the subject matter. He began with a small segment of the South, the state of Georgia, and in time he spread his interest to include the whole region. He chose as his first major line of approach, politics and federal relations, he progressed through the transportation media of canals and railroads to plantations and slavery, his greatest contribution, and at the time of his death he was on the point of a greater synthesis and interpretation of all the forces which entered into the development of the South. Just as he gained strength and courage by his earlier detailed writings, which entitled him to deal in broader generalizations later, so did he develop his style from a strictly factual, straightforward flow into a diction tinged with artistry. Yet he never departed from his historical faith that though some writers might produce a true picture by breathing in their nostrils "the ether in which the stars hold their courses," he must for the most time content himself by breathing "mundane atmosphere." "But only when the wind is in a

[1] For an appraisal of Professor Phillips' place in American historiography, see Wood Gray, "Ulrich Bonnell Phillips," in W. T. Hutchinson, ed., *The Marcus W. Jernegan Essays in American Historiography* (Chicago, 1937), pp. 354–373.

rare quarter," said he, "would I give rein to Pegasus if I could. In the main I am content to delve rather than to try to soar." [2]

Practically all of Professor Phillips' writings lay in the antebellum period of the South, but he promised himself in his latter days the possibility of coming on down with his "consolidated social and political themes" from "that epochal year" 1861, where his last published work ended.[3] He did not say how far he would come, for certainly he himself had not then decided.

Professor Phillips was a prolific writer.[4] His first important work, *Georgia and State Rights*,[5] appeared in 1902, and the last of his books to be published in his lifetime, *Life and Labor in the Old South*,[6] was brought out in 1929. This last volume he had planned as the first of a series of three on the history of the South. The second, he stated, would "trace the course of public policy to 1861," and a third would carry the whole story forward to an unstated point. Though he had not completed in every detail his second volume, he had made sufficient progress by the spring of 1932 to give its main content in six lectures at Northwestern University, under the Norman Wait Harris Foundation. He entitled these lectures "The Course of the South to Secession" and he stated that he intended "to examine the conditions and movements which prompted the South to attempt in 1861 to make itself an independent nation." [7]

After his death, Mrs. Phillips allowed the *Georgia Historical Quarterly* to publish these lectures, beginning in the issue for December, 1936 (XX, 4) and continuing consecutively through March, 1938 (XXII, 1). To make them more available, the Committee on the Albert J. Beveridge Memorial Fund of the American Historical Association decided to republish them as a book. They are here presented as they were left by Professor Phillips, with slight editing, and as they were published originally in the *Georgia Historical*

---

[2] U. B. Phillips, *Life and Labor in the Old South* (Boston, 1929), p. viii.
[3] *Ibid.*, p. vii.
[4] For a list of his published writings see D. M. Potter, Jr., comp., "A Bibliography of the Printed Writings of Ulrich Bonnell Phillips," in the *Georgia Historical Quarterly*, XVIII, 3 (Sept., 1934), pp. 270–282; and E. E. Edwards, comp., "A Bibliography of the Writings of Professor Ulrich Bonnell Phillips," in *Agricultural History*, VIII, 4 (Oct., 1934), pp. 199–218.
[5] Published in the *Annual Report of the American Historical Association for the Year 1901* (Washington, 1902), II, pp. 3–224, and also separately. It was awarded the Justin Winsor Prize by the American Historical Association.
[6] This book was awarded a money prize of a substantial amount by Little, Brown and Company, who published it.
[7] From the program announcement.

INTRODUCTION

Quarterly. They represent the nearest approach Professor Phillips ever made to purely interpretative writing. Included in this volume is his article, likewise interpretative along the same lines, "The Central Theme of Southern History," which served as the basis of a discussion at the 1928 meeting of the American Historical Association in Indianapolis,[8] and which was published in the *American Historical Review.*[9]

E. MERTON COULTER

[8] For an account of this meeting, see the *Annual Reports of the American Historical Association for the Years 1927 and 1928* (Washington, 1929), pp. 144–145.

[9] October, 1928 (XXXIV, 1). A few minor changes have been made in the form of this article as well as in the articles republished from the *Georgia Historical Quarterly,* to bring about uniformity.

CONTENTS

CHAPTER	PAGE
I. DAUGHTERS OF ENGLAND	1
II. THE FRAME OF INDEPENDENCE	23
III. THE VIRGINIA DYNASTY	60
IV. A QUESTION OF ETHICS	83
V. AN ANSWER OF RACE	100
VI. THE FIRE-EATERS	128
THE CENTRAL THEME OF SOUTHERN HISTORY	151
INDEX	167

THE COURSE OF THE SOUTH TO SECESSION

CHAPTER I

DAUGHTERS OF ENGLAND

When one state had seceded and six were on the brink, an advocate at New Orleans wrote: "South Carolina, Georgia, Mississippi, Florida, Alabama, Louisiana and Texas are knit by God and their own hearts indissolubly together."[1] These ere long made the nucleus of an independent South. Four others, when summoned to give aid for coercion, cast their lot with the Confederacy, and in three more there were popular stirrings in sympathy. A choice was being made between conflicting loyalties. As in 1776 old allegiance no longer gave accustomed security; new dangers from an old government brought a seeking of separate destiny. Prophets in the past, impressed by contrast of systems and foretelling division, had been contemned in their day; but a culmination of events now seemed to prove them true.

Just after the peace of 1783 a British captain said to an American general: "When all of you are in your graves, there will be wars and rumors of wars in this country: there are too many different interests in it for them to be united under one government. . . . One of these days, the Northern and Southern powers will fight as vigorously against each other, as they have both united to do against the British."[2] About the same time a European diplomat said: "This republic has been born as it were a pigmy. . . . But a day will come when it will be a giant, a veritable awe-inspiring colossus in these regions."[3] How many people made forecasts in one of these lines or the other cannot be known. In the main they doubtless troubled themselves little with continental questions and less with the century to come. Efforts were but casual to pry the future, to discern whether mutual forbearance was to maintain accord and lead to peaceful power or, in default of this, division was to bring mortal strife. Private citizens handled their personal affairs in the manner

[1] *Daily Crescent*, New Orleans, Jan. 3, 1861.
[2] George Hanger, *Life, Adventures and Opinions* (London, 1801), II, 426–427.
[3] The Count of Aranda to the King of Spain, 1784, quoted by W. R. Shepherd in the *Political Science Quarterly*, XXXIX, 55.

to which they had been locally bred; public functionaries were equally prone to routine and averse to novelty. In any generation few suspected that mere custom was pregnant with crisis; and, so complex are the causes and effects in the course of human events, one may still doubt that this particular conflict was predestined by divergence of institutions.

* * *

Prior to the Revolution there were plentiful quarrels within the several colonies and between sundry neighboring jurisdictions; but as to regional interests the sole conflict arose over the molasses trade. In this, New England wanted a free market in which to buy cheap materials for the making of rum, while Barbados and Jamaica sought a monopoly for their own output. The West Indians won a restrictive act from the British Parliament in 1733, but the Yankees found solace in so copious a smuggling as virtually to nullify the law. The continental communities from New York to Georgia were onlookers in this matter, not participants. As to commerce and industry in general, each community tended to its own affairs with a minimum of neighborly contacts. The Chesapeake settlements, the rice coast, and the sugar islands alike sent the main volume of their produce across the Atlantic. Pennsylvania, New York, and New England, producing much the same goods as the Old World, found their chief markets in tropic lands whether on American or African shores.

As to contrasts other than economic, there were not many to be found. Negro slavery was a matter of course in every colony, differing in volume from place to place but not essentially in law. Indian relations were on much the same basis everywhere, trade implying peace and land-hunger provoking war. The white population from Barbados to Maine was much of a kind in its predominant lower-class British origin. A sprinkling of upper-class Englishmen, however, had come to every tidewater settlement; and well-to-do citizens, distinguished for their genteel bearing, were a constant feature in every prospering colony. On the far-flung seaboard fine manners and coarse, high dialect and low, were separated by the lines of social strata far more than by those of geography. The most impressive regional differentiation, in fact, came from religion; and here the contrast lay not between any North and South as such but between New England and all the rest.

The Puritans differed from other British and American religionists mainly in the degree of their zealotry and the firmness of their purpose to make every mundane institution subserve the purposes of their church.[4] With the Bible as the basis of law, civil authority had as a main function the support of ecclesiastical power. No provincial proprietor nor any royal government was to be tolerated except under duress; life in the large and in the small was to be ruled by and for the tried supporters of the true faith. The carrying of this into local affairs explains the prominence of the village or "town" as an institution. About the "meeting house" the homesteads must be closely clustered, that the people might be regimented in congregations. Round about lay the land for tilth, fenced into great fields but each field parceled into strips of individual ownership without partitioning fences. Beyond these lay the meadows and the woodland whether held for common use or parceled among individuals. The town meeting and the selectmen, civil counterparts of the congregation and the deacons, determined the seeding of the fields and apportioned the use of the commons. That every man's life should impinge always upon his neighbors' was a matter of course in these close-knit, isolated communities where faith, morals, crops, and pasturage were debated and controlled as things of joint concern.

The social influence of this régime was not altogether what might have been expected. Instead of eloquence in debate, a taciturnity prevailed as each man's defense against an excessive public knowledge of his private affairs. The strictness of Sabbath-keeping on land was offset when sailors went to sea by the rule of "no Sundays off soundings"; the rigidity of sex morals was relaxed in bundling; and the horse-trading deacon or the whittler of wooden nutmegs for sale became symbolic of Yankee shrewdness. The stringency of theocratic control defeated its own purposes. The village system, furthermore, proved inconvenient for husbandry. When the land of a single farmer lay in a dozen widely scattered strips, much of his time was lost in going from job to job, and he could not watch the needs of his crops nor guard them against injury. No sooner was the system established, in fact, than by purchase and exchange fields began to be consolidated and the pristine plan to be superseded. When New England expanded beyond its limits of the seventeenth century, neither full-fledged Puritanism nor the character-

[4] Nowhere short of Mormon Utah has another commonwealth been constructed systematically for control in the interest of a specific religion.

istic village system was carried into the new spaces. In New York, New Jersey, Pennsylvania, and the West, farm steadings were scattered in much the same fashion as in the South.

The New England village was in essence an English manor without a lord. In early Maryland there were manors by name, with lords authorized to rule them. In Virginia the early unit of representation was the borough, a name which implies a nucleated settlement. James City and Charles City loomed so large in prospect that their names in full were bestowed upon the counties which came to comprise them. But the manors and boroughs alike were evanescent in the face of the dispersive influence of topography and economy. Except for the parish with its varied but usually subordinate functions, the county was the one unit of local government throughout the South;[5] and the county had no consultative apparatus. The legislature at the colonial capital was the sole deliberative assembly within each province. In the local exchange of opinion on public affairs a farmer left his lonely cabin, a planter his isolated steading, only on occasions not officially scheduled for the purpose. The locations of the churches and court houses, often aloof in the forest, were symbols of the slightness of organization.

These conditions need not imply that discussions were infrequent or languid. Church attendance was habitual with all who dwelt within riding distance. Before and after service the parishioners read the public notices on the door and chatted of things in general; and the homeward path of a family group was likely to lie in a detour to some friendly house for dinner and an afternoon of talk. Court days once a month brought larger, more masculine and less decorous assemblage. To the bench went the "squires" of the county to constitute the court; to the bar went such as were charged with offenses or had witness to give or civil causes to plead. The rest formed at will an audience in the room or a crowd outside for sport, politics, or business. Affairs of the law might be finished in an hour, but the throng remained until nightfall and festive spirits filled the tavern till the small hours. The mere knowledge that many men would assemble at the time and place caused others to go thither. One might have a slave to sell or an overseer to hire, another a stallion to show or a colt to test at the standard quarter-mile.[6] A third

[5] In Louisiana the counties are called parishes.
[6] Before blooded horses began to be imported, about 1730, racing speed could hardly be maintained for a greater distance. In the backwoods, "quarter races" continued in vogue until the nineteenth century.

might merely wish to send a letter to a distance and in default of postal service go on court day to find anyone who, dwelling in the proper direction, would relay the missive when opportunity came.

On court day a candidate would literally mount a stump and harangue those of his fellow citizens within reach of his voice. To draw a crowd and engage good-will a friend of the speaker might use a neighboring stump as a table for dispensing liquor. Turkey shootings, gander pullings, horse races and cock fights, one or all, could hardly await the court's adjournment; and the justices of the peace, knowing this and wishing to miss no sport, were none too patient with long-winded pleas.

Election days and militia musters, neighborhood hunts and barbecues, log rollings, house raisings and husking bees, even weddings and funerals with liquors provided, augmented the means of exchanging news and gossip, of discussing affairs great and small, of concerting opinion or sharpening divergencies. The complete privacy of daily life increased the relish of weekly or monthly congregation and the disposition to make the meetings worth while. Hence, perhaps, the chatty sociability and the fondness for oratory which became Southern characteristics.

* * *

The social order grew, as it usually does, without a plan, and with no remark of its distinctiveness except when travelers brought discussion of contrasts with distant regions. To stay-at-homes all things of habit were matter of course. Old-timers possessed the lore of preceding trial and error and the knack of prevailing practices. Newcomers in the main were indentured servants, if not Negro slaves, who must do as they were told; and even if some came as freemen they consciously had much to learn in a local adaptation. Native youths grew adult, adopting accustomed ways, their elders assisting with precepts and warnings. Even pioneering had its patterns; and few desired pioneer status for long. Normal people wanted establishment, and establishment was attained.

This meant not merely a means of steady livelihood and a convenient provision of handicraftsmen and of commerce, but a body of law and an apparatus for changing the law when occasion arose and for preventing change by distant authority against the local will. A predilection for liberty and for politics was an inheritance from England, strengthened by the crossing of the sea. The settlers in Virginia looked upon their colony as a mere camp until the House of Burgesses was instituted in 1619; and their distress at the crown's displacement of the London Company was not relieved until the continuance of the House was assured. Marylanders, with sanction from the crown and Lord Baltimore, quickly developed an assembly in their turn, and used it steadily to whittle down the proprietary prerogatives. Carolinians maintained a constant obstruction to the fantastic "fundamental constitutions" of John Locke until the wearied proprietors ceased their insistence; and then the people took the first occasion to cast off the proprietary yoke and procure from the crown a more liberal government for South and North Carolina separately, with provision in each for a fully functioning assembly. The Georgia settlers in their belated turn groaned under the benevolent autocracy of the trustees, envying the liberties of their neighbors and protesting continuously till the thwarted trustees resigned their charter and the crown applied what had long since become the standard pattern of a royal province.[7]

Thus each colony became something of a commonwealth, a daughter of England emulating considerably the motherland's constitution. In each there was an elected house controlling the public purse and participating in all sorts of legislation. In each also there was an appointed council usually sitting as an upper house of legislature, and a governor likewise appointed by the crown, or in the case of Maryland by the proprietor. The council might reject any measures adopted by the lower house; the governor might veto what both houses had agreed upon; and the crown or the proprietor might disallow what a governor had approved. But the governor was often under pressure from below, because his pay depended upon assembly votes; and the remoteness from England tended usually to minimize imperial interference with provincial enactments. There were thwartings and grievances from time to time, and even a rising in arms by Bacon against Berkeley in Virginia; but in the main, until the time of George III, these colonies were contented daughters ordering their own houses under the protection of a distant, powerful, but easy-going mother.

This adherence to the mother was the more willing by reason of dangers from French, Spanish and Indians on the flanks and in the rear of their homes. And these menaces gave the chief occasion for

[7] Delaware showed so little Southern impulse at any time that she will not often be mentioned herein.

joint enterprises among the sisterhood, as when South Carolina gave armed assistance to North Carolina against the Tuscaroras and to Georgia under Oglethorpe against the Spanish. There was at no time in the southerly group a definite regional union such as the short-lived New England Confederation; and when apparatus for continental concert was offered by the Albany Congress it met as chill a reception below the Potomac as above. The sisters, diverse as they were in age, size, employment, and predilection, were, outside of New England at least, much more attached to the mother than to one another.

At the same time certain traits of maternal policy were irksome, partly because they denied the daughters' maturity. For example in 1751, when Virginia's age approached a century and a half, the crown vetoed an act of hers prohibiting the construction of wooden chimneys and the keeping of hogs in the village of Walkerton, because in the Privy Council's opinion it was "highly unjust and improper" to permit any person finding hogs at large in the town to kill them. If such pettish interference from distant Westminster was rare, it was frequent enough at the hands of carpetbagger lordlings who were vested with provincial authority. Such arrogant and inept functionaries as Boone and Montague in South Carolina, Martin in North Carolina, and Dunmore in Virginia did more damage in the critical years than the wisest imperial ministry could well have repaired. When a placeman as governor was buttressed by placemen in his council, as in South Carolina, chronic feud was not far to seek.

In some regards a persistent immaturity invited restraint. A common instance of this was paper money, which the colonials called bills of credit. This device, which came into vogue early in the eighteenth century, enabled any government in time of stress to meet its expenses without the trouble of raising hard cash. The paper was generally made legal tender for the payment of all debts; and its depreciation, often speedy, permitted citizens to discharge personal obligations at reduced cost. Inflation was hard to stop, because its continuance gave advantage to the farmers and other speculators in the colony at the expense of creditors whether local or British. Merchants of London and Liverpool, Bristol and Glasgow protested, and sundry steady-going colonials reinforced their demand that the British authorities intervene. In response, during the middle decades of the century, royal governors were instructed to veto further legal-tender issues; then an act of Parliament forbade such issues in New England, and a further act extended the prohibition over all the colonies. This, in the esteem of loudly protesting inflationists, was a tyrannous invasion of colonial rights, while in the judgment of others it was a salutary check upon fraud. The strongest repercussions were perhaps in Rhode Island and South Carolina, where inflation was greatest; in Massachusetts and Virginia, where self-restraint had prevailed in public finance, there was no special complaint. The question had no regional bearing; and of itself did not evoke apparatus of intercolonial concert.

It was on the other hand an actual and conscious maturity which at various times prompted Virginia, both Carolinas, and Jamaica to legislate in restraint of slave imports. The crown, safeguarding British commercial interests, invariably disallowed such acts, thereby grieving conservative colonials who desired to prevent a drain of money in payment for a sort of property which might become a social menace, but rejoicing those who sought more slaves for their personal service and profit. Here again, there was no concert among the colonies concerned.

* * *

In general it is hard to find an episode in southerly latitudes prior to George III in which the people of even a single province were solidly opposed to a transaction of the crown. George II's veto of Virginia's "tuppenny act" is almost the only instance.

"A competent and sufficient provision for the clergy will be the only means to supply this dominion with able, faithful and orthodox ministers whereby the glory of God may be advanced, the church propagated and the people edified." Thus runs the preamble of a Virginia statute of 1696, duly sanctioned by the crown, which directed the vestry of each parish annually to levy and pay to the incumbent minister 16,000 pounds of tobacco. For nearly sixty years this law remained effective without serious protest and with but a single slight revision. Tobacco was the commonest medium for all payments, and its use for tithes was a matter of course. The price in sterling money fluctuated usually between a penny and twopence per pound, and it seemed fair enough that salaries should rise and fall in automatic accord with general prosperity. The clergy, with other officials, had merely a chronic mild grievance that the tobacco paid them was of the lowest permissible grade.

But 1755 brought a crisis of crop failure. After the product of the preceding year had gone to market it became evident that in broad zones hardly a leaf would be harvested, and anyone bound to deliver tobacco would be at the mercy of him to whom it was due. In October the assembly responded with a preamble:

> Whereas by reason of the great drought a very small quantity of tobacco is made, so that the inhabitants of this colony are not able to pay their public, county and parish levies and the officers' fees and other tobacco debts in tobacco for this present year, according to the laws now in force; for remedy whereof, and to prevent the sheriffs and other collectors of the public dues from taking advantage of the necessities of the people and exacting exorbitant prices for tobacco due or payable to them from the poor and needy,

it passed an act permitting all persons to commute their debts and dues for the current fiscal year by paying twopence in lieu of each pound of tobacco.

This temporary statute served its purpose and expired without ado. Accordingly when 1758 brought another crop shortage the two houses, by almost unanimous votes, adopted another one-year "tuppenny act," with a preamble, "it being certainly expedient at all such times to prevent as much as possible the distress that must attend such a scarcity." [8] Perhaps this intimation of a permanent policy made more stir than the simple repetition of the taxpayer's relief. The clergy protested in convention and the Bishop of London, within whose diocese the colonies were included, championed their cause. Richard Bland, Virginia's foremost lawyer, replied in a pamphlet asserting a right of the colony to pass necessary legislation without interference; and others used all means available to argue the justice of Virginia's action and show the strength of her will. But the crown disallowed the statute after its expiration, whereupon sundry clergymen entered suit in their counties to recover the difference between what they had been paid under the invalid law and what they would otherwise have received in tobacco.

One of the cases came to jury trial in Hanover County in 1763, with young Patrick Henry as attorney for the defense. The court had already declared that the plaintiff was entitled to damages, and the jury's function was merely to ascertain the just amount. Expert

---

[8] William W. Hening, ed., *Statutes at Large of Virginia*, III, 151; VI, 568; VII, 240. A third tuppenny act, for a three-year duration, was adopted in 1769 (Hening, VIII, 381). The royal approval of this was a conciliating gesture too late for generally placative effect.

evidence, furthermore, had been heard to the effect that the prevailing local price of tobacco during the year in question had been sixpence per pound. Mathematics would thus indicate an award of some £288 sterling. Henry, conceding the law, denied the right of this. Government, he declared, was a mutual compact binding the subjects only so long as the sovereign gave justice and protection; the "tuppenny act" was a good law, and its disallowance in the interest of a rapacious clergy was an act of misrule, a piece of tyranny which the subjects had no obligation to obey. Ignoring a remark of "treason" from the plaintiff's attorney, he said that a people restrained in making their own laws was in bondage, and the chain ought to be broken. The jury, he concluded, had a chance to make such an example of the plaintiff that others would be deterred from challenging Virginia's authority. The means at hand was to grant damages in conspicuously nominal amount. He recommended a farthing; and the jury, slightly more generous, awarded one penny.[9] It may be wondered that neither he nor they hit upon "tuppence" as the cream of a grim jest. Perhaps all were too intensely earnest for a sardonic indulgence.

Henry had borrowed his essential doctrines from Bland; but his rampant fervor, his ringing phrases, and his torrential speed in uttering them were his own. He had owed this opportunity at the bar to his father, who was a magistrate on the bench; all things afterward he owed only to the people, who flocked to his eloquence and then to the polls. From his Piedmont county of Louisa he was elected to the House of Burgesses in time to flame against the Stamp Act as a stroke of British oppression. An agent of the French government visiting Williamsburg happened to hear Henry's great speech in support of his own passionate resolutions, and wrote in his diary:

Shortly after I Came in one of the members stood up and said he had read that in former times tarquin and Julus had their Brutus, Charles had his Cromwell, and he Did not Doubt but some good american would stand up, in favour of his Country, but (says he) in a more moderate manner, and was going to Continue, when the speaker of the house rose and Said, he, the last that stood up had spoke traison, and was sorey to see that not one of the members of the house was loyal Enough to stop him, before he had gone so far. upon which the Same member stood up again (his name is henery) and said that if he had afronted the speaker, or the house, he was ready to ask pardon, and he would shew his loyalty to his majesty King G. the third, at the Expence of the last Drop of his blood, but what he

[9] William W. Henry, *Patrick Henry* (New York, 1891), I, 39–42.

had said must be atributed to the Interest of his Countrys Dying liberty which he had at heart, and the heat of passion might have lead him to have said something more than he intended. . . .[10]

Whether this item, discovered in recent years, or the traditional account concluding "If this be treason make the most of it" be nearer to Henry's own words is not a vital matter. He and many another were skirting the borders of treason; and there were few Virginians to do more than deprecate his haste and vehemence. Then and for a decade afterward there was divergence merely between the pugnacious who wanted speed and the peaceable who counseled caution in prosecuting a cause to which all were committed.

* * *

In the British empire something of a crisis must have come in this period, even without the young king's personal ambition to rule or the maladroitness of his ministers. The recent great war against France, waged in Asia, Europe, and America, had exposed a lack of central control and had loaded Britain with debt. The several colonies had participated with men and money more or less, but a laggardness of theirs in meeting requisitions had been embarrassing and costly. With a view to future contingencies a systematic imperial revenue and a definite integration of commerce and policy were sought. Hence the Stamp Act, the Townshend Tariffs, and the rest of the royal and parliamentary program of the 'sixties and 'seventies. A vigorous opposition in Parliament sought with but intermittent success to prevent or at least to temper this exaltation of central authority.

But on American shores the recent treaty which eliminated France from Canada and Spain from Florida had canceled all need of military protection and left mere loyalty to combat any sense of griev-

---

[10] *American Historical Review*, XXVI, 4 (July, 1921), p. 745. The report continues as to the next day:

"*May the 31th.* I returned to the assembly today and heard very hot Debates stil about the Stamp Dutys. the whole house was for Entering resolves on the records but they Differed much with regard the Contents or purport therof. some were for shewing their resentment to the highest. one of the resolves that these proposed, was that any person that would offer to sustain that the parlement of Engl'd had a right to impose or lay any tax or Dutys whats'r on the american Colonys, without the Consent of the inhabitants therof, Should be looked upon as a traitor, and Deemed an Enemy to his Country. there were some others to the same purpose, and the majority was for Entring these resolves, upon which the Governor Disolved the assembly, which hindered their proceeding." (Pp. 745-746.)

ance. The New Englanders were as usual the most alert against encroachments of power, for their colonies had always had the greatest degrees of autonomy and the sharpest divergences of interest and sentiment from those of England. Accordingly Massachusetts led the resistance to consolidation, though Virginia and South Carolina were quick in accepting the general challenge. Maryland and North Carolina moved with the main mass, while New York and Georgia brought up the rear. Jamaica, Barbados, and the Floridian and Canadian provinces did not appreciably participate at any stage. The West Indies had their market improved by the stiffening of trade control in regard to sugar and molasses; and if they felt anger at any concomitant measures, their isolation from sister colonies and their helplessness in the face of naval power in case of war must have made them quiescent. East and West Florida had only the tiniest clusters of white people, and these were mostly not of English stock. Quebec, with a French population habituated to despotism, was barely beginning an orientation to the British régime; and Nova Scotia, voided of her Acadians, was but now receiving her pioneer British replacements.

Georgia had special grounds for contentment with things as they were. Her escape from the stringent restraints of the trustees into the lax control of the crown in the 'fifties had brought a surge of prosperity to replace languishing poverty; her small population was now freed by British power from the militant menace of Spain; and in Sir James Wright she had a sagacious governor who bracketed his fortunes with hers by investing in a dozen rice plantations. Some pique may have been felt at such interventions as the royal veto in 1759 of an act exempting immigrants from other colonies from debts incurred by them before coming to Georgia; but her quiescence was undisturbed until settlers in the present Liberty County, who had come from New England, carried her into the "continental" movement in time for her delegates to sign the Declaration of Independence.

The status of Maryland as a proprietary jurisdiction, while assuring no placidity of politics, exempted her from quarrels with the crown over local questions and thus from the commoner sort of preliminaries to the struggles against the new imperial program.

North Carolina's deficit was not of quarrels but of integration. Having drawn thin settlement of diverse origins and habits into the region of Albemarle Sound, the Cape Fear coastal district and the wide uplands, respectively, and possessing very poor channels of interior trade or communication, she could attain cohesion only when some crisis was peculiarly notorious and vivid. Her generally distraught condition is illustrated by the deeds and disasters of her so-called Regulators.

These pioneers in the Piedmont, earning the plainest of livings from toil in their crude crops, had little money with which to pay their taxes or the quit-rents which in the northerly zone were due to Lord Granville. But arrearage rendered any citizen's property liable to distraint and loaded him with fee-charges from rapacious officers of the law. Before the end of the 'fifties complaints were put on record. In 1767 George Sims particularly denounced Samuel Benton who had recently been a member of the legislature from Granville County. At the time of election he "was universally esteemed a person calculated for what is called a poor mans Burgess, and indeed he has proved a poor mans Burgess, he forgot that you sent him to do your business, Gentlemen, . . . and all his transactions below have been for the benefit of that dear self of his. . . ." In consequence he had now become colonel of militia and clerk of the county court, ruling and, with his confederates, robbing the people. Sims exclaimed:

> Does not daily experience shew us the gaping jaws of ruin, open, and ready to devour us? Are not your lands executed, your negroes, horses, cattle, hogs, corn, beds, and household furniture? Are not these things, I say, taken and sold for one tenth of their value? Not to satisfy the just debts which you have contracted; but to satisfy the cursed exorbitant demands of the Clerks, Lawyers and Sheriffs, . . . [who] laugh at us for being such simpletons as to suffer it? . . . But, let us appear what we really are, To wit, free subjects by birth, endeavouring to recover our native rights according to law, and to reduce the malpractices of the Officers of our Court down to the standard of law.[11]

Protests bringing no relief, disorders ensued in these northerly counties, and the disorder increased when repression was applied. A succession of rescues from arrest evoked a riot act from the legislature, and in turn armed rallies by the backwoodsmen. Against these Governor Tryon in 1771 led an expedition of militia, officered

---

[11] George Sims, "An address to the People of Granville County," in the *American Historical Review*, XXI, 2 (Jan., 1916), pp. 329, 330, 331. Samuel Benton was a grandfather of Thomas H. Benton, senator from Missouri. The senator's other grandfather, Thomas Hart, was a contemporary sheriff of a neighboring county, who when investigated was found "not a farthing out in his accounts." Archibald Henderson, *ibid.*, p. 362 n., citing *North Carolina Colonial Records*, VIII, 233.

by scores of prominent lowland citizens. The large assemblage of Regulators which was confronted on the Alamance Creek found itself leaderless; for when a parley came to naught, Hermon Husband, hitherto the moving spirit, abandoned the field in obedience to his Quaker scruples, and James Hunter when invited to take command replied, "We are all freemen, and everyone must command himself." A fusillade in which nine men were killed on each side was followed by the rout of the Regulators, the hanging of seven captives, and the outlawry of many who had made escape. The sequel was a stampede north, west, and south from the invaded region. Governor Martin, who soon came to replace Tryon, adopted a policy of placation which won the good-will of the remaining ex-Regulators to the crown but did not reconcile them to the rule of the lowland colonels and legislators. Hence a prevalence of Toryism in some upland areas during the War of Independence.

These Regulators in North Carolina drew their designation from a more truly regulating movement in the 'sixties in the Piedmont of South Carolina. The settlers there had no courts and usually no legal officers nearer than Charleston. When horse-thieves and other disturbers of peace and property were to be dealt with, orderly citizens must needs become vigilantes and apply frontier justice. While the governor sought to repress lynch law, the assembly welcomed a proposal to relieve the need of it by circuit courts to supplement the single existing "general court" at the capital. This purpose was blocked by the monopoly control of sheriff's functions by Richard Cumberland, a London playwright, who held office as provost-marshal of the province and operated by deputy. As a fruit of negotiation the colony brought a relinquishment of office by Cumberland and persuaded the crown to abolish the sinecure; and thereupon the needed courts were created.

This gesture of good-will from the lowlands had a special timeliness of outcome. By chance the judge available for the circuit of the inland courts, when they were organized in 1773, was William Henry Drayton, who had stood loyal to the crown through the troubles of the 'sixties, but was now fired with opposition to the coercive acts being applied to Massachusetts. Not content with magisterial routine, he charged the grand juries to consider the tyrannous pretenses of Parliament; and in response the jurors pledged their "lives and fortunes" to the defense of colonial rights.

* * *

With a partial exception in Virginia, where Piedmont settlements were old enough to have attained integration and where the high talents of Henry and Jefferson made special contribution, the voice of protesting America was the voice of the seaboard. It was there, if anywhere, that the stamps and the taxed glass, paper, paints, and tea were to be bought. There stood the few towns; there ships came and went, overseas or coastwise, bearing news as well as cargoes; there presses issued gazettes and assemblies held session; there alone could the strokes of Britain be countered by prompt action. There also was counsel moderated by men of established place and vested interests, men accustomed to look behind and before, to the right and the left before deciding upon their course. Near salt water, from Boston to Savannah, dwelt John Adams, Hancock, and Quincy in Massachusetts, Jay and Livingston in New York, Franklin, Dickinson and Wilson in Pennsylvania, Dulaney and Carroll in Maryland, Washington, Page, Nelson, Mason, Wythe, Pendleton, the Randolphs and the Lees in Virginia, Davie, Caswell and Iredell, Drayton, Middleton, Rutledge, and the Pinckneys in the Carolinas, Hall and Habersham in Georgia, widely diverse in personal proclivities, variously grouped on particular questions, but remarkably homogeneous on general public policy. There also dwelt James Otis and Samuel Adams in Massachusetts and Christopher Gadsden in South Carolina, who with Henry were the van of irritation.

As a rule protest and resistance found origin at Boston, to be confirmed elsewhere; but in sundry details initiative was assumed in other colonies, with Virginia contributing much and acting with special weight of influence.

Remonstrance by the House of Burgesses against the Stamp Act had been followed by paralyzing demonstration at Williamsburg, and by Richard Henry Lee's launching of an association in his county to boycott British goods until the act was repealed. Parliament's compliance ere long relieved the tension, but the Townshend taxes quickly revived it. A stringent protest by the Burgesses in 1769 caused the governor to dissolve the House, whereupon its members convened in a private place and adopted a boycott resolution. Parliament again yielded to pressure by repealing the taxes except for threepence a pound on tea, which was retained as a mere symbol of British authority. Now came a lull in which citizens might review the procedure and consequences, refurbish their theories, and debate in their own minds and with one another the prospects of eventual accord within the empire or further struggle for colonial rights. Virginia planters, farmers, and merchants appear to have been remarkably at one in hope for peace and resolve to resist on occasion. British tea meanwhile was generally boycotted, but otherwise affairs had returned fairly near to the normal.

The train of decisive events began in 1773 when a glut of tea on the East India Company's wharves in London prompted a seemingly subtle device to break the residual deadlock. While not changing the requirement of tax in the colonies, Parliament permitted the company to draw back a tax of a shilling per pound previously required in England on tea destined for America, thus reducing the gross levy to ninepence less than it had been before the Townshend tax was laid. The company thereupon sent cargoes at bargain prices to the principal American ports. But all along the western shore tea had equally become a symbol to be rejected. At most places its entry was prevented peaceably; but at Boston citizens disguised in Indian war paint flagrantly dumped the stuff into the harbor. Parliament now resorted to coercive measures, forbidding all waterborne traffic into Boston and providing for red-coat regiments to be quartered there, changing the Massachusetts charter in the interest of prerogative, and requiring that certain offenders be brought to England for trial. American repercussion to this was equally prompt; the cause of the Bay Colony was to be the cause of the continent.

Everywhere appointive governors were ousted,[12] legislatures converted themselves into conventions or "congresses," committees of correspondence and of public safety took over administrative authority, and a Continental Congress, with members extra-legally

[12] A preliminary was described by a Virginian in a letter of May, 1775: "I don't doubt you have heard of the great disturbance our Governor has occasioned by taking the ammunition and locks of the guns out of the magazine in Williamsburg privately in the night and putting them on board of a man of war, . . . which occasioned in about four days after upwards of 1000 men to assemble together in Fredericksburg, among which were 600 good riflemen. There was a council of war held three days, Saturday, Sunday and Monday. The evening of the third day we were all drawn up in ranks and discharged on some promise of the governor about delivering of the powder. If we had continued there one or two days longer we would have had upwards of 10,000. All the frontier counties of Va. were in motion, even Hampshire, Fincastle, Barkley. There were expresses from Fredericksburg to meet every company to let them know there was no occasion for their marching. Fredericksburg never was so honoured with so many hearty men since it was a town, every man, rich and poor, with their hunting shirts, belts, tomahawks, and fixed off in the best manner." H. E. Hayden, *Virginia Genealogies*, p. 705. Lord Dunmore, the baffled governor, said that in opposition to British policy "the men of fortune joined equally with the lowest and meanest," and among them "the laws of Congress" got marks of reverence which they never bestowed on their legal government.

chosen, began to legislate provisionally for the colonies at large. The whole continent was in flux, old governments overthrown and new rulers uncertain but unrestrained. A mere local group might act at its own discretion. Thus the public safety committee of Mecklenburg County, North Carolina, meeting at Charlotte on May 31, 1775, considering all royal commissions in the colonies to be suspended, provided for local courts, taxation, and militia control, to be valid "until Instructions from the General Congress of this Province . . . shall provide otherwise, or the legislative body of *Great Britain* resign its unjust and arbitrary Pretensions with Respect to *America*." By a curious twist in a participant's memory many years afterward, this committee was converted into delegates elected by militia companies, the date of its action shifted to May 20, and its resolutions transformed into a declaration repudiating British allegiance and asserting in Jeffersonian phrase "That we . . . are and of right ought to be a sovereign and self-governing Association, under . . . no power other than that of our God and the General Government of the Congress; to the maintenance of which independence, we solemnly pledge to each other our mutual cooperation, our lives, our fortunes, and our most sacred honor."[13] There can be no doubt that this rhetoric and this utter intransigeance are an imputation from a later time. None the less, men in this and other localities were spontaneously filling the gap left by the collapse of royally constituted authority and were prepared to carry on till further notice.

As protest merged into resistance, the county committees, whose members were generally men of local trust and prestige, were of notable service in maintaining order and concerting policy. By publication of names of men as enemies of America, by seizures of goods, and even by imprisonment or banishment of persons, these committees coerced opponents of the boycott and established a full control of trade, press, and speech. In that sense only was the second Continental Congress warranted in saying "Our union is perfect" when announcing, July 6, 1775, its recourse to military force.

"Our cause is just. . . . Our internal resources are great, and if necessary, foreign assistance is undoubtedly available," the Congress declared in the same connection. The "cause" was as yet the re-

[13] A. S. Salley, Jr., "The Mecklenburg Declaration: The Present Status of the Question," in the *American Historical Review*, XIII, 1 (Oct., 1907), p. 27; W. H. Hoyt, *The Mecklenburg Declaration of Independence* (New York, 1907).

covery of exemptions within the British empire, and the immediate purpose was to bring Parliament, as twice before, to repeal its aggressive enactments. Parliament replied instead by an act in December declaring the colonies in rebellion and ordering a blockade of all their ports. This in turn drove Americans to consider more explicitly a French alliance; and this implied an assertion of independence, for France would hardly give aid in a quarrel over mere details of colonial status. Thus the sequence of events blazed an always opportune trail to the declaration of what Americans in general had sought to avoid.

* * *

When in the Course of human events, it becomes necessary for one people to dissolve the political bands which have connected them with another, and to assume among the Powers of the earth, the separate and equal station to which the Laws of Nature and of Nature's God entitle them, a decent respect to the opinions of mankind requires that they should declare the causes which impel them to the separation.

We hold these truths to be self-evident, that all men are created equal, that they are endowed by their Creator with certain unalienable Rights, that among these are Life, Liberty, and the pursuit of Happiness.

These Fourth of July phrases of Jefferson are not of distinctive American origin; they certainly have no savor of the *South* before his time. They were borrowed from British philosophy, notably the works of John Locke, and somewhat amended for use in this emergency.

In the preceding month a Virginia convention, acting on advice from the Congress, had adopted a state constitution, prefixing a bill of rights by George Mason which asserted "That all men are by nature equally free and independent, and have certain inherent rights, of which, when they enter into a state of society, they cannot, by any compact, deprive or divest their posterity; namely the enjoyment of life and liberty, with the means of acquiring and possessing property, and pursuing and obtaining happiness and safety." Other fledgling states, mostly Northern, echoed Virginia and the Congress, making inherent liberty as a natural right a seeming dogma for all American patriots.

But such assertions were justificatory of what was being done, not explanatory of the past nor necessarily prophetic of the future. They were a device newly borrowed to replace prior appeals to colonial

DAUGHTERS OF ENGLAND

charters and the rights of British subjects, which had served the preceding occasions none too well and would clearly not apply to the present need. In fact, individual liberty, whether inherited by the colonists as Englishmen or inherent in all men, was not an issue. The concrete question, having arisen over finance and commerce, concerned home rule—the right of a community to restrict or cast off extraneous control. Theoretical rights of all men as individuals were used for what they were worth as "fundamental principles," which means a philosophical gloss, in a campaign for community interests.

The participants had as their objective not anarchy but continuing order with a shifted control. Engaged in war already, they did not scruple to suppress or expropriate and expel the new crop of Tories which assertion of independence created; and not many felt keen qualms in continuing to hold Negroes in a bondage which denied them both liberty and the possession of property.

These rebels, nevertheless, were not sardonic or insincere, but opportunist, using expertly what came to hand. Some of them, Jefferson and Mason conspicuously, sought a remodeling of the local order in accord with their adopted principles; and where occasion existed in the Southern states the church was disestablished and entail and primogeniture abolished. These changes were not of huge importance. Religious toleration had previously become so complete that disestablishment meant mainly the relief of taxpayers from the burden of supporting an Anglican clergy. Primogeniture and entail had found little use in colonies where land was very cheap and homesteads often shifted.

The state constitutions adopted in this period did not much broaden the suffrage, redistribute representation, or diminish property qualifications for office. There was turmoil enough in the mere exigencies of war. Citizens were generally content with a concentration of public endeavor upon resistance to the British efforts at conquest.

Even in this they were naturally much more willing to spend their breath and their ink than their blood or their money. An illuminating if not fully typical document is preserved in the Virginia archives—a petition addressed to the legislature in 1780 by two sergeants and nineteen enlisted men of Amherst County militia. This

Humbly Sheweth

That your Petitioners are of the Number of those who were lately Ordered into Service on the Southern Expedition—That with a Conscious Shame & heartfelt Sorrow we most sincerely lament and Deplore the shameful Timmidity which marked our behaviour at the Unfortunate Battle of Cambden, as well as its unhappy Consequences—That as to our Conduct (amongst Others) on that important Occasion We dare not pretend to justify Ourselves—yet by way of alleviating in some degree our Guilt we humbly offer to the Consideration of your Hon[ble] House the following Facts—That your Petitioners were the first Militiamen of this State who were ever Order'd into service at such a distance as South Carolina—That on our Arrival at Hillsborough we staid but a few days to Rest before we march'd to the South, from which time (except a few days Halt which we made at Deep River) we were March'd almost Night & Day and kept on half allowance of Flour for Eight or Ten days before the Battle—That from these Circumstances, and being wholly unacquainted with Military Discipline, which we had not time to learn; Greatly Exhausted by Fatigue at that hot Season, which we had not been inured to; Dispirited for want of Rest & Diet; and Panick-struck by the Noise and Terror of a Battle which was entirely New to most of us; We (amongst Others, Officers and Privates) were so unhappy as to abandon the Field of Battle Notwithstanding all the efforts of our Gallant Generals & the Example of our brave brethren the Regulars—To Extenuate our own Guilt by accusing Others we disdain to do and dare not Attempt—yet we humbly beg leave to Represent to your Hon[ble] House That had our inferior Militia Officers been experienced in Military Discipline or Capable of encouraging us by their Example as well as Orders and particularly had we not been drawn up in such Close Order but had more space to Act, And Lastly been Permitted to Fire on the Enemy before we receiv'd their Fire, or before we came so near, We verily believe the Event had been Otherwise— —But to Proceed— —On our return to Hillsborough finding that all our Blankets & Cloathing (except what little we had on) were entirely lost, being destitute of Money or other means of supplying Ourselves at that place, we Petition'd our Officers for furloughs to go home in Order to provide such as we could—This they refused—but at the same time most of those who went from our own County with us—not only did not forbid, but advised & encouraged us so to do—When we had accordingly return'd to our own County We apply'd Ourselves to the County Lieut., informing him of the Cause of our Coming and of our Resolution of returning to our Duty as soon as we could provide a few Cloaths to supply our immediate wants—Who indulged us with Furloughs for about 20 Days which were then prolong'd to this present Instant being the 9th of Octo[r].

Accordingly having met this day in Order to Proceed to Camp, there to serve out the Remainder of our Term and to make good the time we have lost—To our Astonishment and Grief We are told by Authority That we are to be turn'd Over to the Regular Service for Eight Months. . . . We are moreover inform'd that Pay-Rolls have been made Out during our Absence in which none were Included but those who were then

DAUGHTERS OF ENGLAND

Present— — —In these Alarming unhappy Circumstances We have no Other Resource but to Petition your Honourable House for Redress— Which we most humbly Beg and Pray— . . . That having been Order'd into Service early in the Summer, Great Part of our last Crops have been lost, by which our Familys and Stocks are likely soon to be Reduc'd to great Distress—That should our Term of Service be prolong'd to Eight Months—Besides looseing great part of the last, We must be depriv'd of any possibility of making any the year to come—That in this Case most of us being already very poor and many of our Familys large tho weak, It must Compleat our Ruin & Theirs—We have always understood That the penalty of Eight Months service inflicted by the Act was on such only as should Refuse to pay due Obedience thereto by Marching when Order'd —But we humbly beg leave to Represent That we never did Refuse but did Actually go and have Served a Considerable part of our Term & always intended & still do faithfully to serve Out & make Good the whole—In which time we yet hope By the Mercy of Divine Providence (as we now joyfully hear that we are to have Regular Officers) That we shall by our future Conduct not only retrieve our own Reputation as Citizens of a Free State But also the losses & Dishonour which our Country has sustain'd by our former Pusillanimity—Wherefore we most humbly hope & pray that your Honble House will Order that we shall be reliev'd by the next Succeeding Divisions of our County (if Wanting) when our Term of Service as at first Appointed is made Good (We being totally unprovided for a Winter Campaigne) And that our pay (without which we cannot Subsist) may be paid agreeable to Justice and Equity. . . .[14]

Such men might have served well under Sumter, Marion or Pickens whose method was that of brief campaigns intermitting farm work. Of mere militia little more could have been expected; farmers embattled occasionally could not prevent even the sluggish Hessian mercenaries from penetrating the country almost at will.

The governments of all the states below the Potomac became fugitive at some time in the latter half of the war, wide zones were devastated, many slaves carried away, plantation routine suspended, public finance greatly demoralized, and every community distraught. Eventual victory was due to the great staunchness of Washington and a group about him, to the half-heartedness of British generals, and to the vigor of the French intervention. The glory was to come in retrospect; incompetence and misery almost prevailed at the time.

But independence was achieved, and with it a measure of continental unity. This was quite against a prognostication made by Thomas Bannister to the Council of Trade and Plantations in 1715:

[14] Virginia State Library, Manuscripts Division, A 845. As an illustration of the very common use of dashes, capitals, ampersands and elevated letters this text is reproduced with a minimum of editing. In various other quotations, I have made the texts easier for modern reading.

I am senseable it has been the policy of some Ministers to curb the forwardness of the Plantations least they should grow too big for the Kingdomes they belong to. . . . But the notion is wild and ungrounded of the Plantations ever setting up for themselves. Different schemes, interests, notions, religions, customes and manners will forever divide them from one another and unite them to the Crown. He that will be at the trouble of reviewing only the Religion of the Continent, and consider how tenacious each sect is, will never form any idea of a combination to the prejudice of the Land of our Forefathers.[15]

But exigency put such philosophizing to scorn. Gadsden, rampant in the Stamp Act Congress, had written upon return to Charleston: "The friends of liberty here are all as sensible as our brethren to the northward, that nothing will save us but acting together. . . . There ought to be no New England men, no New Yorker, etc., known on the Continent, but all of us Americans." [16] And sagacious Franklin said after the war: "Motives of common safety, when they had once assumed a hostile position, cemented the jarring interests of the colonists, and for the time subdued their inveterate jealousies."

A blundering British upset of equilibrium between central and local authority had split the empire and prompted a coalition of the thirteen units of detachment as a means of making independence valid. What form and measure their union would assume and whether the cement would prove lasting remained to be seen.

[15] *Calendar of State Papers, America and West Indies, 1714–1715*, p. 225. The writer used the word *plantation* in the sense of "colony."

[16] R. W. Gibbes, ed., *Documentary History of the American Revolution: consisting of Letters and Papers relating to the Contest Chiefly in South Carolina . . . 1764–1776* (New York, 1855), p. 8.

CHAPTER II

THE FRAME OF INDEPENDENCE

Samuel Johnson said in 1781 for Boswell's enlightenment and ours that a high Tory would exalt government with such excess as to make it unintelligible, while a violent Whig would allow to every man so much liberty that there would not be power to govern anyone; but a wise Tory and a wise Whig would agree in effect, though the one approached any question with a prejudice in favor of establishment while the other preferred innovation. Such groupings in politics, which in continental Europe are described as extreme right, right center, left center and extreme left, are of common occurrence all round the world, though their cleavages are sometimes obscured and the left objectives, while of equalitarian tendency, are quite varied in detail.

In America the stroke for independence had been initiated by the extreme left, violent Whigs in Johnson's phrase, men who contemned authority in general. Royal intransigeance in the crisis drove all moderates into support of independence, the right center continuing to cherish order while sanctioning the transfer of its control from eastern to western shores. But high Tories in America, identifying establishment with British authority, got a local monopoly of the Tory name which thereby became in American speech a stigma.

In the latter half of the war-time, while the British held Savannah and Charleston as bases, the harshness of belligerence was little short of savage. John Rutledge when governor of South Carolina and at the same time a fugitive beyond her borders wrote that the British endeavor was "to break every man's spirit, or if they can't, to ruin him." Accordingly they had hanged many patriots for breach of parole and "burnt a prodigious number of houses and turned a vast many women, formerly of affluent or easy fortune, with their children, into the woods." [1] Interior Tories, banded under Thomas Brown or David Fanning, supplemented the red-coat maraudings,

[1] *South Carolina Historical and Genealogical Magazine*, XVIII, 1 (Jan., 1917), p. 44.

while the patriot "partisans" retaliated where they might. Plantations were specially tempting to forayers, for the slaves thereon were moveable assets of pronounced value. The proprietors of such estates in an invaded region were under pressure to save their fortunes from seizure by professing loyalty to the local conquerors or by declaring personal neutrality and bespeaking the invader's protection. Many citizens of some prominence took one or another of these recourses during the long British occupation of the seaboard, liberating their persons or safeguarding their property at the cost of their patriot repute.

When the war was nearing its end, with the red-coats driven back upon the ramparts of Charleston, the South Carolina legislature in a session at Jacksonborough pronounced a confiscation of the property and a banishment of the persons of those whom it named as loyalists, and laid a capital tax upon those additionally listed as having accepted British protection. In the peace treaty Britain bespoke a mitigation of loyalist hardships, and South Carolina tempered her laws in some degree; but sundry local zealots were none the less determined upon spoliation and revenge. This was one of several questions to vex the politics of the state for a span of years.

Heavy debts and taxes, how to dodge or shift them or how to pay them if they must be paid, formed part of the complex. The Charleston mob of artisans and shopkeepers, echoed and imitated by many farmers at a distance, clamored for sweeping confiscations and quick sale of seized properties, that traitors might be punished, the public treasury be replenished, and patriots be afforded estates and equipment at bargain prices on long credit. Impatient at the law's delay, bands in town and country committed violence upon undesired neighbors, to spread a terror and impel a flight. Magistrates and the governor issued appeals and warnings against lawless deeds, and Christopher Gadsden, more sober than when a Liberty Boy long before, added his voice on the side of moderation.[2] Gadsden's place as leader of the rampant element was taken by Alexander Gillon, a facile Dutchman who had come to Charleston as a ship captain, prospered there as a merchant, procured a commodore's commis-

---

[2] As an index of his changing attitude Gadsden had remarked in 1778: "I am afraid we have too many amongst us who want again to be running upon every Fancy to the meetings of the Liberty Tree. Query whether there is not a disease amongst us more dangerous than anything that can arise from the whole herd of contemptible, exportable Tories." Edward McCrady, *History of South Carolina in the Revolution, 1775-1780* (New York, 1901), p. 271.

sion from South Carolina during the Revolution, made prize of some British merchant ships, and himself been taken prisoner at sea. Returning to Charleston, he now created the Marine Anti-Britannic Society and took charge of the Whig Club of Six Hundred, using both organizations to foment enmity to loyalists and opposition to rule by the wealthy. These nabobs, a club circular said, hoped "by destroying the republican equality of citizenship, . . . for which the middling and the poor had shed their blood in profusion, to introduce family influences into the government, and thereby establish in their own hands an odious aristocracy over their betters."[3]

Such crass appeals of course evoked censure and a rally in opposition, increasing the cleavage of the commnowealth into factions, the one styling itself Democratic Whig, the other contenting itself without a name.

A mere lapse of time, aided by mitigative legislation, reduced the loyalist question to the scale of neighborhood adjustments. Meanwhile the bursting of a post-war financial boom directed public attention to projects of relieving private debtors from keen distress. Judge Henry Pendleton, in charges to the grand juries in his upland circuit, described the progression of speculative policy. Instead of patient and frugal industry at the war's end, he said,

a happy speculation was almost every man's object and pursuit. . . . What a load of debt was in a short time contracted in the purchase of British Superfluities, and of lands and slaves for which no price was too high if credit for the purchase was to be obtained; these fatal effects too were accelerated by . . . the act for prescribing the payment of old debts by instalments of one, two and three years; had this act totally abolished all old debts, men could not with more avidity have run on contracting new ones. [In consequence a panic had now come, with a collapse of commodity prices,] the loss of public credit and the most alarming deficiencies in the revenue and in the collection of the taxes; the collection of new debts as well as old in effect suspended, while the numerous bankruptcies which have happened in Europe amongst the merchants trading to America, the reproach of which is cast upon us, have proclaimed to all the trading nations to guard against our laws and policy, and even against our moral principle.[4]

The panic was quite severe, and for several years it kept the commonwealth in a welter of competing palliatives. Ralph Izard had

[3] *South Carolina Gazette*, September 16, 1784, quoted in Allan Nevins, *The American States during and after the Revolution, 1775-1789* (New York, 1924), p. 402.
[4] *Charleston Morning Post*, December 3, 1786.

proposed in 1785 that the drain of capital from which the community suffered be stopped by prohibiting the importation of African slaves; but Gillon procured instead an authorization of paper currency to be lent to citizens, and then a new stay-law, giving more grace for the payment of debts. In the legislature Dr. David Ramsay, opposing the moratorium, denied the state's authority to change the terms of private contracts and argued that prior stay-laws had merely promoted irresponsibility. But Gillon threatened more drastic measures if this were defeated, and John J. Pringle, Speaker of the House, declared the popular demand so strong that rejection would be perilous. Further disputes of such tenor in the legislature and the press prolonged the factional cleavage into the 'nineties.

Added to the turmoil of war and of returning peace, the community was experiencing sharp changes in plantation industry. Separation from Britain had cut off an imperial bounty on indigo, making its production so unprofitable that the planting of it was abandoned. In the same period the locale and method of rice culture were shifted from inland fields irrigated with impounded brookwater to alluvial strips on the tidal rivers. These new fields with richer soil and more copious water yielded heavier crops and better profits, but the clearing, dyking, and elaborate ditching of them required an outlay involving credit beyond the local resources. Since the London money market was no longer available in full measure, arrangements were made with banks and merchants in the northerly commercial states. Numerous planters, ordinarily cautious, were therefore embarrassed in the panic, along with many chronic debtors among the farmers and in fellowship with casual speculators.

But a common condition of debt, instead of producing identical policy, left undiminished an old cleavage between opportunists eager for temporary relief at some cost of reputation, and conservatives cherishing continuity and respecting the rules of business by which their fathers had prospered. On the one hand were mainly the "middling and poor" to whom Gillon appealed, on the other hand patricians habituated to rule by grace of allies among merchants, mechanics, and farmers of sober cast. The Liberty Boys had shaken the grip of the well-to-do; their successors, the Democratic Whigs, now threatened to break it and use the state for purposes which conservatives thought pernicious. At this stage of stress in local politics, with financial relief soon to come from cotton culture

THE FRAME OF INDEPENDENCE

but as yet unsuspected, the problem of reorganizing the United States intervened.

* * *

The War for Independence had been conducted by the Continental Congress as an improvised agency functioning on the sufferance of the several states and depending upon them uncertainly for the sinews. Articles of Confederation were framed by the Congress in 1777 to give a formal character to the union, only to meet a four years' delay in ratification; and no sooner were these Articles in force than they began to prove ineffective. Without a president or an adequate judiciary, without authority to levy taxes or control commerce or currency, the union was no more than a league of little republics whose petty graspings and bickerings gave prospect of a complete central paralysis. As early as 1780 Alexander Hamilton saw the danger which by the middle of the decade was becoming visible everywhere. Something of individual freedom and state authority must be yielded if the common interests were to be saved and the general welfare promoted.

In sequel to a conference at Mount Vernon and in compliance with advice from a convention of several states at Annapolis, Congress invited all the states to send delegates to a convention to meet at Philadelphia in May, 1787, to propose amendments to the Articles of Confederation. South Carolina, like nearly all her sisters, responded by deputing her most capable public men. The first in repute among her delegates was John Rutledge, a conservative planter who had been a guide in affairs from the beginning of the Revolution. Another was Charles Cotesworth Pinckney, brother of Thomas Pinckney who was then governor of the state. Sons of a colonial chief justice, they had been reared by their talented mother, who in girlhood as Eliza Lucas had introduced indigo culture while managing her father's rice plantation.[5] Quiet grandees in their pri-

---

[5] Her aristocratic precepts must have been much like those of record from a Virginia mother to her son upon his election to the legislature: "I hope you are come into the Assembly without those trammels which some people submit to wear for a seat in the House,—I mean unbound by promises to perform this or that job which the many-headed monster may think it proper to chalk out for you. . . . I think, from long observation, I can venture to assert that the man of integrity, who observes one equal tenor in his conduct,—who deviates neither to the one side or the other from the proper line,—has more of the confidence of the people than the very complaisant time-server, who calls himself the servant —and, indeed, is the slave—of the people. I flatter myself, too, you will act on a

vate lives, much in the mold of George Washington, they were on call throughout their long lives for conservative, responsible public service. Another delegate was a facile young cousin of these, Charles Pinckney, whose talents were on this occasion, though not always, applied to high purposes. The fourth was Pierce Butler, a loquacious, engaging Irishman who had come to the colony as a British army officer before the time of stress, had resigned his commission and acquired a plantation by marriage, and now yielded to no man in zeal for interests of the United States unless they conflicted with those of the South.

At Philadelphia they were agreed in advocating a fully effective government. As to specific provisions they insisted merely upon a reckoning of slaves in the ratio of representation and a denial to Congress, at least for the time being, of power to prohibit importation of slaves. This they said was a *sine qua non* of ratification by the two southernmost states, although those commonwealths were likely themselves to stop the trade in the near future.[6]

Returning home with acceptable compromises in both regards, the delegates found the planters warmly favorable to the convention's handiwork; and Gillon's endorsement made the seaboard almost unanimous. Rawlins Lowndes, an aristocratic individualist, stood almost alone as a conspicuous exception.

But upland farmers mostly wanted no strong government anywhere unless they had a clear prospect of controlling it; and in the legislature their representatives furnished a minority supporting Lowndes's argument against calling a convention to ratify. His theme was: "The security of a republic is jealousy. . . . Let us not,

---

more liberal plan than some members have done in matters in which the honour and interest of this State are concerned; that you will not, to save a few pence to your constituents, discourage the progress of arts and sciences, nor pay with so scanty a hand persons who are eminent in either. . . . Your weight in the House will be much greater if you do not take up the attention of the Assembly on trifling matters nor too often demand a hearing. To this I must add . . . that temper and decorum is of infinite advantage to a public speaker, and a modest diffidence to a young man just entering the stage of life. . . ."—Letter, 1784, of Anne Nicholas, daughter of Wilson Cary, to Wilson Cary Nicholas, in William Meade, *Old Churches, Ministers and Families of Virginia* (Philadelphia, 1878), I, 184, 185.

[6] From that year, indeed, until 1803 South Carolina prohibited slave imports. In 1805 a new prohibition was voted by the lower house but was defeated by a majority of one in the senate. Georgia, whose delegates echoed the South Carolinians on this point, permitted the trade until 1798 when prohibition was laid both by statute and by the state constitution. The other states, whether by prohibitory taxes or explicit prohibitions, forbade slave imports continuously till the congressional prohibition became effective in 1808.

THE FRAME OF INDEPENDENCE

therefore, receive this proffered system with implicit confidence, as carrying with it the stamp of superior perfection. . . . It has been said that this new government was to be considered as an experiment. . . . What, risk the loss of political existence on experiment!" He sincerely believed that when this new Constitution should be adopted, "the sun of the Southern States would set, never to rise again; . . . that the interest of the Northern States would so predominate as to divest us of any pretensions to the title of a republic." Using the matter of the slave trade as one of his talking points, he pictured a time when the magnitude of congressional power would reduce the South Carolina legislature "to the confined powers of a corporation." To the plea that affairs in future would be managed by great men incapable of mistake or prejudice he replied with skepticism: "If, at any future period, we should smart under laws which bore hard upon us, and think proper to remonstrate, the answer would probably be, 'Go: you are totally incapable of managing for yourselves.' "[7] Against the drastic change now proposed, and until a more moderate one could be framed, he wished to preserve the sovereignty of the states in the existing framework of union by which independence had been won.

Edward Rutledge in reply said "the wings on which we were carried so triumphantly through the war" were the firm spirit of the people, the armaments of an ally, and financial aid from abroad;

and not this wretched Confederation, which is unable, by universal acknowledgment, to obtain a discharge of any part of our debts in the hour of the most perfect domestic tranquillity. What benefits, then, are to be expected from such a constitution in the day of danger? Without a ship, without a soldier, without a shilling in the federal treasury, and without a nervous government to obtain one, we hold the property that we now enjoy at the courtesy of other powers. Was this such a tenure as was suitable to the inclinations of our constituents? It certainly was not. They had called upon us to change their situation, and we should betray their interest and our own honor if we neglected it.

As to the menace of harm from a powerful government: "If the gentleman would show the power that could do no harm, he would at once discover it to be a power which could do no good. To argue against the use of a thing from the abuse of it, had long since been exploded by all sensible people."[8]

[7] Jonathan Elliot, ed., *Debates on the Federal Constitution* (Philadelphia, 1866), IV, 271, 272, 274.
[8] Elliot, ed., *Debates*, IV, 275, 276.

Lowndes had cited the treaty with Great Britain as recognizing the states to be severally independent. Charles Cotesworth Pinckney, countering this, declared that independence was properly dated from the Declaration of Independence, which

> sufficiently confutes the honorable gentleman's doctrine. . . . The separate independence and individual sovereignty of the several states were never thought of by the enlightened band of patriots who framed this Declaration; the several states are not even mentioned by name in any part of it,—as if it was intended to impress this maxim on America, that our freedom and independence arose from our union, and that without it we could neither be free nor independent. Let us, then, consider all attempts to weaken this Union, by maintaining that each state is separately and individually independent, as a species of political heresy which can never benefit us but may bring on us the most serious distresses.[9]

On the same side spoke Pringle, Ramsay, Gillon, Robert Barnwell and sundry others, asserting the worthlessness of the old frame, the wholesomeness of the new, and the groundlessness of Southern fears. Lowndes, repeatedly taking the floor but finding only one vocal supporter, at length admitted defeat, saying that "he spoke merely to point out those dangers to which his fellow-citizens were exposed—dangers that were so evident that, when he ceased to exist, he wished for no other epitaph than to have inscribed on his tomb, 'Here lies the man that opposed the Constitution, because it was ruinous to the liberty of America.' "[10]

Thirty years were to pass before this proposed inscription was refreshed in memory by Robert J. Turnbull with warm praise.[11] Its utterance by Lowndes marked his own exit from public life. The commonwealth, particularly the lowlands, wanted not in that time of confidence to hear a Cassandra's voice. In convention, which was duly held, ratification was carried by two-thirds majority, a nearly solid vote from the lowlands overwhelming a mainly upland opposition.

* * *

[9] *Ibid.*, p. 301.
[10] *Ibid.*, p. 311.
[11] *The Crisis: or Essays on the Usurpations of the Federal Government. By Brutus* [R. J. Turnbull] (Charleston, 1827), p. 144: "Those who remember Mr. Lowndes as well as I do can bear testimony to his virtues as a Patriot. . . . He was identified, soul and body, with the *Colony* and the *State* from which he received so many honours; and it was his strong attachment to that State, whose independence he contributed to rear, which caused him to struggle to the last against a form of Government, which, in his view, would bring it back again to a colonial dependence upon sections of the Union, who were opposed to our peculiar interests by education and by prejudice."

As a delegate at Philadelphia Pierce Butler had endorsed a suggestion of obliterating the states and creating a unitary republic. But as a senator in Congress he lost at once his illusions of national harmony. In the first session he wrote to James Iredell:

> I find locality and partiality reign as much in our Supreme Legislature as they could in a county court or [a] State legislature. . . . I came here full of hopes that the greatest liberality would be exercised; that the consideration of the *whole* and the general good, would take place of every object; but here I find men scrambling for partial advantages, State interests, and in short, a train of those narrow, impolitic measures that must, after a while, shake the Union to its very foundation. . . . I confess I wish you [i.e., the state of North Carolina] to come into the confederacy, as the only chance the Southern interest has to preserve a balance of power.[12]

A fear of injury to his community through predominant Northern selfishness was making Butler a trenchant Southern partisan and inclining him in defense to restrain the powers of Congress within the strict scope of the Constitution. Ralph Izard, his colleague, did not share Butler's new fears nor join in his reaction, but, like Thomas and C. C. Pinckney, Gabriel Manigault, and many another opulent rice planter, gave adherence to the Federalist party of Alexander Hamilton supporting a government of broader powers than the text of the Constitution implied. Some of these men held bonds of the United States and of South Carolina whose value was much enhanced by Hamilton's funding and assumption program; and as a group in politics they approved Hamilton's general purpose of arraying the rich to control public policy.

Among the Charleston mechanics the Democratic Whigs were still disposed to meet any challenge of the grandees. On Genêt's arrival in 1793 with greetings and appeals from republican France, they formed clubs to promote liberty, equality, and fraternity. Had not Gillon been within a year of his death he might have gone to sea with a French letter of marque to prey once more upon British trade.

Interior farmers, more slowly committing themselves, mostly took side against Hamilton's party of "the rich and the good." Stimulated in this course by Jefferson's appeals, they were organized by Charles Pinckney, who, parting from his two cousins and most of

[12] August 11, 1789. J. G. McRee, *Life and Correspondence of James Iredell* (New York, 1857, 1858), II, 264, 265.

his neighbors, grasped a politician's opportunity to get a following.

An opposite shift was made by Robert Goodloe Harper, a young Virginian and a graduate of the College of New Jersey, who went to Charleston to study law and then to the Piedmont of South Carolina in search of clients and a career. Harper's first reaction to the French Revolution was warmly sympathetic. But excesses at Paris and extreme disorders in Haiti turned him so strongly to the cherishing of order that he took the side of Britain in the war abroad and of Hamilton in the party strife at home. In the latter half of the 'nineties he was prominent among the Federalists in Congress. Harper was fond of printing pamphlets, addressed nominally to his constituents, to set forth his views upon each major question which arose. When at the century's end he married a daughter of Charles Carroll and made his home in Maryland the South Carolina Federalists who lost their most eloquent leader.

The Pinckney brothers were never campaigners, but dignitaries whom the party put forward at one time or another for a major national post. One such occasion was in 1800 when C. C. Pinckney was a running-mate of John Adams against Jefferson and Burr. Under the constitutional provision then effective there was no separate balloting for the two offices to be filled. Each elector casting two ballots for President, the candidate receiving the highest electoral vote was elected President and the one receiving the next highest Vice-president, if these votes were a majority of the whole number cast. Under the South Carolina law, as continued until after 1860, electors were not chosen by popular vote but by joint ballot of the two houses of the legislature. Charles Pinckney, then a Senator from South Carolina, thought it more important for him to manage maneuvers at Columbia for a month at the end of 1800 than to discharge his duties at Washington. A current local project was to bracket Jefferson and C. C. Pinckney in a straddle ticket at the cost of Adams and Burr. C. C. Pinckney refused to sanction this, whereupon Charles procured enough persuadable votes to make a majority for Jefferson and Burr. In repeated letters implying local commitments, he reported all this to Jefferson and asked that no federal appointments in South Carolina be determined until after conference with him. In reply he must have received an intimation of censure upon his lobbying, for in a last obsequious letter he retracted his request.[13] Fate showed him little kindness thereafter. His plunging in plantation ventures brought bankruptcy; and in politics, instead of becoming as he hoped a power in the national administration, he held for brief terms the ministry to Spain, the governorship of South Carolina, and a seat in the lower house of Congress. Failing the brilliant promise of his youth, maturity made him no more than a political hack, intermittently employed.

Meanwhile Jefferson as President was meeting exigencies which required him and Congress to use the powers which he had previously said the government did not rightfully possess. Some of his measures, including the purchase of Louisiana, impinged upon the Northern interests or sentiments, and the Federalists in that section generally took up the preachment of strict construction which the Republicans were mostly willing now to leave in abeyance. But in South Carolina the Federalists, instead of sharing in this exchange of doctrines, held firmly to their former views and accepted a dwindling of numbers as their sons increasingly became Republicans.

* * *

In an important internal problem South Carolina was attaining accord. This was the regional apportionment of legislative representation, which in colonial times and in early statehood was heavily skewed in favor of the seaboard. After a decade of interior demand, the legislature in 1789 ordered an election of delegates to a convention to meet in the following year and revise the state constitution. The seats in this body, however, were apportioned no more generously to the uplands than in the legislature which had ordered its convening. As a sop to the interior the convention transferred the seat of government to the new town of Columbia where the Broad and Saluda rivers flow together at the Piedmont's edge. It also made some small changes in the property qualifications for suffrage and office-holding. But as to representation it merely reduced the size of the lower house without making material change in the regional ratios. Furthermore it continued the provisions by which the elections of governor and numerous other officials were vested in the legislature.

[13] "South Carolina in the Election of 1800," in the *American Historical Review*, IV, 1 (Oct., 1898), pp. 111–129.

In the same year the first federal census reported a population of 28,664 whites and 79,216 colored in the seaboard localities, which were assigned twenty seats in the senate and seventy in the house, as compared with 111,534 whites and 29,697 colored in the rest of the state, which had only seventeen senators and fifty-four assemblymen. One fifth of the whites in a zone of stabilized population were to control both houses as against four fifths in a much larger area where the population was known to be fast increasing.

A clamor was a natural consequence, with Robert Goodloe Harper converting it into an orderly, argumentative campaign. A Representative Reform Association was organized, which in 1794 issued a printed *Address to the People of South Carolina;* and one "Appius," who was presumably Harper, followed it with a series of public letters. These writings admitted that no frauds, abuses, or oppressions had as yet been committed by the state government; but, appealing to natural rights, they contended for doctrinal equity and future security against a rule of the many by the few. Some had said that property must be protected against assaults by the poor; but wealth itself gave prestige and influence, and if property was to be represented at all a control of one house would surely be sufficient. The two zones were analyzed as essentially diverse. On tidewater the fertile tracts were as a rule too malarious to be cultivated by whites at all; there was no opportunity for men without large capital, and such whites as were not rich were likely to be very poor; the trend of private life was to luxury and aristocracy, and of public policy to favor a free exchange of specialized local produce for articles of consumption from foreign sources. A lavishness in social habit, furthermore, promoted a sentiment for high salaries to public officials and large expenditures by the government. In the uplands, on the other hand, where Negro slaves were not a necessity but a mere convenience, where as a rule white men tilled their own fields and their modest fortunes were much alike in value one with another, and where lack of navigation made expedient a diversity of production, a preference prevailed for simple manners, low taxes, public frugality, and encouragement of manufactures. The more numerous community should rightfully be vested with control of one house if not of both.

Timothy Ford and Henry W. Desaussure issued pamphlets in reply. Of a theoretical state of nature and a social compact in the forgotten past of mankind they were skeptical; if inherent liberty was a right, and this were applied in South Carolina, the hundred thousand blacks would be freed, with such ruin as had now befallen Haiti. The lowland planters, if they were to prevent huge disaster, must maintain a system which their forefathers had established. These planters were no foes of citizens' rights; their daily contrast of slaves' lives with their own made them value freedom the more highly. Their peculiar system did not menace the scheme of upland life; their wealth was a resource taxable for benefits willingly shared; their rule would continue to be honest, enlightened, and equable. But they were not willing to have their commerce restrained, and they could not risk interference with slave property.[14]

Ford's argument concluded with a plea to the people of the middle zone, saying that an extension of the plantation system then in manifest progress ought to give them a fellow feeling for the seaboard citizens. This inland thrust of plantation slavery, in fact, was destined ere long to relieve the sectional tension within the state. The new culture of cotton for export, greatly stimulated by Whitney's gin as the last of an epochal series of inventions in textile processing, made slave labor worth its current price wherever good land was within two or three days' haul to navigation. The culture spread swiftly through the middle districts and the lower half of the Piedmont; and where cotton went slaves were sure to go —not in proportions like those in the rice area, but at least in great enough numbers to modify the social and political atmosphere. A realization of this interior change quieted seaboard fears to such extent that in 1808, by virtually unanimous vote in both houses of the legislature, a new distribution was made.

This assigned one senator to each district and parish except Charleston, which was to have two; and as to the lower house it provided for periodic distribution on a combined basis, one half in ratio to white population, one half in ratio to taxes paid. For the time being this gave to the seaboard, where most of the "parishes" clustered, twenty-two senators and fifty-four assemblymen and to the interior, where "districts" were the prevailing units of local administration, twenty-three senators and seventy assemblymen. Calhoun in after years described this act as having set up a method of government by concurrent majorities, each house con-

[14] These pamphlets of 1794 and 1795 are summarized by William A. Schaper, "Sectionalism and Representation in South Carolina," in the *American Historical Association Report for 1900*, I, 408–417. The lowland spokesman at this time conveniently ignored pleas that control of one house be yielded to the interior.

trolled by one interest in the commonwealth and neither capable of legislating without the other's consent. Mathematically as between the maritime and interior regions this was nearly true; but in actual bearing it did not apply; and had the seaboard citizens felt a continued absence of interior sympathy they would surely not have given tame sanction to the plan. Inland sentiment, while more or less jealous of planters' wealth, polish, and ostentation, had never indeed been hostile to slavery; and now the spread of the plantation pattern year by year was assimilating the people, nearly to the foot of the mountains, to the philosophy characteristic of a slave-holding community.

Nevertheless a full accord upon this matter of representation, which had vexed the state for three decades, was a notable achievement, permitting a domestic placidity and clearing the way for united action against any threat from outside. The same trend was promoted by an act of 1801 establishing a college at Columbia to be supported by public funds. But for the time being no pressure of external circumstance gave occasion for drastic policy.

* * *

South Carolina's original scope of territory stretched west and south almost without limit; but Georgia's founding made a barrier of the Savannah River, and Georgia soon hampered the trade of outsiders with such Indians as dwelt within her chartered borders. At a later period, when lands for the culture of rice were in great esteem, the thought spread among South Carolinians that, since the Altamaha River was Georgia's farther limit, tracts beyond that stream might be granted them by their own colony. But the crown spoiled this prospect by broadening Georgia's area to the St. Marys River. Finally the common revolt from the British authority seemed to give the elder sister a possible chance to recoup by annexing the younger. Late in 1776 the legislature of South Carolina resolved that a union with Georgia would promote strength and safety, and at the beginning of the next year a commission went to Savannah to propose it. The officials there showing disapproval, but some citizens expressing favor, William H. Drayton as the spokesman of the visitors procured a hearing by the convention then framing Georgia's first constitution. Remarking the identity of climate, products, and interests, he said that injurious disputes would come over such matters as the navigation of the dividing river if the two should remain separate, and a rival city would rise on the left bank to ruin Savannah's commerce; but merger would assure the stream's improvement, reduce the costs of government, and cause wealthy Carolinians to develop the Georgia lands. The convention rejected the proposal at once; and when Drayton persisted in posting broadsides and circulating petitions derogatory to the Georgia functionaries, Governor Treutlen by proclamation offered a reward of £100 to anyone who should seize him and procure his conviction of unlawful practices. Drayton, dropping the dignity which he sometimes wore, closed the contretemps by thumbing his nose: "I respect the people of Georgia; but, most *wise* rulers, kissing your hands, I cannot but laugh at some folks. Can you guess who they are?"[15]

While the later decades brought no more bickerings of moment between these kindred commonwealths, no warmth of cordiality linked them. Their policies, though generally parallel, diverged on various occasions; and each made some point of not serving as the other's catspaw.

Georgia's assertion of a will to rule herself was not accompanied at once by much demonstration of capacity. The brevity of the previous experience of her people in sharing the responsibilities with a royal governor was no doubt partly responsible, and also her shortage of such families of wealth, culture, and prestige as plantation prosperity had given to South Carolina. Her tidal strips of alluvium adapted to rice were quite limited; and, prior to the cotton era, the prevailing social tone even on the seaboard was that of plain people. Inland, of course, this was more strongly the case, for the lands procured by cession from the reluctant Creeks and Cherokees, extending far up the Savannah River valley, had until 1790 a width of no more than thirty or forty miles. The life was that of new settlers in a wilderness, and politics tended to be crude and fumbling.

The convention which gave Drayton a fruitless hour vested control of the state in a single chamber of many members. Confusion followed, not wholly due to the British invasion; and a few years of peace proved the need of a new frame of government. By curious device in 1788 the legislature selected "three fit and discreet persons" from each county to convene and consider needful changes. A constitution framed by this body was published and referred to an elected convention, which offered amendments; and the document

[15] Charles C. Jones, Jr., *History of Georgia* (Boston, 1883), II, 275-278.

as amended was ratified by yet a third convention. The fruit of all this was novel but not satisfactory. In the choice of a governor, for example, the house of representatives was to name three men; and the senate, now created as a second chamber, was to select one from among the three. Another convention made revisions in 1795, and yet another in 1798, with a constitution at last resulting which stood the test of six decades. In the course of these proceedings control of the legislature by the seaboard gave place to preponderance of upland members; and the seat of government was moved to the inland village of Louisville. Another transfer in 1804 shifted it to the new town of Milledgeville on the edge of the Piedmont, where it remained until Atlanta became the capital in the late 'sixties.

A New England impulse, conveyed by Lyman Hall and Abraham Baldwin, prompted the chartering in 1785 of a state university, which opened its doors at Athens in the distant uplands in 1801.

Exploitation of wild lands, whether for public or private benefit, was a matter of avid concern. Sundry speculative projects of large scale applied to regions remote from Georgia's routine jurisdiction and involved relations with distant capitalists. An enterprise of 1784 looking to the Tennessee River valley about Muscle Shoals coming to naught, a group of incipient corporations in 1789 negotiated with the Georgia government for the purchase of yet more westerly tracts where the Yazoo River drained lands in Choctaw and Chickasaw tribal possession. The promoters failed on this occasion to deliver the purchase prices; but soon a new group of companies, with shareholders dwelling as far away as New England, made fresh overtures which the governor and legislature accepted. By this transaction, completed in 1795, Georgia sold in four tracts to as many "Yazoo" companies most of the territory now comprised in the states of Alabama and Mississippi, the purchasers assuming the burden of ousting the Indians and adjusting the claims of any prior white settlers. The price, half a million dollars in total, was promptly paid to the treasury. But a spread of information that legislators and the governor had been bribed with money or shares of stock speedily roused a strong demand for the cancellation of the sale. James Jackson resigned a seat in the federal Senate and procured election to the legislature as the leader of the campaign. A vehement rescinding act was passed in 1796; the records were expunged, and when the corporations refused to take back their money, the Georgia convention of 1798 put into the state constitution a denial of the sale's validity. This incident, which made the name "Yazoo" a term of reproach, weaned the commonwealth from its desire to handle a distant region. In 1802 Georgia ceded to the United States all title and jurisdiction in lands beyond her present western boundary, in consideration of a money payment and a pledge that Indian claims to the remaining lands in Georgia would be extinguished at federal expense as soon as it could be done peaceably at reasonable cost.

The Yazoo question and the contract of 1802 were to have repercussions in after years. Meanwhile Georgia's modest area of settlement was extended by sundry Creek and Cherokee cessions, and in each instance, from 1804 until 1835 when the last parcel was distributed, the state pursued a very democratic method of her own in transferring the land from public into private possession. Each successive tract was divided into numbered units of size adapted to simple farming, and by lottery these were distributed among heads of families in the state's population. Any recipient, upon payment of a mere survey fee, was free to cultivate or sell his land as he saw fit. The system was intended to give advantage to men of small means as against capitalists, though tracts of plantation size could of course be consolidated by purchase. In a political phase, by giving every citizen the prospect of a lottery chance in every cession to be procured, it kept the Georgia government under pressure to prevent the federal authorities from forgetting the pledge of 1802.

As to the federal Constitution the Georgia delegates at Philadelphia, while seldom taking the floor, modestly facilitated the framing; and her convention ratified it with instant unanimity. The contemplation of a frontier need of military support impelled a sanction of central strength. But episodes of the time gave evidence that this implied no meek abdication of authority beyond the clear meaning of the text.

A case in point is the suit of Chisholm, a citizen of South Carolina who sought in the Supreme Court of the United States to receive a sum of money from the state of Georgia. When the state government was notified of this in 1792, it replied by denial of the court's jurisdiction.[16] A majority of the bench thought otherwise and au-

[16] In the Virginia convention which ratified the Constitution Mason and Henry had argued, as a hostile contention, that under it a state might be sued by a citizen of another state; Madison and Marshall had concurred in denying the possibility.

thorized a writ for the plaintiff. The vehemence of many Georgians may be seen in a bill passed by the lower house of the legislature: "And be it further enacted, that any Federal marshal attempting to levy on the territory of this State, or on the treasury, by virtue of an execution by the authority of the Supreme Court of the United States, for the recovery of any claim against the said state of Georgia shall be guilty of felony, and shall suffer death, without benefit of clergy, by being hanged." [17] The senate did not concur, probably because the Eleventh Amendment was in process of adoption to safeguard the several states against suits in federal courts by citizens of other states.

As to political parties, there had been factional conflict at the war's end, as everywhere, concerning loyalist property; but alignments did not clearly persist into later years. In the 'nineties the Federalist party procured virtually no adherents on the Georgia seaboard, and not enough in the interior to warrant a campaign at any time. All the prominent public men styled themselves Republicans, though they were not notably harmonious among themselves. Cotton culture and the plantation pattern brought a smoothing of manners, though Georgians for long were likely to prove rugged on occasion.

* * *

North Carolina was as yet and for long a loose commonwealth of yeomen, if not of yokels, varied by a thin easterly sprinkling of immigrant planters, merchants, and lawyers. The tone of two factions which persisted for a quarter of a century may be gathered from the "Creed of a Rioter" which young James Iredell ironically wrote in the stress of 1776:

1. I am a sworn enemy to all gentlemen. I believe none in that station of life can possibly possess either honor or virtue.

. . .

3. I impute to *gentlemen* all our present difficulties. If they had not been so cunning as to foresee distant evils, we never should have dreamt of them.

. . .

5. Let every man take care of himself is my maxim. The public interest is too troublesome to attend to. What care I who the devil is miserable, if I am not so?

. . .

[17] U. B. Phillips, "Georgia and State Rights," in the *American Historical Association Report for 1901*, II, 27.

6. . . . I think I have a right, if I can, to shift distresses from my shoulders, and put them on those of my neighbors.

. . .

8. As I have the utmost confidence that all my own opinions are right, I despise every man who differs from me. I am sure he must be a tory.

. . .

10. . . . I am of opinion that our affairs would prosper much better, if gentlemen who read and consider too deeply for us, were totally banished from all public business, and if those who neither read nor think at all (and consequently cannot injure us by the excess of those practices) were entrusted with the management of our present arduous concerns. . . .[18]

Iredell, born of aristocratic but impoverished parents in England, had procured a post in the royal service at Edenton on Albemarle Sound. There he studied law under the guidance of Samuel Johnston, an outstanding attorney, married a daughter of Johnston, and embraced the right-center politics of the family, which, while warmly sanctioning American independence, advocated restraints upon "the fury of democracy." A conservative coterie was formed, including William Hooper and Alexander Maclaine of Wilmington, Richard D. Spaight of Newbern, and William R. Davie of Halifax; but for many years it could prevail in few matters. The chief sway of the populace lay with men who talked of liberty rather than moderation and responsibility. Such were Willie Jones, a polished and wealthy planter on the Roanoke River who followed zealously the doctrines of Thomas Jefferson; Thomas Person, a man of like status in the same region but more headstrong than Jones; David Caldwell, an upland Presbyterian preacher who turned his talents also to medicine, teaching, and politics; and the genial, plausible Timothy Bloodworth, who was a quack in theology, medicine, and government in or out of his blacksmith, wheelwright, and watch-repair shop at Wilmington. A third group, including Richard Caswell, William Blount, Abner Nash, and Alexander Martin, straddled issues when expedient and sought personal advantage in land speculation.

When resolving upon independence in 1776, the provisional assembly directed the citizens to send delegates to a convention, choosing them with "the greatest attention," seeing that the constitution to be framed, "as it is the Corner Stone of all Law, so it ought to be fixed and Permanent, and that according as it is well or ill Ordered,

[18] McRee, *Iredell*, I, 335, 336.

it must tend in the first degree to promote happiness or Misery of the State." [19] The resulting instrument, with a schedule of maxims [20] attached as a bill of rights, continued operative until 1835, but promoted no happiness during the war. The governor, having little further function than "to sign receipts for his salary," was powerless for good or evil, and the legislature showed itself more eager in mulcting loyalists and issuing legal-tender paper money than in meeting patriot responsibilities. When peace came, although Jones turned very moderate for a time, there was little abatement in the "phrenzy of misguided political zeal—avarice cloaked in the cover of patriotism—or private passion and prejudice under pretence of revenging the wrongs of the country." [21]

Refusals by Jones and Caswell to go to the Philadelphia convention gave the North Carolina delegation there a coöperative temper without diminishing the sentiment for local liberty at home. When the state's convention met in July, 1788, to consider the new federal frame, ratification by ten other states had already settled the vital question of its going into operation. But advice from Jefferson was at hand, that the residue of states withhold ratification in order to impel adoption of amendments. By vote of 184 to 84,[22] after full debate, this convention adopted a resolution intimating an eventual ratification but proposing meanwhile a long bill of rights and twenty-six amendments to "the most ambiguous and exceptionable parts of the said Constitution of government." [23] Toward the end of the next year, when some of these proposals were in train for adoption and when isolation from the reorganized Union was beginning to be quite inconvenient, a second North Carolina convention ratified the constitution by a large majority.[24]

A placative policy by those who had campaigned for the constitution procured seats for several of them in Congress, where their first impulse was to be chary toward the use of doubtful powers. Hamilton, however, captured most of them in due time; and the

[19] W. L. Saunders, ed., *Colonial Records of North Carolina* (Raleigh, 1890), X, 696.
[20] Of which the twenty-first reads: "That a frequent recurrence to fundamental principles is absolutely necessary to preserve the blessings of liberty."
[21] Hooper to Iredell, May 1, 1784, in McRee, *Iredell*, II, 100.
[22] Nearly all of this minority, which advocated prompt ratification, came from the northeasterly region about Albemarle Sound. Iredell's argument was of such tone and quality that Washington the next year appointed him to the bench of the Supreme Court.
[23] Elliot, ed., *Debates*, IV, 242-247.
[24] At the instance of Johnston and Iredell the University of North Carolina was chartered in 1789, and began operation at Chapel Hill a few years later.

THE FRAME OF INDEPENDENCE 43

Federalist party, with particular strength in the region about Wilmington, controlled one of North Carolina's electoral votes in 1796 and four in 1800. Thereafter, the Republicans, with Nathaniel Macon as their chief guide, held almost undisputed sway.

* * *

At the time of the Declaration of Independence North Carolina's great space beyond the barrier of the Blue Ridge had but a nucleus of settlement at the northeastern point of what is now Tennessee. In that frugal and simple community were sturdy James Robertson and romantic John Sevier, who must have remained obscure farmers and Indian fighters had they not become linked in large enterprises with men of wealth, political influence, and impulse to procure great unearned increments from the wilds of the West.[25] Grouped in several corporations and alliances, these included Blount, Caswell, Nash, Martin, and Richard Henderson of North Carolina and Patrick Henry, Dr. Thomas Walker, Arthur Campbell, and other Virginians, mostly venturing their money and credit, not their persons, in western exploitation. Henderson, procuring from the Cherokees a pretense of title to the Cumberland River valley, enlisted Robertson to lead a band of pioneers through the farther wilderness and build a village which was named in honor of Nash. Blount and Caswell arranged with Sevier to stake out large tracts on warrants bought by them from soldiers of North Carolina to whom the state had issued them with lavish hand. Other areas were bought at nominal prices directly from the state.

But Indians were a menace, roads were needed, and an assured outlet for produce down the local streams and the Mississippi to the Gulf was essential before any throng of settlers would buy these lands at a profit; and meanwhile taxation must be kept at a minimum. The speculators thought a transfer of jurisdiction to Congress would enhance their prospects; and seaboard North Carolinians were quite willing to let go the transmontane districts whose pleas for aid in Indian campaigns made them "a pest and burthen" to the commonwealth. Accordingly an act of 1784 offered to cede

[25] The sentiments of plain pioneers concerning these operations of engrossment may be seen from a memorial of citizens of Botetourt County, Virginia, in 1777: "We have settled in the west and defended it for years against the savage, in consequence of which we hoped to have obtained a just and equitable title to our possessions, without being obliged to contribute large sums of money for the separate emolument of individuals." Charles H. Ambler, *Sectionalism in Virginia from 1776 to 1861* (Chicago, 1910), p. 43.

the Tennessee region to the United States on certain conditions. Surprising occurrences ensued. Arther Campbell, a speculating rival of the Blount-Caswell-Sevier group, envisaged a huge new commonwealth, to reach from the Ohio perhaps to Florida, with membership in the Union and control of its own public lands. At his impulse a convention at Jonesboro proclaimed the "State of Franklin" and adopted for it a duplicate of North Carolina's constitution. But Sevier turned the tables by procuring election as governor of Franklin while still holding a general's commission in the North Carolina militia. An upland reaction in the parent state now brought a repeal of the cession act before Congress could accept the transfer; and the Franklin authorities, refusing to relinquish their project, became technically rebels. But with Caswell and Sevier, intimate allies, holding office as governors of North Carolina and Franklin, the conflict had a sham character until Caswell was replaced by Samuel Johnston whose eye was not to land-grabbing but to the supremacy of law. Marches and counter-marches, arrests and escapes ensued, until in 1788 the pretended State of Franklin collapsed and with it a vague plan for connection with Spanish Louisiana in case the hope of statehood in the Union should be thwarted.[26]

In 1790 North Carolina renewed her offer of cession, stipulating as before that her land grants and warrants be validated, that slavery be not abolished in the region without the consent of the inhabitants, and that in due time one or more states be created therein. Congress accepted at once, and Blount procured appointment as governor of the territory. Statehood, under the name of Tennessee, was accomplished in 1796, without an enabling act of Congress, with a constitution patterned upon that of North Carolina but providing for popular election of governor instead of choice by the legislature, distributing representation in ratio to population instead of equally among counties, and eliminating property qualifications for resident voters.

Blount, who was at once elected to the national Senate,[27] was a Federalist like most other speculators of large scale; but Tennessee

[26] In some contrast with prior accounts, I am here following the narrative of Thomas P. Abernethy, *From Frontier to Plantation in Tennessee* (Chapel Hill, 1932).

[27] After brief service there Blount was expelled for conspiring to promote a British attack upon Florida and Louisiana. He died at the century's end. Sevier's geniality and his old-time fame as a warrior, rather than any rating in statecraft, gave him repeated elections as governor of Tennessee and in old age a seat in Congress.

THE FRAME OF INDEPENDENCE

gave her presidential votes to the Republican ticket in 1796 and again in 1800.

* * *

Virginia in her great generation had a marvelous number of highly talented men contributing to shape American destiny. Towering in repute for sagacity and sheer character was immortal Washington, capable of hot anger and vehemence but firmly controlled by his iron will, relishing most a quiet plantation life but zealous for the common good and responding always to calls into heavy service. Less only to "the father of his country" in title to fame was Jefferson, a cosmopolitan aristocrat of exquisite taste with special mastery of architectural design, an earnest promoter of education and science, and an enlightened friend of the people.[28] Alert in seeking "fundamental principles" of government and society, and eager to propagate his findings, his aversion to hurly-burly did not prevent him from holding a long succession of onerous offices or from becoming the head of a shouting political party. Madison was yet more definitely a scholar in politics, moderate in doctrine, keen for wholesome order and constant in its' pursuit. Marshall, of lank person and lax posture like Jefferson, had, like Washington, a soldier's discipline in the war and shared with him and Hamilton a firm predilection for national strength and consolidation. Genial and cogently persuasive, never a searching student of the law but ever shrewd in public policy, his lasting achievement was that of a statesman in ermine, "the most legislative of judges." Henry alone among those of persisting fame depended upon that gift of "soul-stirring" oratory which is often said to have been the chief accrediting of public men of the Old South. In addition to these major figures a crowd of less distinguished men showed capacities which must have brought more celebrity had not some of them lacked ambition or had they lived and labored in another commonwealth where their lights were not dimmed by such brilliant comparisons.

In the Virginia state constitution of 1776 the colonial requirement of land-holding for the suffrage was continued, and likewise the assignment of two assembly seats to each county regardless of size, wealth, and population. A senate was added; and the two houses

---

[28] These words had a special and specific pertinence in the philosophical circles of his time, but a limited meaning of neither "enlightened" nor "friend of the people" is needed when discussing the sage of Monticello.

in combination were given virtual control over the executive and the judiciary. The governor, elected annually by the legislature, was additionally restrained by a council of state.

This constitution of hasty design continued in force until 1830, despite a fire of criticism which Jefferson promptly began [29] and the upland people almost continually maintained. Jefferson, followed by Madison, wanted a more effective separation of powers as a check upon impulsive policy as well as a more equable distribution of representation; but Henry, as well as the lowland conservatives, opposed any change.

The government had its full share of tribulations during the war, especially when the red-coats came while Jefferson was governor; and the first years of peace were no more placid than in the sister states. Problem crowded upon problem—loyalist property, planters' debts to British merchants, entail and primogeniture, church disestablishment, road and river improvement, commercial and fiscal reorganization, western lands, foreign and interstate relations. Every project had vigorous advocates and opponents; and although the cleavages upon diverse questions were somewhat various, regional alignments were always palpable.

* * *

The greatest problem among the leaders of thought came to be that of enhancing central authority. Washington wrote to Madison, "No morn ever dawned more favorably than ours did; and no day was ever more clouded than the present. . . . We are fast verging to anarchy." [30] And in the course of sundry replies Madison advocated a central veto power over the legislation of the states like that which the crown had held over the colonies. Without it, he said, "the States will continue to invade the National jurisdiction, to violate treaties and the law of nations and to harass each other with rival and spiteful measures dictated by mistaken views of interest." [31] Henry's thoughts had been moving in the same direction until their course was reversed by a regional crisis.

The Spanish government, possessing both banks of the lower Mississippi and fearing the thrust of American settlement into the center of the continent, proclaimed in 1784 an exclusive right of

[29] Thomas Jefferson, *Notes on the State of Virginia* (Boston, 1832), query XIII.
[30] W. C. Ford, ed., *Writings of Washington*, XI, 81. November 5, 1786.
[31] Gaillard Hunt, ed., *Writings of Madison*, II, 345, 346. April 16, 1787.

THE FRAME OF INDEPENDENCE 47

navigating the river and sought from the United States a sanction of this for twenty-five years in exchange for commercial advantages in Spain's home ports. Congress responded to the overture for a treaty by authorizing John Jay to negotiate, but instructed him to deny the claim of Mississippi monopoly. Jay, meeting an impasse, asked for a relaxation of this part of his instructions; and after a bitter debate it was granted by vote of the seven easterly states against the six of the South. Such a victory was defeat in effect, for the Articles of Confederation stipulated approval by the delegations of nine states in the ratification of any treaty; and Jay, seeing no prospect of such a sanction, let the negotiation die.[32] But Henry, with others, was put upon a somewhat lasting alert against Eastern and Northern selfish power, and he took pains to spread an impression among the settlers on the western waters that strengthening of the Union would menace their prosperity.

In the convention at Philadelphia Madison, despite his very small stature and weak voice, was the floor leader in behalf of the Constitution as it was given form. Washington as the presiding officer, while scrupulously self-contained, was a powerful agent in its favor; and the delegates, confident of his becoming the first executive, "shaped their Ideas of the Powers to be given to a President, by their opinions of his Virtue."[33] George Wythe and John Blair were quiet advocates; but George Mason and Edmund Randolph withheld their signatures from the completed instrument, and Henry had refused to serve as a delegate, saying that he would countenance no project of centralization. These three, with many another, wanted a second federal convention to modify the handiwork of the first, or else wanted rejection outright.

The question as to whether Virginia would ratify was doubtful and momentous. Including as yet all the great stretch of Kentucky, and containing more people than all the states to the southward, her prestige as a commonwealth and a mother of statesmen was immense. At the polls a majority of perhaps two-thirds—very large in the populous Piedmont—was against ratification; but the heavy allocation of delegates to the little counties in the Tidewater [34]

[32] When much more water had flowed to the Gulf and the current of trade was clearly not to be stopped, a treaty comporting with Southern wishes as to navigation and boundaries was negotiated at Madrid in 1795 by Thomas Pinckney.
[33] Pierce Butler, in Max Farrand, ed., *Records of the Federal Convention of 1787* (New Haven, 1911), III, 302.
[34] The delegates from the Potomac and Shenandoah regions were also committed to ratification.

almost equilibrated the convention and made its decision hang upon influence and argument. Partisans of yea and of nay went to Richmond primed for battle and for blandishment. Except for Washington, whose reticence kept him at Mount Vernon, in touch by frequent letters, and for Jefferson, who was absent on a long diplomatic sojourn in France, all the talent of the state met upon the floor. The proceedings were memorable.[35]

Partly thrust and parry upon specific points, but mainly debate upon general implications and prospects filled a fortnight. Those who defended the new plan excelled in tactics and team work; the strength of attack lay chiefly in Henry's ardor and eloquence. His vocal allies, Mason, Monroe, Benjamin Harrison, and William Grayson, made good points without pressing them home; but Henry, now closing his career of public debate, proved himself still "perfectly master of 'Action, Utterance and Power of Speech to stir Men's Blood.' "[36]

To challenge at once the Constitution's legitimacy, Henry moved a reading of the Virginia legislation preceding the Philadelphia convention. The aged but adroit Edmund Pendleton countered:

Mr. Chairman, we are not to consider whether the federal Convention exceeded their powers. . . . This Constitution was transmitted to Congress by that Convention; by the Congress transmitted to our legislature; by them recommended to the people; the people have sent us hither to determine whether this government be a proper one or not. . . . Although those gentlemen were only directed to consider the defects of the old system, and not to devise a new one, if they found it so thoroughly defective as not to admit a revising, and submitted a new system to our consideration, which the people have deputed us to investigate, I cannot find any degree of propriety in reading those papers.

Henry withdrew his motion, but soon attacked the first three words of the Constitution as a key to the whole tenor:

And here I would make this inquiry of those worthy characters who composed a part of the late federal Convention. . . . What right had they to say, *We, the people?* . . . Who authorized them to speak the

[35] *Debates and Other Proceedings of the Convention of Virginia, Convened at Richmond on Monday the Second Day of June, 1788, for the Purpose of Deliberating on the Constitution Recommended by the Grand Federal Convention. . . . Taken in short hand by David Robertson . . . of Petersburg* (Richmond, 1805). A not quite accurate reprint of this exploit of early stenography fills the third volume of Elliot's *Debates*. A spirited summary is in Albert J. Beveridge, *Life of John Marshall* (Boston, 1916), I, 357–480.

[36] Gouverneur Morris, a lobbying visitor, quoted in Beveridge, *Marshall*, I, 433.

THE FRAME OF INDEPENDENCE 49

language of *We, the people,* instead of, *We, the states?* States are the characteristics and the soul of a confederation. If the states be not the agents of this compact, it must be one great, consolidate, national government, of the people of all the states. . . . That they exceeded their power is perfectly clear. . . . I wish to hear the real, actual, existing danger, which should lead us to take those steps, so dangerous in my conception.

Reply came as a bombshell from Henry's own rear, for Washington had privately persuaded Governor Randolph that ratification was imperative in prevention of anarchy. Randolph now revealed his conversion:

"As with me the only question has ever been between previous and subsequent amendments, so will I express my apprehensions, that the postponement of this Convention to so late a day has extinguished the probability of the former without inevitable ruin to the Union; and the Union is the anchor of our political salvation." Experience had proved, he said, that the Confederation was fatally lacking in cement; the just calls of Congress for quotas of money were not answered by the states; public credit was gone; commerce languished; justice was trampled underfoot; and we were contemptible in foreign eyes.

After meeting in Convention, the deputies from the states communicated their information to one another. On a review of our critical situation, and of the impossibility of introducing any degree of improvement into the old system, what ought they to have done? Would it not have been treason to return without proposing some scheme to relieve their distressed country? [As to] "We, the people," I ask, why not? . . . If the government is to be binding on the people, are not the people the proper persons to examine its merits or defects? I take this to be one of the least and most trivial objections that will be made to the Constitution; it carries the answer with itself.

Mason replied to Randolph that whether the Constitution were good or bad, it clearly provided a national authority, with a taxing power "calculated to annihilate totally the state governments" and with a judiciary so compelling as to make it doubtful, in view of human thirst for power, "whether a consolidated government can preserve the freedom and secure the rights of the people." Madison, Pendleton, and "Light Horse Harry" Lee rejoined with assurances against federal aggrandizement.

Henry refused to let his fears be lulled. "Here is a revolution [37]

---

[37] As Beveridge remarks, this is the word reported by Robertson but Elliot misprinted it "resolution."

as radical as that which separated us from Great Britain." Not only is the sovereignty of the states to be relinquished, but freedom of the press, trial by jury, and all immunities are to be made insecure. "Guard with jealous attention the public liberty. Suspect every one who approaches that jewel. Unfortunately, nothing will preserve it but downright force. Whenever you give up that force, you are inevitably ruined!" The danger is not from abroad, as the nationalists think, but from domestic tyrants. "A standing army we shall have, also, to execute the execrable commands of tyranny; and how are you to punish them? . . . Will your mace-bearer be a match for a disciplined regiment?" After much more, he concluded for that day: "I have, I fear, fatigued the committee; yet I have not said the one hundred thousandth part of what I have on my mind, and wish to impart." Day after day he thundered other fractions of his thoughts, as the many details of the Constitution were considered.

In equally persistent reply Madison stressed the drastic need of effective authority, denied the prospect of invasive or oppressive government, and besought a trust in the virtuous moderation of the men whom an enlightened and alert people would elect in representation.

Marshall, more plausibly than truly, said: "In this country there is no exclusive personal stock of interest. The interest of the community is blended and inseparably connected with that of the individual. When he promotes his own, he promotes that of the community." In this best of possible countries, granting ratification, in the best of possible worlds, he denied all menace except from foreign foes; and he warned the Kentuckians in particular that a feeble government could not protect their navigation. Neither from Congress, the President, or the courts, he said, was infringement of rights to be feared.

Contemning such cult of smugness, Mason spoke of ulterior motives: "There are many gentlemen in the United States who think it right that we should have one great, national, consolidated government, and that it was better to bring it about slowly and imperceptibly than all at once. . . . I know, from my own knowledge, many worthy gentlemen of the . . . opinion." Here Madison interrupted to demand whether this implication was intended to fit him; and Mason, exonerating all the Virginia delegation at Philadelphia, dropped the pregnant theme.

Henry appealed to state pride:

THE FRAME OF INDEPENDENCE

> Is the government of Virginia a state government after this government is adopted? I grant that it is a republican government, but for what purposes? For such trivial domestic considerations as render it unworthy the name of a legislature. . . . Does it not insult your judgments to tell you, Adopt first, and then amend! . . . You agree to bind yourselves hand and foot—for the sake of what? Of being unbound. You go into a dungeon —for what? To get out. Is there no danger, when you go in, that the bolts of federal authority shall shut you in? Human nature never will part from power.

He appealed to Southern fears as to slavery. Those in authority, he said, "will not reason with you about the effect of this Constitution. . . . They will construe it as they please. . . . Among ten thousand *implied powers* which they may assume, they may, if we be engaged in war, liberate every one of your slaves." In its general defense and welfare clauses, the Constitution "speaks to the point: they have the power in clear, unequivocal terms, and will clearly and certainly exercise it. As much as I deplore slavery, I see that prudence forbids its abolition. . . . The majority of Congress is to the north, and the slaves are to the south. In this situation I see a great deal of the property of the people of Virginia in jeopardy, and their peace and tranquillity gone." He appealed also to the fears of Kentuckians as to the Mississippi, for the votes of their fourteen delegates might control Virginia's decision.[38]

But, continuing to voice, as he said, the sentiments of the yeomen, Henry saw toward the end that he was contending in vain against firm rebuttal, expert maneuver, and the heavy pressure of Washington's influence. At a late stage he said that if ratification without prior amendment were voted, he would "go home" and await a volcanic outburst of the people's fury. Randolph begged him to withdraw his threat of secession: "Such an idea of refusing to submit to the decision of the majority is destructive of every republican principle. It will kindle a civil war, and reduce everything to anarchy and confusion. To avoid a calamity so lamentable, I would submit to it, if it contained greater evils than it does." Madison, echoing this, added a pledge that the friends of ratification would labor in good faith to procure through subsequent amendment such of Henry's "long train of alterations" as were not "palpably and insuperably objectionable." And Henry, conscious of "being overpowered in a good cause," agreed not to bolt: "I will be a peaceable

[38] It was actually the change of sides by four Kentuckians and a few others which made ratification possible.

citizen. My head, my hand, and my heart, shall be at liberty to retrieve the loss of liberty, and remove the defects of that system in a constitutional way."

The proponents of ratification then offered a resolution written with concession and finesse by George Wythe:

Whereas the powers granted under the proposed Constitution are the gift of the people, and every power not granted remains with them, [no official or branch of the government of the United States has authority to modify the scope of power or to restrain,] among other essential rights, liberty of conscience and of the press. . . .

And whereas any imperfections which may exist in the said Constitution ought rather to be examined in the mode prescribed therein for obtaining amendments, than by a delay, with a hope of obtaining previous amendments, to bring the Union into danger—

Resolved, That . . . the said Constitution be ratified. But in order to relieve the apprehensions of those who may be solicitous for amendments,—

Resolved, That . . . whatsoever amendments may be deemed necessary be recommended to the consideration of the Congress which shall first assemble under the said Constitution. . . .

In substitute a resolution was offered that previous to ratification a declaration of rights together with amendments "ought to be referred by this Convention to the other states in the American confederacy for their consideration." This was defeated by vote of 80 ayes to 88 noes, and the original motion was then adopted by 89 against 79. Finally a committee comprising the leading speakers on both sides of the debate was appointed to recommend amendments, and a long schedule of sharply restrictive changes which it reported was adopted as Virginia's proposals to Congress.

Henry had his way, for what it was worth, in the session of the legislature which followed upon the convention's heels. By large majorities it asserted that freemen's rights were unsafe under the Constitution and urged Congress, in prevention of "those grave disorders which must arise under a government not founded on the confidence of the people," to call a second convention to make changes. It furthermore elected to the federal Senate, over Madison's candidacy, two men who had opposed ratification; and when fixing districts for elections to Congress it gerrymandered the state against the Constitution's friends. At the polls in 1789, however, the citizens elected Madison over Monroe to Congress, and otherwise gave evidence that opposition to the routine functioning of the Constitution

THE FRAME OF INDEPENDENCE

would not be sanctioned by them. Henry, having no more obstructive resources, went to sulk in his tent; but, unlike Achilles, his final emergence was on the side of the Trojans.

Madison in Congress, to the sharp chagrin of Hamilton and Marshall, showed a firm adherence to the restraints of the Constitution as expounded by him in *The Federalist* and at Richmond and as confirmed by the Tenth Amendment. With his help Jefferson took the lead of those contending for administration in the strict spirit in which the Constitution had been ratified. Henry, the guide of Jefferson's novitiate, had repudiated him once for all in 1781; and Madison he never liked or approved. But Marshall was a personal favorite even when an antagonist in policy. Now, in his resentful old age, Washington's offers of high office, which he declined, made him responsive to Marshall's blandishments; and in 1798 he stood as a Federalist candidate for the Virginia legislature. He defeated young John Randolph, a worthy foeman on the hustings, but died before the time came to play his reversed rôle at Richmond.

* * *

Maryland in this period gave echo to Virginia, with voice less reverberant and emphasis different in detail.

The gentry had strength to shape a constitution in their interest in 1776 and to prevent its replacement for sixty-five years. Not only did this require large property holdings in qualification for office, but it guarded the senate from popular pressure by providing indirect election at five-year intervals. At the polls in each county two persons were to be chosen, and one in each of the cities, Baltimore and Annapolis, all to meet as an electoral college, to choose the fifteen senators—six dwelling east of the Chesapeake and nine living west of the bay. As intended, the senate proved a moderating factor, usually thwarting the projects of the lower house for loyalist spoliation, test acts, and paper money. Samuel Chase and Luther Martin, equivalents of Patrick Henry in a minor field, were foiled repeatedly, while the grandee Carrolls, Tilghmans, and Howards held main sway.

A characteristic issue concerned facilities for education. In 1782 the legislature founded Washington College at Chestertown on the Eastern Shore, granting it an annual subvention. Delegates from the Western Shore soon asked an equivalent, and St. John's College at Annapolis was established on a similar basis, the two to constitute the University of Maryland. A clamor against this budgeting of £3,000 a year arose from plain people saying that men sending sons to college ought to pay the full costs of education, and especially from innkeepers objecting to the tax on liquor-selling by which the money for the colleges was to be raised. Repeal was not accomplished.

In larger affairs, Maryland set on foot a movement by which Congress took over the western land claims of the several states, and she shared with Virginia the shaping of events which initiated the revamping of the Union. Among her delegates to the Philadelphia convention, however, Luther Martin and John F. Mercer withdrew in protest; and Martin at home wrote a vigorous memorial censuring the convention's extra-legal procedure and contending that the Constitution would emasculate state authority and imperil the liberties of citizens. The three who signed the Constitution, Daniel Carroll, Daniel of St. Thomas Jenifer, and especially James McHenry, defended it before the legislature against Martin's attack.

After lively discussions in the Baltimore press and on the stump, the citizens chose delegates favorable to ratification everywhere except in Ann Arundel, Harford, and Baltimore counties; and one of this contingent, William Paca, was content for Maryland to ratify if at the same time she would propose amendments. But before the convention assembled at Annapolis in April, 1788, the majority members agreed that, since opinions were already ripe, and since quick ratification would exert wholesome influence in other states, they would abstain from all debate. The minority, thus getting no replies to its arguments, talked itself out in a few days, whereupon ratification was carried by 63 votes against 11. After this the majority relaxed enough to let a committee consider Paca's amendments. But a wrangle over details embroiled this committee; and the convention adjourned without further action.[39]

Those who supported ratification were generally broad constructionists in the sequel, giving Maryland a prevailingly Federalist complexion; and when McHenry was made Secretary of War by Washington his alliance with Hamilton was almost a matter of course. More surprisingly Samuel Chase turned his coat in the

[39] The fragmentary records, including newspaper controversies, are analyzed by B. C. Steiner, "Maryland's Adoption of the Federal Constitution," in the *American Historical Review*, V, 1, 2 (Oct., Dec., 1899), pp. 22-44, 207-224.

THE FRAME OF INDEPENDENCE

middle of the 'nineties, but, unlike Patrick Henry, he took a seat on the bench of the Supreme Court in reward, adding a native truculence to the proverbial zeal of a proselyte. His rampant partisanship when in magisterial robes provoked John Randolph to procure in 1804 a vote of impeachment by the House of Representatives, but the Senate refused a conviction. Luther Martin also strangely turned Federalist before the century's end and printed savage onslaughts upon Jefferson. More light than is yet available would be welcome upon the mental histories of Henry, Chase, and Martin as belated converts to nationalism.

* * *

Kentucky's effective beginnings fell with the period of the American Revolution—an evidence, if any were needed, that among thousands of citizens the search for better lands was of keener concern than the redress of grievances or the vindication of continental independence.

The first project of government was of "Transylvania," impelled by Richard Henderson in 1775 in furtherance of his company's great speculation in lands.[40] On this occasion delegates of the two or three hundred settlers in the Bluegrass region met at the Boonesborough stockade and adopted laws to create courts, organize militia, fix official fees, prohibit Sabbath-breaking and profanity, improve the breed of horses, preserve the grazing, and check the destruction of game. But James Harrod, Benjamin Logan, and George Rogers Clark held aloof or turned against the premature project; and Clark traveled across the mountains to counter Henderson's plea for Transylvania's recognition. The Virginia assembly needed no hostile persuasion. It promptly destroyed the would-be commonwealth by making it a Virginia county. The land claim of Henderson's company was likewise denied except for a large tract about Green River as a solace.

Indian warfare, incited by the British, fills the Bluegrass chronicle for the next half-dozen years, while nevertheless a strong influx of settlers was rapidly swelling the population. The county was duly subdivided, and representatives increasingly took seats in the Virginia legislature. These voiced the local needs of roads and ferries and a fortification on the Ohio River where war-paths came from

[40] Henderson's purchase of Cherokee hunting grounds, extending nominally to the Ohio River, has been mentioned in the discussion of Tennessee.

the direction of Detroit. In intended compliance Clark, who held a general's commission from Virginia, was instructed to fortify; but he built works at Louisville only, which lay too far west for protective effect. His failure to block the line of danger was the first and chief persisting grievance of the Bluegrass people against Virginia's government.

But mere location on "western waters" beyond the mountains was more cogent than any concrete grievance in prompting a movement for separation. Virginia was wisely not averse to her daughter's membership in the sisterhood of states, though she was disposed to make stipulations concerning public lands and a sharing of her own public debt. Long parleys ensued, involving sessions by ten conventions in Kentucky between 1784 and 1792 before fruition was reached. Part of the delay came from Indian hostilities, part from Congressional procrastination, part from the desire of many citizens for complete independence rather than membership in the Union. Relations with Spain and her huge, almost empty, province of Louisiana were part of the complex, and James Wilkinson was the self-appointed chief negotiator.

Suave and fluent, acute and enterprising, Wilkinson, after a checkered career in the Continental army, migrated in 1784 to the new zone of opportunity. He was avid for both wealth and fame, ambitious, in his own words, to become the "Washington of the West." The time seemed propitious. Thirty thousand people, including many slave-holders, were settled in and about the Bluegrass; and so many more were coming every year that old-timers could prosper by merely supplying fresh arrivals with foodstuffs and breed-stock. The pioneer phase was ended; planters, merchants, and politicians were taking charge with a sharp eye to commercial outlet, for outlet downstream there must be if prosperity was to continue.

The Spanish government was aware that its own tenure of New Orleans and its hinterland was made precarious by the surge of people into the Kentucky-Tennessee region. Obstruction of exports might slacken the migration slightly; liberal policy might engage good-will; and a shrewd combination or alternation of these programs might even convert Protestant western Americans into subjects or allies of His Most Catholic Majesty. Wilkinson with a plausible tongue in his cheek went to New Orleans for a long visit

THE FRAME OF INDEPENDENCE 57

in 1787 to capitalize this dilemma for his own advantage.[41] His proposal was that Spain engage friendship among influential Kentuckians by giving them special privileges of export, or that she make upper Louisiana so attractive by means of generous land grants, religious freedom, and political and commercial privilege that Kentucky would be depopulated by stampede across the Mississippi; and in either case he proposed himself as the sole agent of Spain in Kentucky and Tennessee, vested with monopoly control of downstream trade in order that he might create a clique among the citizens with a view to separation of the district from the United States. He suggested also that a salary would be welcome. Miro and Navarro, governor and intendant of Louisiana, forwarded Wilkinson's memorial to Madrid with warm endorsements. After much deliberation the Spanish ministry made Wilkinson its agent, eventually with a stipend but never with such powers as he desired; and it proclaimed a welcome to all comers into Louisiana and West Florida with full toleration of such religions as they might bring. An experiment in liberalism already made in the neighborhood of Natchez was a favorable precedent in this departure from Spain's historic policy.

As to settlers who should continue to dwell upon Ohio tributaries, traffic to New Orleans was now permitted under mild taxation, and Spain stood ready for negotiation if they should secede from the Union; but she refused to give aid or incitement in advance of a stroke for independence. With Judge Harry Innes and Benjamin Sebastian as his chief colleagues, Wilkinson continued an endeavor to play Spain against the United States for personal profit until commercial rights on the Mississippi were assured in 1795 by Thomas Pinckney's treaty.

Meanwhile Kentucky was admitted in 1792 as a state in the Union, with Virginia's consent and without an intervening territorial status. Her constitution of that year was the first in America to vest suffrage in all adult male freemen. As a restraint upon popular impulse it provided for election of governor and senate by an electoral college on the Maryland pattern; but this was deleted before the century's end. A more lasting provision forbade the legis-

[41] Wilkinson was not in purpose a traitor to the United States, but merely a frontier diplomat of more shrewdness than honesty. R. S. Cotterill, *History of Pioneer Kentucky* (Cincinnati, 1917), p. 214; A. P. Whitaker, *The Spanish-American Frontier, 1783–1795* (Boston, 1927), *passim*.

lature to pass laws for emancipating slaves without procuring the prior consent of their owners and making full compensation for their value. Kentucky was destined never to have a large ratio of Negroes in her population, but her prevailing sentiment was firm that such blacks as there were should not be freed from restraint nor their property value be destroyed.

* * *

If this chronicle were more detailed it would show still greater variety among people, states and localities. Men when they thought of public affairs at all were, as usual, thinking of many things in a complex of pressures. They were citizens of the several states and of the United States, residents of some distinctive region, possessors or not of lands or slaves, bonds or stocks or merchandise; they were debtors or creditors or both at once, they were planters, farmers, merchants, manufacturers, lawyers, carriers, artisans, or several of these combined; they were plain or pretentious, frugal or lavish, vigorous or indolent, cautious or impulsive, partisan or neutral. They were of all sorts and conditions, reflecting in their public responses an endless diversity of predilection, circumstance, and contact. They combined in large numbers to support any program only by compromise among themselves or by yielding to argument or emotional appeal. When like met like, a cohesion was probable unless prevented by personal grudge, as of Henry against Jefferson. When unlike met unlike, alliance was yet possible by bargain or by defensive combination against some third element of common and stronger dislike.

In the welter which followed the stroke for independence, doctrines and projects and the men who promoted them rose and fell. The pendulum of policy swung and swung again. In 1776 it reached extreme left in the preamble of the Declaration; in 1787 it swept far to the right in the Constitution, but not as far as the Federalist party soon carried it. Statesmen and the people corrected this in due time, for the many local communities which were now combined into one body politic were prevailingly moderate. Men talked much of "fundamental principles" whether of the left or of the right, and somewhat honestly considered their opponents obsessed.[42] But in sober consciousness men were aware that liberty and

[42] For example one Alexander Kelly wrote from Virginia in 1802 to his brother in Kentucky: "I am now keeping bachelor's hall and expect to remain in that

property were combined in the popular esteem, that continuity was cherished as against revolution, and that conflicts of debate were concerned with emphasis, devices, and matters of detail. In short, mutual trust exceeded mutual distrust between men, states, and regions.

As regards Negro slavery in particular, prophecy, true or false, was required for anyone in the eighteenth century to foresee or pretend to foresee disturbance through government action. The few, such as Rawlins Lowndes and Patrick Henry, who viewed with alarm the prospect of a Northern destruction of the South's régime were manifestly seeking something with which to produce a dread, using a stalking horse for a purpose which was not itself derived from a contemplation of race relations. Their colleagues and constituents refused to become perturbed. By general agreement, explicit or implicit from Florida to Canada, Negroes were a permanently inferior caste, and property in slaves, like property in general, was quite secure within any commonwealth as against extraneous interference. Holders of slaves and dwellers in zones of heavy black population were therefore free to function in politics as if their possessions and their neighborhoods were of no peculiar type.

The prevailing unconcern of the rice planters was eloquent of social and pecuniary confidence. Charleston, the forum of parishes crowded with Negroes in huge ratio, was then and afterward the point at which any fever in the Southern pulse would first and most palpably be felt. The Pinckneys, the Rutledges, and the rest could not have shared in the ratification of the Constitution or in the broad construction of it had they believed federal or national authority to carry menace to the local structure. As yet, indeed, the South as a conscious entity was emergent only now and then, here and there. It had no prior coherence, no constitutional status, and seemingly no cogent occasion to procure specific establishment. For the time being and until further notice public attention in the main was otherwise absorbed.

---

line untill I explore the rich lands of Kentucky etc., which I shall shortly do, unless am prevented by the hostile and overruling conduct a people in them parts, term'd Democrats, who as I am inform'd have shut their ears and lock'd up their senses to the sound reasonings of a moderate Federalist, I say moderate because the term is justly applied, whereas to show me a moderate democrat would be almost an impossibility, or rather, a wonder of wonders." *William and Mary College Quarterly*, XVII, 28.

CHAPTER III

THE VIRGINIA DYNASTY

E Pluribus Unum! The many states had formed a "more perfect union"; and Alexander Hamilton was reshaping it again as a paradise for investors and speculators in bonds and stocks. Madison in the House and Jefferson in the cabinet challenged the bill for the United States Bank as exceeding the constitutional authority; but Hamilton and his lieutenants persuaded Washington and Congress that what was expedient was "necessary and proper." The national debt was funded as another item in the program; and with Jefferson's aid in trading a few votes to procure a Potomac location for the future capital city, Congress assumed the revolutionary debts of such states as still owed them. To complete the series a tariff was enacted, essentially to furnish revenue but in some particulars explicitly protective. An architect of nationality was laying the base of a colossal structure, cementing it with money-baron appetite for profits and privilege. The land-barons and the plain farmers were dubious at best about all this; the localists and individualists of every stripe resisted at every stage but without avail. Hamilton, his groundwork mightily done, withdrew from office, though not from politics; John Adams followed Washington in the presidency; the Federalist party through the Sedition Act made forthright opposition a crime; and partisan judges clapped editors and pamphleteers into jail. The country needed a redeemer. Jefferson was at hand.

Hamilton's preferred pattern for America, as he said in the Philadelphia Convention, was that of Great Britain with king, lords, and commons, or at least with life-time service for President and senators. He wanted to merge the several states completely, thus avoiding at once and always embarrassment from pretense of state sovereignty. Failing of these desires, he wrought with the tools permitted him to make his country a power on the model of Western Europe, with a standing army, strong navy, varied and ready resources—authoritative in a hemisphere, capable of holding its own and gaining more. He was not far from Napoleonic a little

THE VIRGINIA DYNASTY

before Napoleon's imperial phase. But his personal ambition for exploits as a commander in the field was thwarted when Adams avoided war with revolutionary France.

Jefferson, after his one repented bargain, pulled an opposite oar, not for the sake of opposition [1] but because the destiny he desired for the country was in another direction. Knowing the capitals and courts of Europe, he liked them not, but he loved the life and simple order of his own wholesome neighbors amid the Virginia hills. His hope was for a federation of such communities, great enough to fend off external threats, enlightened enough to cultivate science and art, sturdy enough to cherish free manhood rather than wealth or prestige, firm enough to keep its government frugal. With some rhapsody he had said in his *Notes on Virginia:*

> Those who labour in the earth are the chosen people of God, if ever he had a chosen people, whose breasts he has made his peculiar deposite for substantial and genuine virtue. . . . Corruption of morals . . . is the mark set on those, who not looking up to heaven, to their own soil and industry, as does the husbandman, for their subsistence, depend for it on casualties and caprice of customers. Dependence begets subservience and venality. . . . The mobs of great cities add just so much to the support of pure government, as sores do to the strength of the human body.[2]

His imaginative ambition for a commonwealth of orderly freedom was cherished as long as he lived. Possession of land by most of the voters he thought essential. Happily the wilderness had space, in his reckoning, to supply homesteads for the prospective increase of the population for a century or two; and by generous administration of the public domain he would facilitate every man's becoming a proprietor. A stake in the country and a self-reliant farmer's life would give the typical citizen a disposition to choose wise officials and watch their conduct. To make the watching more effective Jefferson would vest all feasible functions in the local governments, entrusting only the necessary residue to the higher and more distant functionaries. Furthermore he wanted "checks and balances" at every point in the governmental structure to prevent magnification of office, abuse of power, and infringement of the people's liberty. In theory, therefore, he was not a sheer democrat, wishing merely that the people's will or impulse prevail; he was instead a federative republican, strongly concerned with safeguarding the

[1] In fact, with regret at its embarrassment of Washington.
[2] Query XIX.

liberty of citizens even against the mass of the citizens themselves.

All this, he thought, was not likely to be set up at one time for endless enjoyment by posterity, but if and when the structure sagged it was to be rebuilt and improved by the successive generations. He doubted that Europeans or South Americans could construct such a happy system at all; but in the people of the United States he had a staunch confidence, and for them a fervent hope.

His philosophy was not distilled from the distinctive Southern order, for it gave no sanction to racial caste and specifically none to Negro slavery. It was derived rather from the libertarian theories then current in Europe and was reinforced in his mind by contemplation of an idealized American West. Its appeal to Southerners lay in its exaltation of agrarian virtues, its live-and-let-live regional implications, and its engaging universality. Its impingements upon slavery were diminished by Jefferson himself when politics made quietism expedient.

* * *

The sage of Monticello was not by predilection a party man; his addiction to thinking vigorously for himself makes it obvious that he would prefer unrestraint for his own expressions. It was the force of circumstance, under the shaping hand of Hamilton, which gave his course a party channel. He could not check or conquer the prevailing trend of policy except by making a phalanx of a multitude. This required colleagues and allies, conference and correspondence, give and take. It required a flood of editorials, pamphlets, and oratory, none of which he furnished in person.

Mute as to public speech, by reason of a very weak voice, but eloquent with his pen and captivating in conversation, Jefferson used assiduously the talents he had. Few Virginians of prominence except Marshall and Henry, and Washington when persuaded by Hamilton, could resist his arguments and his charm. His flights of optimistic fancy might not be followed, but his concrete plans found ready support. Madison was his right-hand man, and Monroe not much less. John Taylor and Spencer Roane lent special zeal for the rights of the states as a safeguard of liberty. William B. Giles, the most powerful debater in Congress before John Randolph's arrival, was a ready colleague against Northern and Federalist aggrandizement. The Nicholas brothers and scores of others with lesser talent or authority were willing workers in the field. Some of these had a democratic fervor, invigorated by the French Revolution; some were incensed by Britain's infringements of neutral rights at sea; the strongest, it seems, were prompted by concern for liberty and local autonomy, or by loyalty to Virginia, or by repugnance to Northeastern money-jobbing spoliation. Several of these promptings, as in Jefferson's own case, might impel one man; and, as Randolph proved, a spirit of aristocracy need not keep one aloof.

Madison had little concern with social theory but much with concrete statecraft. Studious and scholarly by habit, he relished his participation in formative affairs. Thanks to his own copious journal of proceedings in the Philadelphia convention, which was not published until 1819, he was the best informed of all men upon what the specifications of the Constitution meant in the minds of those who had phrased it. A joint author of the *Federalist* essays and a strong advocate of ratification on the hustings and in the Virginia convention, he was acquainted in full with the arguments for and against adoption and with the pledges by which majority qualms in pivotal states had been sufficiently quieted. The Constitution itself did not provide quite as much concentration of power as he had wished; and a knowledge of this led Hamilton to think that Madison would in coming years work, like himself, to procure a broad construction of its terms. But Madison was no Machiavelli. He cherished the Union and in good faith its Constitution as understood by those who had established it. Abiding by his own pledges, he would not sanction an assumption of unintended powers except in case of great need. Like a gyroscopic stabilizer on a great ship, he functioned to keep the trim against the buffets of a stormy sea. Hamilton and his followers delivered the buffets; Madison consistently countered them. His force may be measured by the chagrin of the Federalists. Hamilton said in 1792 that had he not expected Madison's continued alliance he would not have accepted the Secretaryship of the Treasury;[3] and in the middle of the decade Henry Lee wrote: "Better would it have been for the harmony and happiness of the United States if Mr. Madison, governed as he is at present, had originally been an opposer of the Constitution. Less weight and influence would have attached itself to his character; and conse-

[3] Hamilton to Edward Carrington, May 26, 1792, in H. C. Lodge, ed., *Works of Alexander Hamilton* (New York, 1886), VIII, 248–265.

quently the power he deservedly enjoys in the public opinion would be less operative in their decision on public questions." [4]

Monroe shared Madison's general outlook, pursuing a variant course only now and then. The chief of these occasions was when he opposed the ratification of the federal Constitution. It was on the ground of this item of record, and a slightly stronger adherence to strict construction in after years, that Randolph, Taylor, and some others preferred Monroe to Madison for the succession to Jefferson in the presidency. Monroe, however, had something of a chronic lethargy which reduced him to minor significance among his extremely vigorous colleagues.

* * *

John Taylor in the course of service in the Virginia legislature presumably found himself confused with other Johns in the large Taylor family. In identification he might have styled himself "of Hazelwood" according to the patrician practice exemplified by Charles Carroll of Carrollton and John Randolph of Roanoke. Instead, he appended "of Caroline," using the name of the county he represented. This was a gesture symbolizing his esteem for locality. To the same effect he used "A Citizen of Virginia" as an anonym in the first edition of his *Arator* essays. He consistently advocated home rule, with minimum rule for citizens an objective. He was a staunch and studious agrarian individualist, powerful on any floor but impatient when away from his home, his crops, and his books. A sentinel on constant alert, he preferred the pen to the tongue because writing could be done on the plantation, while speaking required sojourn elsewhere. A reluctant senator and state assemblyman from time to time, he was an eager contributor at all times to doctrines and plans of wholesome policy. Having opposed the federal Constitution when its ratification was pending, he was the first and long the leading philosopher of strict construction. All the others, including Jefferson and Madison, were in greater or less degree his pupils. His very dislike of public office made him free to maintain identical views through the decades till his death in 1824, while sundry contemporaries were turning somersaults in response to concrete exigencies. His conservatism in regard to slavery and his

---

[4] Lee to Iredell, January 21, 1795, in McRee, *Iredell*, II, 436. Like Henry, Chase, and Martin, Lee had about-faced since 1789.

THE VIRGINIA DYNASTY

disapproval of free Negroes, which we shall note again, combined with his predilection for agriculture and his antipathy to centralization in qualifying him to be a principal pioneer of Southern policy.

Entering the Senate in 1792, Taylor challenged the program of consolidation at all points, and upon resigning the seat after two years he continued the battle in pamphlets.[5] Discussing the Bank and the public debts, he showed, by mention of names, that most members of the two houses who supported Hamilton's policy were security-holders legislating in their own interest. Generalizing from this, he described the Federalist party as an embodiment of special interests bent upon rapacious and endless exploitation. He charged it also with creating useless offices in a system of patronage and with increasing taxation for expenditure in special, not general, interests. He called upon owners and cultivators of the soil, as the truly productive element, to stop this mulcting of themselves and crush the machinations before the "mischievous precedents" were "matured into . . . fundamental rules."

To prevent a tyranny by cliques and corporations, he thought it essential to guard against concentration of power. Hence his desire that the functions and authority of the several states be cherished as checks upon the central government and as protectors of regional welfare. In the federal system he considered that the state legislatures had "at least as good a right to judge of every infraction of the Constitution, as Congress itself,"[6] and on occasion he wanted an effective exercise of that right.

The vigor of Taylor's regional championship gave ground for surmise that he would favor a dismemberment of the Union. Rufus King of New York and Oliver Ellsworth of Connecticut sounded him upon this one day. Southern and Eastern interests, they said, were so incompatible that the Union could not survive; and plans for peaceful separation ought to be framed in avoidance of unfriendly procedure to the same end. Taylor concurred only as to

---

[5] *An Examination of the Late Proceedings in Congress respecting the Official Conduct of the Secretary of the Treasury* (1793); *A Definition of Parties, or the Political Effects of the Paper System Considered* (Philadelphia, 1794); *Enquiry into Principle and Tendencies of Certain Public Measures* (Philadelphia, 1794). Taylor's career is narrated in Henry H. Simms, *Life of John Taylor* (Richmond, Virginia, 1932); his doctrines are well analyzed in "The Political Ideas of John Taylor of Caroline" by Roy J. Kimmel, a Master of Arts essay, 1931, of which a typescript is on deposit in the library of Yale University.

[6] Taylor, *Enquiry into Principles*, p. 55.

preference for peaceful policy. He said that means were available to settle such inter-sectional questions as were then at issue, and he refused to participate in a separatist project.[7]

King and Ellsworth were expecting the control of Congress to pass into Republican hands. When the next few years continued the Federalists in power instead, and when impacts of the great war in Europe intensified American animosities, Congress adopted and President Adams approved the Alien and Sedition Acts which contemplated a sharp repression of political dissent. While these acts were pending, Taylor, then a member of the Virginia legislature, began to consider some counter-stroke. A letter of his to a congressman remarked a local tendency to estimate the separate mass of Virginia and North Carolina with a view to their separate existence. He spoke of this discussion as either not unwise or not unusual, according to diverse reading of a blurred script. The recipient showed the letter to Jefferson, then Vice-president, who wrote to Taylor with a calming purpose:

It it true that we are completely under the saddle of Massachusetts and Connecticut, and that they ride us very hard, cruelly insulting our feelings as well as exhausting our strength and subsistence. . . . But our present situation is not a natural one. The republicans through every part of the Union say that it was the irresistible influence and popularity of General Washington, played off by the cunning of Hamilton, which turned the government over to anti-republican hands, or turned the republicans chosen by the people into anti-republicans. [Time will erelong bring a change, Jefferson wrote.] Be this as it may, in every free and deliberating society, there must, from the nature of man, be opposite parties, and violent dissensions and discords; and one of these, for the most part, must prevail over the other for a longer or shorter time. Perhaps this party division is necessary to induce each to watch and delate to the people the proceedings of the other. But if on a temporary superiority of the one party, the other is to resort to a scission of the Union, no federal government can ever exist. [If New England were cut off, Jefferson wrote, a Pennsylvania and a Virginia party would arise in the residual confederacy; and so also if the Union should comprise only Virginia and North Carolina.] Seeing, therefore, . . . that we must have somebody to quarrel with, I would rather keep our New England associates for that purpose, than to see our bickerings transferred to others. They are circumscribed within such narrow limits, and their population so full, that their numbers will ever be the minority, and they are marked, like the Jews, with such a perversity of character, as to constitute, from that circumstance,

[7] Gaillard Hunt, ed., *Disunion Sentiment in Congress in 1794: a confidential Memorandum, hitherto unpublished, written by John Taylor of Caroline, Senator from Virginia, for James Madison* (Washington, 1905).

the natural division of our parties. . . . Better keep together as we are, haul off from Europe as soon as we can, and from all attachments to any portions of it; and if they show their power just sufficiently to hoop us together, it will be the happiest situation in which we can exist.[8]

In reply Taylor declined to be solaced. A reversal of control, he said, would not stop the course of usurpation. "A Southern aristocracy oppressing the Northern states would be as detestable as a Northern domineering over the Southern states." The need of the times was a restraint of power. "The right of the state governments to expound the Constitution might possibly be made the basis of a movement toward its amendment. If this is insufficient, the people in state conventions are incontrovertibly the contracting parties, and possessing the infringing rights, may proceed by orderly steps to attain the object."[9] Doubtless with a purpose of guiding some such transactions, Taylor had now procured again a seat in the Virginia legislature.

* * *

Jefferson believed that the "monarchizing" tendencies of the "Tories," as he now styled the Federalists, could be thwarted and a "Whig" control of the government be procured by the spread of pertinent information among the people and by some specific stroke to signalize the crisis. On the one hand he caused the launching of numerous Republican local newspapers. On the other hand he maneuvered for a stroke to be made with seeming spontaneity from some quarter distant from himself. Pursuing Taylor's idea, he framed a set of resolutions with an intention of arranging for their introduction into the legislature of North Carolina. But John Breckinridge, a prominent Republican assemblyman of Kentucky, learned of the document while on a Virginia visit and procured it for his commonwealth's use. These resolutions asserted that the general government of the United States was created by compact among the several states which by the Constitution delegated to it certain definite and specified powers, reserving each state to itself the residual mass of authority; that whenever the general government assumes undelegated powers, its acts are void and of no force; that the general government is not the judge of its own powers, but

---
[8] P. L. Ford, ed., *Works of Thomas Jefferson* (Federal Edition, New York, 1904), VIII, 431, 432, 433 (June 1, 1798).
[9] *John P. Branch Historical Papers*, II, 273-276 (June 25, 1798).

each state, as a party to the compact, has a right to judge of infractions and of the mode and measure of redress; that numerous proceedings of the general government had evinced a disposition to stretch the meaning of certain phrases in the Constitution, and in some time of tranquillity this ought to be restrained by amendment; but some recent legislation by Congress, including the Alien and Sedition Acts, called for immediate redress as unwarranted infringements of liberty; that as a means of reclaiming the constitutional rights of the states and the people, and thereby preserving the Union in accordance with the plain intent and spirit of the compact, the senators and congressmen from Kentucky were enjoined to use their best endeavors to procure the repeal of the obnoxious acts, and all the sister states were called upon to concur in the pronouncement and the program.

When these resolutions, after slight revision, were introduced into the Kentucky House of Representatives in November, William Murray, a member from Franklin County, was almost alone in expressing opposition. If it were true, he said, that Congress had committed improprieties in its legislation, it was equally improper for a state legislature, with powers restricted by the state constitution, to usurp a function of censorship and pronounce void statutes of the United States. Breckinridge in reply said: "I consider the General Assembly as the grand inquest of the commonwealth. They are bound in duty, as well as by oath, to support their own as well as the Federal Constitution; and all attempts to violate either, from whatever quarter offered, demand their earliest consideration and reprehension." The resolutions were soon adopted, with negligible dissent in the House and none in the Senate.[10]

In furtherance of the same purpose Madison, with advice from Jefferson, framed a set of resolutions to much the same effect, though with a stronger assertion of loyalty to the Union. These were introduced into the Virginia House of Delegates by John Taylor in December. A debate ensued which was currently thought important enough to warrant stenographic report and publication. Sundry members in opposition expressed faith in the sagacity of

[10] Jefferson's authorship was kept a strict secret for many years. His rough draft and his fair copy are in Ford, ed., *Works of Thomas Jefferson*, VIII, 458–479. The resolutions as adopted are, like those of Virginia, printed in many publications. The speeches of Murray and Breckinridge are reprinted from the Frankfort *Palladium* of November 13 and 20, 1798, in E. D. Warfield, *The Kentucky Resolutions of 1798* (New York, 1887), pp. 87–95. Warfield contends fallaciously that Breckinridge contributed a substantial element of authorship in these resolutions.

Congress and alarm that Virginia's action might produce tumult and armed conflict. Those in support viewed with dread a prospect of Federal oppression and praised the resolutions as a completely placable appeal to reason. Taylor as the chief protagonist virtually confessed a party purpose: "Are the republicans," said he, "possessed of fleets and armies? If not, to what could they appeal for defence and support? To nothing, except public opinion. If that should be against them, they must yield." [11] No speaker on either side alluded to the provision which the Virginia legislature had made at the beginning of that year for the construction of a state armory. The silence on this point is evidence that all concerned were quite convinced that hostilities against the United States were not in contemplation.[12] The resolution, after the deletion of a few especially stringent words, was adopted by votes of 100 to 63 in the House and 14 to 3 in the Senate.

The logic which had produced the Kentucky and Virginia Resolutions was inverse to that which the documents themselves displayed. The need was to restore freedom of speech on public matters. The legislature of a state having no specific standing for championing personal immunity as against Congress, argument was required in behalf of such a standing; and this argument involved an exaltation of the several states as creators of the Union and as authoritative interpreters of the Constitution as a compact. Quite excluded from the phrasing, but clearly known to politicians of every stripe, was the purpose of making capital for the Republican party.

All of the states lying northward of the Potomac made adverse replies, for the very good reason that their legislatures in 1799 were controlled by Federalist majorities. Most of these merely declared the Alien and Sedition Acts to be wholesomely valid and asserted that a state legislature was without authority to pronounce them void. The Vermont legislature alone denied the contractual theory of the Constitution: "The people of the United States formed the federal constitution, and not the states or their legislatures." Not

[11] *Debates in the House of Delegates of Virginia, upon Certain Resolutions before the House, upon the Important Subject of the Acts of Congress passed at their Last Session, commonly called the Alien and Sedition Laws* (Richmond, 1798), p. 124.
[12] Some historians have assumed a connection of purpose between the Armory Act and these resolutions. Philip G. Davidson; in his "Virginia and the Alien and Sedition Laws," *American Historical Review*, XXXVI, 2 (January, 1931), pp. 336–342, has demolished the surmise.

all the Federalists were willing to say this, for it meant the burning of a bridge which might be valuable as an exit in case the tide of sectional strife should be reversed. For example William Cobbett, the foremost of their journalists, remarked in reply to a Virginia pamphleteer:

> Does he imagine, that the industrious and orderly people of New England will ever suffer themselves to be governed by an impious philosopher or a gambling profligate [*i.e.*, Jefferson], imposed upon them by Virginian influence? . . . The New Englnders . . . know their own value; they feel their strength, and they will have their full share of influence in the federal government, or they will not be governed by it. It is clear, that their influence must decrease; because every man has a vote, and the middle and southern states are increasing in inhabitants, five times as fast as New England is. If Pennsylvania joins her influence to that of New England, the balance will be kept up; but, the moment she decidedly throws it into the scale of Virginia, the balance is gone, New England loses her influence in the national government, and she establishes a government of her own.[13]

Both sides, indeed, wanted avoidance of a severe constitutional crisis; and by mutual forbearance the question of ultimate authority was allowed to subside. Jefferson, having attained his limited objective, counseled his lieutenants to maintain a passive firmness. The Kentucky legislature in the fall of 1799 declared again that the several states, having established the Constitution and "being sovereign and independent, have the unquestionable right to judge of the infraction," and explicitly *"That a Nullification by those sovereignties, of all unauthorized acts done under color of that instrument is the rightful remedy"*; but as to the Alien and Sedition Acts it merely made a solemn protest. The Virginia legislature soon afterward adopted a voluminous committee report, written by Madison, which rebutted all the replies by the Northern states. This was rather a disquisition on the nature of the Union than a piece of crisis-propaganda, and it concluded with a mere iteration of Kentucky's protest. It was to serve in after years, however, as a manual for those who sought grounds of restraining central aggrandizement. The culminating passages were as if in reply to John Marshall's future pronouncements from the bench:

[13] Frank M. Anderson, "Contemporary Opinion of the Virginia and Kentucky Resolutions," *American Historical Review*, V, 1, 2 (Oct., Dec., 1899 [sic]), pp. 45–63, 225–252. The quotation of Cobbett, from the *Country Porcupine*, April 1, 1799, is given by Anderson on p. 50.

THE VIRGINIA DYNASTY

The Constitution of the United States was formed by the sanction of the states, given by each in its sovereign capacity. . . . It follows of necessity that there can be no tribunal above their authority to decide, in the last resort, whether the compact made by them be violated; and, consequently, that, as parties to it, they must themselves decide, in the last resort, such questions as may be of sufficient magnitude to require their interposition. . . .
But it is objected that the judicial authority is to be regarded as the sole expositor of the Constitution in the last resort. . . . On this objection it might be observed, *first,* that there may be instances of usurped power which the Constitution would never draw within the control of the judicial department; *secondly,* that if the decision of the judiciary be raised above the authority of the sovereign parties to the Constitution, the decisions of the other departments, not carried by the forms of the Constitution before the judiciary, must be equally authoritative and final with the decisions of that department. [Any "last resort" authority which the Federal judiciary has, therefore,] must necessarily be deemed the last in relation to the authorities of the other departments of the Government; not in relation to the rights of the parties to the constitutional compact, from which the judicial as well as the other departments hold their delegated trusts.[14]

The states to the southward abstained from action for or against the Virginia-Kentucky pronouncements. The presidential campaign, which had evoked the whole maneuver, called for no more constitutional ado, for its result was known to hang upon voting in the city of New York, where syllogisms were of no concern but where the power of Tammany Hall and the manipulations of Aaron Burr were to be decisive.

* * *

When promoting his candidacy by private correspondence Jefferson wrote a personal platform. He wanted the Constitution preserved in its original intent, the reserved rights of the states respected and the powers of Congress not absorbed by the President; he was for a rigorously frugal and simple government, and against a multiplication of officers in order to make partisans; he wanted no standing army and a minimum navy.

I am for free commerce with all nations; political connection with none; & little or no diplomatic establishment. And I am not for linking ourselves by new treaties with the quarrels of Europe; entering that field of slaughter to preserve their balance, or joining in the confederacy of kings

[14] Hunt, ed., *Writings of Madison,* VI, 349–352.

to war against the principles of liberty. I am for freedom of religion & ... freedom of the press. ... And I am for encouraging the progress of science in all it's branches; and not for raising a hue and cry against the sacred name of philosophy; for awing the human mind ... to believe that government, religion, morality & every other science were in the highest perfection in ages of the darkest ignorance, and that nothing can ever be devised more perfect than what was established by our forefathers.[15]

To much the same effect was his inaugural address; and his actual administration was in consonance. With Madison and Gallatin in the cabinet, Nathaniel Macon Speaker of the House, Randolph chairman of the Ways and Means committee, and similar talent in control of the Senate, the team work was excellent for several years, and the prevailing spirit magnanimous. Some abuses committed by the Federalists were corrected, but no reprisals were made on behalf of party or of region. If the South was in the saddle, no spur was on its heel, and the reins were softly held.

Mildness of purpose, however, could not assure a placid course of policy when the renewal of tremendous war in Europe set commerce askew, made American sailors liable to impressment on British warships, and put the political map of the whole western world at hazard.

Transactions in France had brought repercussions in the United States, and somewhat particularly in the South, before the turn of the century. On the one hand, approval of the French Revolution had impelled the forming of Democratic clubs in all the towns from Savannah to Boston, and these had facilitated the creation of the Republican party, which the Federalists insisted upon styling Democratic or Jacobin. On the other hand, there came upon all citizens who had a Negro problem in mind a conservative reaction in consequence of extreme disorders in the French colony of Haiti. First the free Negroes and then the slaves took arms against the whites, to slaughter whom they could and expel the rest. Hundreds of refugees took ship, with any slaves they might carry, to Norfolk, Charleston, Savannah, New Orleans, or Havana, spreading tales of horror and maxims against extending to Negroes anywhere the principles of *liberté, égalité, fraternité*. This influx of personnel and of knowledge emphasized the precariousness of white life amid black

[15] Letter to Elbridge Gerry, January 26, 1799, in Ford, ed., *Works of Thomas Jefferson*, IX, 18, 19.

masses and tended to stiffen the restraints under which the Negroes in the South passed their lives.

Meanwhile France, controlled by Bonaparte, utilized a brief peace with Britain for a campaign to resubjugate the Haitian blacks, and also procured a retrocession of the huge province of Louisiana from the palsied hands of Spain. But Toussaint L'Ouverture plus yellow fever destroyed the French forces in the island, and the resumption of British war made Louisiana impossible to hold. When, therefore, the American minister, prompted by Jefferson, offered to purchase the left bank of the Mississippi in assurance of a commercial outlet, Bonaparte offered to sell the whole of Louisiana instead, and a treaty to that effect was quickly drawn and signed.

* * *

This astonishing acquisition brought, soon or late, immense changes from prior expectations in the status and orientation of the United States, internal as well as external. It paved the way to Texas, Oregon, and California; it furnished Missouri and Kansas as grounds of inter-sectional strife. Though it seemingly gave chief increment to the South, it brought ultimate preponderance to the North, for "Louisiana" was a triangle with its apex on the Mexican Gulf and its base on the Canadian border.

These matters were mostly hidden to men of the day. The considerations impressive at the time were that the area of the United States was to be doubled; a wilderness procured into which cumbering Indian tribes might be shifted; all fear of restraints on the Mississippi trade relieved; the center of political gravity transferred perhaps across the Appalachian Mountains; and incidentally that the purchase itself was of questionable constitutionality.

That Jefferson was an expansionist is evidenced by his desire to possess New Orleans and Mobile, and perhaps by his dispatch of Lewis and Clark to spy the land as far as Oregon. He was also a constitutionalist; and the Constitution said nothing whatever of annexation. This was doubtless an oversight of the framers, for the prior Articles of Confederation had contained authorization, and the general purpose in 1787 was an increase of central power. But a strict constructionist was barred from seeking warrant in a hypothesis as to what the framers would have done had an oversight not occurred. Small accretions, Jefferson thought, might be made as rectifications of boundary; but a million square miles, occupied in part by citizens of un-English language, laws, and customs, was quite another matter.

The occasion was irresistible, and the terms of the treaty gave no time to procure an enabling amendment to the Constitution. Jefferson recommended ratification by the Senate, and he drafted a validating amendment. He wrote privately, and was inclined to say publicly:

> The Executive in seizing the fugitive occurrence which so much advances the good of their country, have done an act beyond the Constitution. The Legislature in casting behind them metaphysical subtleties, and risking themselves like faithful servants, must ratify & pay for it, and throw themselves on their country for doing for them unauthorized what we know they would have done for themselves had they been in a situation to do it.[16]

But, as his advisers were quick to say, an amendment might be defeated by New England, with most embarrassing results. These men accordingly sought warrant in theory. The logic of John Taylor as the strictest of constructionists is of particular note. The several states before forming the Union, he said, had possessed a power of acquiring territory; and this was a right somewhere still existing. The states when federating had merely relinquished to the central government as their agent all functions touching foreign lands and peoples; and that agency, as part of its function, must needs possess authority for annexation in behalf of the states collectively.[17] This was little more than common sense, yet it involved an implication of powers beyond the Constitution's literal text as truly as did any strokes of Hamilton or Marshall.

No one opposed this great expansion but the diminishing diehards of New England, who now conspired with Burr for an easterly secession. Their plans were foiled by the defeat of Burr for the governorship of New York and by Jefferson's landslide in a second election to the Presidency.

Before these episodes were closed, a Massachusetts congressman remarked a prospect of Northeastern solace and advantage. The people of the West, he said, had hitherto been under the control of Virginia and the Carolinas because in their frontier insecurity they

---
[16] Letter to John Breckinridge, August 12, 1803, in Ford, ed., *Works of Thomas Jefferson*, X, 7 n.
[17] *Annals of Congress*, 8th Cong., 1st sess., 50.

THE VIRGINIA DYNASTY

looked to these neighbors for aid and protection. But now that the frontier had been removed, they would seek their own interests. They were competitors with the South in the markets; they would ply their trade with the commercial states; and a Northern and Western coalition in politics was already the theme of conversation.[18]

As to constitutional interpretation another New Englander said in sardonic truth, "we the people care not a pin's point for it." [19] But most of the Northern Federalist politicians had already become strict constructionists, adopting flagrantly the localism of state sovereignty upon being ousted from the central control. The Federalists of the South, however, followed in the main a different course. No regional interests of theirs were in the range of potential menace; and when the Republicans began to take centralizing measures, the Pinckneys, Harper, Marshall, and their fellows found no reasons to reverse their doctrines for the mere sake of opposition. Maintaining until after Monroe's election the skeleton of a party machine, they continued to cast what influence they had in favor of nationality. Marshall in particular never faltered in this resolve. Appointed to his key position as a last act of Adams against the Republicans, he was building a special paradise for the Federal judiciary, and with Hamiltonian plausibility was acclimating Story and other Jeffersonian appointees therein.

As the Republicans multiplied and their opportunities and responsibilities enlarged, they became increasingly diverse among themselves. Those of New England were mostly mere underprivileged people seeking to diminish the local power of the well-born and to relax the control of the Congregational clergy. From New York to Maryland the party was a hodgepodge of the high, the middle, and the low, without a clear purpose beyond immediate selfish expediency. In the West, where lay Jefferson's main theoretical hope, Republicanism as a restraint upon government was being replaced by Democracy as a demand for effecting the people's will regardless of technicalities and implications. For example the Kentuckians, now finding their commonwealth central in an expanded country, were forgetting their stringent resolutions of 1798 and '99. Wanting improved roads and waterways at anyone's cost who

[18] Letter of Nahum Mitchell, Washington, March 12, 1804, to E. H. Robbins, quoted in Everett S. Brown, *The Constitutional History of the Louisiana Purchase* (Berkeley, California, 1920), pp. 145, 146. This monograph is an admirable study of transactions and opinions concerning Louisiana from 1803 to 1812.
[19] Fisher Ames, quoted by Brown, *ibid.*, p. 30.

would furnish the money, they were preparing to embrace Henry Clay's "American System" in due time. In South Carolina young Republicans were effectually the same in doctrine as old Federalists. In Georgia there was more quiescence than usual in Federal relations; and North Carolina's apathy was unbroken. Virginia remained as the chief cherisher of state rights, apart from New England's adventitious adherence; and when loyal sons of hers held sway in the White House, "the mother of presidents" had little ground for perturbation.

* * *

"The capital and leading object of the Constitution was," in the recurrent expressions of Jefferson, "to leave with the States all authorities which respected their own citizens only, and to transfer to the United States those which respected citizens of foreign or other States: to make us several as to ourselves, but one as to all others." [20] The severalness had been emphasized by him in prior years; but external pressure in his second term gave special need of oneness as against foreign impingements; and this continued through most of Madison's time in the White House. The Embargo and other devices of passive resistance failing to restrain invasion of neutral rights by the desperate Old World belligerents, the United States at length made war upon Britain as the chief oppressor of American commerce and seamen. Successive emergency measures were enacted, some of which involved use of doubtful powers.

New England protested with increasing vehemence. The legislature of Connecticut resolved in 1812 "that the state of Connecticut is a FREE, SOVEREIGN and INDEPENDENT state; that we are a confederated and not a consolidated republic"; and in 1814 the Massachusetts General Court resolved:

We spurn the idea that the free, sovereign and independent State of Massachusetts is reduced to a mere municipal corporation, without power to protect its people, and to defend them from oppression, from whatever quarter it comes. Whenever the national compact is violated, and the citizens of this state are oppressed by cruel and unauthorized laws, this legislature is bound to interpose its power, and wrest from the oppressor his victim.[21]

[20] *Writings of Thomas Jefferson* (Monticello Edition, Washington, 1904), XV, 448.
[21] H. V. Ames, ed., *State Documents on Federal Relations* (Philadelphia, 1906), pp. 61, 71.

In the same year Daniel Webster said in Congress when opposing a pending bill:

> The operation of measures thus unconstitutional & illegal ought to be prevented, by a resort to other measures which are both constitutional and legal. It will be the solemn duty of the State Governments . . . to interpose between their citizens & arbitrary power. These are among the objects for which the State Governments exist; & their highest obligations bind them to the preservation of their own rights & the liberties of their people. I express these sentiments here, Sir, because I shall express them to my constituents. . . . With the same earnestness with which I now exhort you to forbear from these measures, I shall exhort them to exercise their unquestionable right of providing for the security of their own liberties.[22]

The Hartford Convention at the turn of the year demanded restraining amendments to the federal Constitution, and called for another convention of aggrieved states to take drastic action in case New England's injuries were not ended within a few months.

What Madison would have done in the face of nullification or secession cannot be said, for peace with Great Britain relieved the crisis before any regional stroke forced his hand. The fact that New England's recalcitrance came in time of war made the rest of the country quite impatient of Yankee protests.

The Virginians in general swam with the current of nationalistic sentiment, and Monroe through two terms in the White House followed Madison's precedent, with Jefferson's advice, in sanctioning sundry measures of broad construction. Randolph, on the contrary, was alert for state rights; and Taylor and Roane were on a special *qui vive* to counter any strokes of Marshall from the bench of the Supreme Court.

* * *

Marshall used every slightest occasion to preach his authoritative gospel and entrench his position. In the case of Marbury *vs.* Madison in 1803 he went out of his way to say that the judiciary could declare void an act of Congress as unconstitutional; and in the made-up case of Fletcher *vs.* Peck, 1810, and again in the Dartmouth College case, he voided acts of state legislatures impairing obligation of contracts. In Martin *vs.* Hunter's Lessee, 1813, he began the

---

[22] C. H. Van Tyne, ed., *Letters of Daniel Webster* (New York, 1902), p. 67. Webster saved himself some later chagrin by keeping this speech out of print. It was found among his papers long after his death.

taking of appeals from state courts in cases involving federal treaties or statutes, and continued it in Cohens vs. Virginia, 1821. In McCulloch vs. Maryland, 1819, he sanctioned the congressional use of all expedient powers as if the government were not federal but national, and he declared that a state law conflicting with a valid national statute was void. In Gibbons vs. Ogden, 1824, he not only destroyed a state's grant of steamboating monopoly, but showed Congress how to stretch its commercial authority to huge dimensions. "All wrong," said Randolph, "but no man in the United States, can tell why or wherein." Taylor and Roane set themselves to prove Marshall's errors and if possible to find means of offsetting them.

Roane, whom Jefferson would have made Chief Justice of the United States had not Adams forestalled him by appointing Marshall, presided over the Virginia supreme court when the Hunter case came before its bench. The case, involving the Fairfax title to large tracts between the Potomac and Rappahannock rivers, had been adjudged in behalf of the Fairfax heirs by a local Virginia court. The supreme court of the state reversed the decision, and on treaty grounds appeal was taken to Marshall's court, which reversed Roane's and issued a mandamus commanding the Virginia supreme court to execute judgment in favor of the Fairfax heirs. Roane and his colleagues with one accord said that the federal courts had no appellate jurisdiction over those of the states, and refused to comply with the mandamus. Marshall's bench, however, triumphed in the end by rehearing the case and ordering the federal marshal in Virginia to put the Fairfax claimants into possession.

In the McCulloch case Roane could make no pronouncement from the bench, since his court was not involved; but as an outraged citizen, using *noms de plume* in the columns of the Richmond *Enquirer*,[23] he made strong protest against the "declaratory doctrines having the effect to change the Constitution." His arguments from the Kentucky and Virginia Resolutions and from Madison's report of 1800 were so cogent that Marshall exhorted his friends in Virginia to make counter-attacks. When these were not forthcoming, he took his court out of its way in the Cohens case to strike at Virginia's pretensions.

Under a Virginia law which made the selling of lottery tickets a

[23] These letters, and another series on the Cohens case, are reprinted in the *John P. Branch Historical Papers*, II, no. 1, pp. 51–121; no. 2, pp. 78–183.

misdemeanor, Cohens was fined by the borough court of Norfolk for selling tickets issued by a lottery licensed in the District of Columbia under an act of Congress. Appeal was taken not to a higher court of the state but to the Supreme Court of the United States. On behalf of Virginia as the defendant her attorneys argued that the federal court had no jurisdiction. The bench ruled in reply that all parties to suits in which rights were claimed under a federal statute might appeal to that court from a state court, regardless of whether a state was the other party. As to Cohens' fine, however, its imposition was upheld on the ground that Congress had explicitly not intended to force the lottery business into states having laws against it.

Roane, again having no official standing since the higher courts in Virginia were not involved, used the newspapers once more for a devastating onslaught.

> This most monstrous and unexampled decision [he wrote] completely negatives the idea that the American States have a real existence or are to be considered in any sense as sovereign and independent States. . . . This decision also claims the right to amend the federal constitution at the mere will and pleasure of the supreme court. . . . It does this at the instance of the petty corporation of the city of Washington, and the statute of Virginia is made to yield . . . by means of the most remote and unwarrantable implication. This decision does not admit the competency of the courts of the states to enforce their own penal laws against their own offending citizens. . . . Nor does it allow them to enforce an act made to promote the morality of their people. . . . It is of no account that . . . Virginia . . . is, indeed, permitted to retain the paltry sum of one hundred dollars. . . . Whenever the actual provisions of an act of Congress and of the ordinance consequent thereon shall show an intention that they should operate within the territories of the states a different decision would be given.

Returning to the case in hand, he said: "The opinion, besides being unusually tedious and tautologous, abounds in defects. . . . It often adopts premises which cannot be conceded, and takes for granted the very points which are to be proved." And one of these points he showed to be in sharp conflict with Marshall's own assertion when advocating that Virginia ratify the Constitution.[24] In

[24] In the Virginia convention of 1788 a member had argued that under the proposed Constitution the states might be subject to suit. Marshall replied: "I hope that no gentleman will think that a state will be called at the bar of the federal court. . . . It is not rational to suppose that the sovereign power should be dragged before a court." Elliot, ed., *Debates*, III, 555.

view of the chain of decisions now culminated, he said of Marshall's domination: "While that high court will scarcely allow that any other government, or any other department of its own government can do right, it acts upon the principle that itself is never in the wrong. . . . It challenges a degree of infallibility scarcely claimed by the arrogant pretensions of the former Popes of Rome." Roane wondered that men who had been appointed as Republicans to be Marshall's colleagues had so fallen under his malign sway that they concurred in such a tyrannous program, and he called upon Republicans at large to rouse from their slumbers and shift the government again, as in 1801, into safe channels. His letters made a notable stir; but his death in the next year ended his part in the fray.

* * *

To the same general purpose but in a more philosophic vein John Taylor continued to ply his pen, producing pamphlets no longer but books in boards and leather. The first [25] and stoutest of this political series was a somewhat rambling sequence of jottings, written through twenty years and provoked partly by the lucubrations of John Adams. It is heavily sprinkled with sagacious apothegms deprecating aristocracy, patronage, war, public debts, privileged banks, executive and magisterial encroachments, sedition laws, passive obedience, party zeal, and government by combination of special interests. For preserving freedom and equity he considered essential a multiplicity of checks within the frame of government. This, he thought, was ideally provided in the United States as intended by the framers of the Constitution, but was now imperiled through loose interpretation and through the grasp of power by parties. The Republicans were merely less of a menace than the Federalists, "outs and ins alternately demagogues and tools. . . . equally proper to delude a nation, and to exalt executive power, which sits in proud superiority, looking down upon the fraud and oppressions caused by itself." In an alternation of parties there was no prospect of reform:

Far from correcting the abuses with which they charge each other, their leaders, trusting to the pernicious doctrine of confidence and authority, will convert their mutual abuses into mutual precedents. Neither parties

[25] *Inquiry into the Principles and Policy of the Government of the United States* (Fredericksburg, Virginia, 1814). The writing was concluded in 1811, so there are no allusions to the War of 1812. Taylor's volume of *Arator* essays, which preceded this, is used elsewhere.

THE VIRGINIA DYNASTY

nor individuals will voluntarily diminish power in their own hands, however vicious they have declared it to be in the hands of others, because if they are vicious, they are willing to abuse it, if virtuous they presumptuously confide in their own moderation.[26]

The lapse of a further decade brought war, a second United States Bank, a protective tariff, a panic, the main series of Marshall's aggressions, and the Missouri crisis in inter-sectional politics. Taylor, now aged but still strong in the gospel of minimum rule, issued three volumes in the last four years of his life.[27] Of this group the first is by far the best. In it he said of sovereignty: "I do not know how it has happened, that this word has crept into our political dialect, unless it be that mankind prefer mystery to knowledge; and that governments love obscurity better than specification. . . . In fact, the term 'sovereignty' was sacrilegiously stolen from the attributes of God, and impiously assumed by kings. Though they committed the theft, aristocracies and republicks have claimed the spoil." Against the "supremacy" claimed by Marshall he contended at every point. On the protective tariff he was equally severe: "It destroys the freedom of labour, and enables government to subject it to the cupidity of combinations or individuals. . . . It corrupts congress and endangers the union, by making a geographical majority an object of solicitude, for the purpose of obtaining geographical advantages."[28] The vice of cultivating regional solidarity in politics, he said, was exemplified in the Missouri question, which would receive no hearing in Congress were there not other grounds for desiring to consolidate sectional sentiment.

The deaths of Roane, Taylor, and Jefferson in rapid sequence marked the passing of a generation; and about the same time the Virginia dynasty was ended. Taylor and Roane, partly because they had little or no federal responsibility, clung to their pristine doctrines through their long lives. Jefferson, Madison, and Monroe, facing concrete occasions when in presidential office, yielded something of theory. They maintained, however, more than lip-service to liberty, governmental checks, and executive self-restraint. They genuinely cherished and exemplified moderation, good-will, and

---

[26] *Inquiry*, pp. 195, 516.
[27] *Construction Construed, and Constitutions Vindicated* (Richmond, 1820); *Tyranny Unmasked* (Washington, 1822); *New Views of the Constitution of the United States* (Washington, 1823). The last two, containing much repetition from his previous writings, have a garrulity which makes them almost unreadable.
[28] Taylor, *Construction Construed*, pp. 25, 26, 252, 253.

patriotism without limit of region. Thereby they were somewhat antiquated before they left the scene. The people now, whether at large or by localities, were taking new guides little acquainted with early landmarks.

But before pursuing the themes of the later 'twenties and the 'thirties, let us note some incidental transactions and local transformations while the Virginians were still at the helm.

CHAPTER IV

A QUESTION OF ETHICS

Ancient Greeks and Romans held slaves; and though their philosophy was in many ways exalted, they seem to have had few qualms as to this practice. In later ages the peoples and powers of Europe knew not slavery, but employed other means of maintaining a safely stratified social order. Then came a special epoch of distant adventure in search of much knowledge and more profit. The seven seas were sailed and their shores exploited. Where gold or silver was found in feeble hands it was taken by glorious conquest; where spices or silks or furs were to be had in trade at bargain prices, commerce was the procedure; where land proved good for tillage, it was appropriated with or without parley; and where labor was wanted for mines or fields, primitive men were liable to be made captive on the spot or brought from a distance as convenience might determine.

By chance the first of these epoch-making voyages was of Portuguese to West Africa, where the commodities available proved to be some ivory, gold, and spice, and many of mankind in slavery. It so befell that some of the slaves when taken to Portugal proved amenable and amiable servants. The use of them was extended to Spain, thence to the West Indies in the time of Columbus, and thence to all suitable shores of America as an aid in wringing a profit from the wilderness. The British were late entrants into the several distant fields, but by their vigor and ingenuity they rapidly made up for their tardiness. Their prompt adoption and improvement of their neighbors' devices were part of the reason for their ultimate predominance in imperial enterprise. Among these devices was Negro slavery, an essential for large prosperity in colonial America.

The race was to the resolute and the resourceful; the battle to the strong and the canny. Creeds Catholic, Anglican, Presbyterian, or Puritan merely prodded men to strive for place in American opportunity; they had, except in a measure among the Quakers, no influence in promoting or hindering the institution of slavery. The godly shared in the transport of Negroes, and they gave thanks for a prosperous voyage or a slave-grown crop as they did for a frontier victory and the capture of a batch of Indians to be ransomed or enslaved. The brutalities of business, like those of war, were a matter of course.

Scruples nevertheless must have been fairly constant in minds here and there. The kind-hearted and the neurotic might be revolted by a scene of coercion or by a tale of such a scene. Any such might raise his voice or seize his pen. Probably protest and answer were fairly continuous from the time when the first Negroes were landed in any port. It happens that the earliest of these to be printed on American soil came from two magistrates of Massachusetts. Though their debate had no manifest sequel for many years, its tone and substance anticipated in striking manner what was to be said on either side in the nineteenth century.

At Boston in 1700 Judge Samuel Sewall issued a sheet entitled *The Selling of Joseph,* implying an analogy between that biblical episode of unfraternal fraud and the bondage of the Negroes in Massachusetts. He drew from Holy Writ: *"God hath given the Earth . . . unto the Sons of Adam"* (Psalms 115: 16),[1] *"And hath made of One Blood all Nations of Men . . ."* (Acts 17: 26). *". . . He that Stealeth a Man and Selleth him, or if he be found in his hand, he shall surely be put to death"* (Exodus 21: 16). *"Therefore all things whatsoever ye would that men should do to you, do ye even so to them: for this is the Law and the Prophets"* (Matthew 7: 12). His own chief assertions were:

> Forasmuch as Liberty is in real value next unto Life: None ought to part with it themselves, or deprive others of it, but upon most mature consideration. The Numerousness of Slaves at this Day in the Province and the Uneasiness of them under their Slavery, hath put many upon thinking whether the Foundation of it be firmly and well laid; so as to sustain the Vast Weight that is built upon it. . . . Originally, and Naturally, there is no such thing as slavery. . . . These *Ethiopians,* as black as they are; seeing that they are the Sons and Daughters of the First *Adam,* the Brethren and Sisters of the Last Adam, and the offspring of God; they ought to be treated with a Respect agreeable.

Sewall's tract brought him not merely "frowns and hard words," as he said, but next year *A Brief and Candid Answer* in print from

[1] The exact words from the King James Version are: "but the earth hath he given to the children of men." Ed.

John Saffin, a colleague on the bench who was himself a slave-holder. With plenty of Scripture cited in opposition,[2] Saffin challenged the pertinence of Sewall's texts: "True, but what is all this to the purpose, to prove that all men have equal right to Liberty, and all outward comforts of this life; which Position seems to invert the Order that God hath set in the World, who hath Ordained different degrees and orders of men, some to be High and Honourable, some to be Low and Despicable; . . . yea, some to be born Slaves, and so to remain during their lives." If emancipation were accomplished, "then the Negroes must all be sent out of the Country, or else the remedy would be worse than the Disease; and it is to be feared that those Negroes that are free, if there be not some strict course taken with them by Authority, they will be a plague to this Country." He concludes:

I may love my Servant well, but my Son better; Charity begins at home, it would be a violation of common prudence, and a breach of good manners, to treat a Prince like a Peasant. . . . It doth evidently appear both by Scripture and Reason, the practice of the People of God in all Ages, both before and after the giving of the Law, and in the times of the Gospel, that they were Bond men, Women and Children commonly kept by holy and good men, and improved in Service; and therefore by the Command of God, *Lev.* 25: 44, and their venerable Example, we may keep Bond men and use them in our Service still.[3]

Such Puritans as had slaves continued to hold them, and such as had ships continued to make slaving voyages on occasion. It was climate, not maxims or argument, which kept slaves few in New England.

Among Anglicans and others, occasional qualms were expressed, as by the second William Byrd of Westover; but in most of the colonial period nearly all who did any campaigning against slavery were Quakers. This radical sect of Protestants, rampant in its first phase but systematically quiet-mannered thereafter, furnished at least one pamphleteer for every decade of the eighteenth century. While uncouth denunciation by Ralph Sandiford and Benjamin Lay gave

---

[2] His citations in addition to Sewall's are: Genesis 9:25–27; 14: 14; 21: 10; Exodus 21: 16; Leviticus 25: 44–46; Joshua 9: 23; Jeremiah 34: 8–22; Psalms 115: 16; Corinthians 12: 13–26; Galatians 6: 10. The same texts did heavy duty at the South in the middle third of the nineteenth century.

[3] Samuel Sewall, *The Selling of Joseph: a Memorial* (Boston, 1700), and Saffin, *A Brief and Candid Answer to a late Printed Sheet entitled "The Selling of Joseph"* (Boston, 1701) are reprinted as discoveries in George H. Moore, *Notes on the History of Slavery in Massachusetts* (New York, 1866), pp. 83–87, 88 n., 251–256.

place to gentle suasion by John Woolman and Anthony Benezet, the purpose was unflagging to bring the Society of Friends itself and then its neighbors and the world to discontinue slave-holding, along with warfare and all other cruelties and vanities in violation of the Golden Rule. There was resistance within the Society by those who loved a well-served fleshpot; but when reinforced by the libertarian philosophy of the Revolution those reformers were able to cleanse their sect from the slave-holding sin throughout the North and to make at least a stir in Maryland, Virginia, and North Carolina. Farther southward Quakerism had little existence or effect.

* * *

In the patriot cause which bore fruit in American independence the vital demand was for home rule—the liberty of communities, not of individuals. It was only for the sake of sentimental reinforcement, of popularization at home and abroad by appeal to "fundamental principles," that leaders of the movement proclaimed that all men were of right entitled to freedom. So earnest were these partisans, however, that many of them embraced the doctrine for its own sake. This impulse, which of course impinged upon Negro slavery, was probably strongest in Massachusetts and Virginia. It was faintest in the Far South.

Dismal experience in Georgia while under Trustee control had caused even the high-minded James Habersham to concur in a prevalent rationalization: "I once thought it was unlawful to keep negro slaves, but I am now induced to think God may have a higher end in permitting them to be brought to this Christian country than merely to support their masters. Many of the poor slaves in America have already been made freemen of the heavenly Jerusalem. . . ."[4] When emancipation from the paternalistic Trustees brought freedom to procure slaves, it was long cherished as a particular boon. One of her delegates in the federal convention said that Georgia considered slave importation to be "one of her favorite prerogatives."

In South Carolina Christopher Gadsden in 1766 deprecated the numerousness of slaves; and a decade afterward Henry Laurens expressed an abhorrence of slavery and a purpose of manumission. But these private remarks had little public echo.

In the North Carolina wilderness it is, as usual, hard to find any

[4] W. B. Stevens, *History of Georgia* (New York, 1857), I, 300.

A QUESTION OF ETHICS

stirring of sentiment. An index of attitude appears in the state's requirement when ceding the Tennessee region that slavery be sanctioned therein.[5]

In Virginia fairly numerous men of prominence were expressing anti-slavery views; and Jefferson expected the younger men who had "sucked in the principles of liberty, as it were, with their mothers' milk" to accomplish emancipation by law. But Washington, taking a general view of the country when the war had ended, said: "The spirit of freedom . . . has long since subsided, and every selfish passion has taken its place. It is not the public, but private interest which influences the generality of mankind; nor can Americans any longer boast an exception."

In Maryland, although Charles Carroll and William Pinkney gave some support to Quaker projects, nothing was put in train but some relaxation in the restraints upon manumission; and likewise in Delaware, although slaves were few, nothing significant was done.

It was only northward of Mason and Dixon's Line that the impulse of the period somewhat slowly wrought a cardinal change in the legal status of Negroes. In Massachusetts this was accomplished by a court decision applying an inherent-liberty clause in the state's bill of rights; elsewhere it was mostly done by legislation providing that children afterward born of slave parents were to become free when attaining specified adult ages. Thanks to the Quakers, Pennsylvania was the first to enact such a law in 1780; New Jersey was the last, in 1804. The process, while discussed with some vigor in each commonwealth, brought no debate of country-wide significance. Negroes throughout the North were too few to create a social problem; their value was too small to maintain an important vested interest; and there was plenty of white labor for all employment available. Each community was merely setting its own affairs in better order, content for its neighbors to use their own discretion. There was nevertheless enough anti-slavery propaganda coming from England and enough interstate agitation to keep some watchful Southerners on guard.

* * *

In the councils of the Union concern arose once in a while with details affecting slavery, but not with the institution in the states

[5] This example was duly followed by Georgia when relinquishing her claims to the Alabama-Mississippi region.

except by mere allusion or when Quaker petitions indiscreetly thrust it forward. On one of these occasions, in 1790, James Jackson of Georgia asked impatiently: "Is the whole morality of the United States confined to the Quakers?" And William Smith of South Carolina said: "When we entered this confederacy we did so from political, not moral motives, and I do not think my constituents want to learn morals from the petitioners; I do not believe they want improvements in their moral system; if they do they can get it at home. . . . We look upon this measure as an attack upon the palladium of the property of our country."

The terrors of slave revolt in San Domingo, resulting from hasty legislation by the French revolutionists, helped to silence agitation in the United States; and Gabriel's attempted uprising in Virginia in 1800 reinforced the French object-lesson.

Nevertheless the eighteenth century had in some degree set the crisis of the nineteenth in train by vesting control of American affairs in a self-governing republic, by disestablishing slavery throughout the North, and by bringing forth resounding denunciations of it. The most effective of these was uttered not by Quakers or Puritans but by the deist Jefferson in 1781: "The whole commerce between master and slave is a perpetual exercise of the most boisterous passions. . . . The parent storms; the child looks on, catches the lineaments of wrath, puts on the same airs in a circle of smaller slaves. . . . Indeed, I tremble for my country when I reflect that God is just; that His justice cannot sleep forever."

Though Jefferson became far more temperate upon this theme in his later years, his flaming words were not allowed to die. A disciple of some importance in the same century was Professor St. George Tucker, who gave each year to his law students in William and Mary College [6] a "melancholy review" of Virginia's persistence in "that partial system of morality which confines rights and injuries to particular complexions"; and he printed a segment of his lectures as a memorial to the legislature, proposing an extremely gradual plan of emancipation.[7] The Senate returned him a "civil answer," but the House of Delegates impatiently laid his pamphlet upon the table.

---

[6] This college in 1791 bestowed an honorary doctorate of laws upon Granville Sharp, a leading English agitator against the slave trade.

[7] St. George Tucker, *A Dissertation on Slavery: with a Proposal for the Gradual Abolition of it in the State of Virginia* (Philadelphia, 1796, reprinted New York, 1861).

A QUESTION OF ETHICS

The problem of disposing of the freed Negroes, whom even Jefferson and Tucker thought must not be retained in the community, caused most Virginians not only to balk at projects of general emancipation but even to disapprove private manumission on any considerable scale.[8] One of these denounced an act of 1782:[8]

> What then has our assembly done? Why, suffered a number of enthusiasts . . . to withdraw their protection, and turn loose amongst us as a scourge, some thousands, perhaps, of the most abandoned, unprincipled wretches on earth, ravaging as they go, and cloaking every species of villainy in others. . . . Let us then petition for an instant repeal of this unadvised, precipitant act, before its bane becomes so diffusive as to bid defiance to every effort. On the success of this or some similar effort depends, in my opinion, our own safety and the salvation of our country.[9]

An intermittent debate upon this question of repeal resulted in a compromise in 1806 which required that any slaves manumitted thereafter depart from the commonwealth within twelve months.[10] Some petitioners in Maryland complained at once that many Virginia "beggarly blacks have been vomited upon us"; and the legislatures of Delaware, Maryland, and Kentucky, followed within the next decade or two by those of Ohio, Indiana, Illinois, Missouri, and Tennessee, forbade influx of free Negroes from other states.[11]

In this period abolitionists were chided from time to time by Southerners when writing upon any theme which brought them to mind. John Drayton in a book describing his commonwealth of South Carolina said that the rice fields could only be cultivated by Negroes, who would not work as freemen. The slaves, he thought, were faring better than the white peasantry of many countries, and immensely better than their fellows in Africa; and they constituted a vested interest beyond the reach of the laws except by consent of their owners or upon fair compensation. Nevertheless men at a distance, ignorant of conditions, were endeavoring to weaken this right of property.

> With as much propriety might we request them to dismiss their horses from the plough. . . . And with the same reason might they be asked to give the money out of their pockets, in order to equalize the situation of

---

[8] As usual in such legislation, the manumitters of any slaves under or over the ages of able-bodied labor must give bonds indemnifying the public against any costs which might result from pauperism.
[9] Letter of "A. B." to the editor, in the *Virginia Gazette*, Dec. 14, 1782.
[10] John H. Russell, *The Free Negro in Virginia* (Baltimore, 1913), pp. 59–70.
[11] *Ibid.*, pp. 71, 72.

every person; as the people of the southern states be requested to make changes in this property. . . . If it be a sin, it is the happiness *of those who are not engaged in it,* to be safe from any of its future calamities.[12]

In Virginia John Taylor of Caroline when discoursing on agricultural improvement remarked upon vagaries of Jefferson and the Quakers. Noting Jefferson's own urbanity as a disproof of truculence in slave-holders, he said:

To me it seems, that slaves are too far below, and too much in the power of the master, to inspire furious passions; that such are nearly as rare and disgraceful towards slaves as towards horses; that slaves are more frequently the objects of benevolence than of rage; that children from their nature are inclined to soothe and hardly ever suffered to tyrannize over them; that they open instead of shut the sluices of benevolence in tender minds.[13]

Negro slavery he considered an economic misfortune "incapable of removal, and only within the reach of palliation." Emancipation would intolerably multiply the free Negroes, who, "cut off from most of the rights of citizens and from all the allowances of slaves," were "driven into every species of crime for subsistence; and destined to a life of idleness, anxiety and guilt." As to the Quakers and their colleagues, he said, if the "religious and philosophical quixottes" should carry their efforts to the full but unintended conclusion, they would, as in Haiti, make "republicans of negro slaves, and conquerors of ignorant infuriated barbarians." Meanwhile he thought the mere agitation was tending to diminish the humanity of the masters and foment malignity among the slaves.[14]

* * *

There were now seeds of sectional antagonism aplenty; but before any growth of this became lush, two matters were handled without much inter-sectional strife: Congress prohibited slave imports,[15] and a society was hopefully launched for an African colonization by free Negroes.

[12] John Drayton, *A View of South-Carolina, as respects her Natural and Civil Concerns* (Charleston, 1802), pp. 144, 145.
[13] *Arator; being a Series of Agricultural Essays Practical and Political in Sixty One Numbers. By a Citizen of Virginia* (Georgetown, D. C., 1813), no. 14. In later editions of these essays, which were first published in a newspaper prior to 1810, Taylor's name is printed on the title-page.
[14] *Ibid.,* nos. 13, 28, 29.
[15] For analysis of debates, votes, laws, and administration see U. B. Phillips, *American Negro Slavery* (New York, 1918), pp. 132-149; W. E. B. Du Bois, *The Suppression of the African Slave Trade to the United States, 1638-1870* (New York, 1904).

A QUESTION OF ETHICS

More or less drastic restraints of the slave trade had been attempted by numerous legislatures in the colonial period, only to meet royal vetoes in the interest of British shipping. The war of independence effectually suspended the traffic; and Virginia, Delaware, and several Northern states embraced the opportunity to enact prohibitions. Maryland followed at the war's end; North Carolina laid a duty in 1787 so heavy that it amounted to prohibition; and in the same year South Carolina began a policy of temporary stoppage which was prolonged by successive acts for sixteen years. Georgia last fell into line with not only a statute but a constitutional clause in 1798; and for five years imports were forbidden in every state.

In prompting these pieces of legislation humane sentiment, which was now being propagated vigorously from England, was reinforced by very concrete considerations of economic and social interest, as is evident in the recurring South Carolina debates. With one voice, though with diverse emphasis, the men of established wealth and conservative attitude—Izard, Rutledge, Ramsay, Pendleton, the Pinckneys, and even Rawlins Lowndes—argued that permission of imports would reduce the prices of slaves already possessed, or at least prevent their values from rising; that it would increase the volume of staple exports and impair the world's market for them; that by draining out money and credit it would keep the community in chronic debt; that it would impair the civilized habituation of plantation groups, heighten the proportion of blacks in the population, and intensify the danger of slave insurrections. In opposition Alexander Gillon was almost a sole spokesman for the privilege of poor men to prosper by purchasing cheap labor on credit. But by the turn of the century Whitney's invention of the cotton gin had so much increased the demand for labor in the back country and the price of slaves in all quarters that a smuggling trade began to paralyze the law; and at the end of 1803 the legislature, by narrow majorities, repealed the prohibition. In the following four years imports into South Carolina, many of whom were at once reshipped to Louisiana, numbered some 40,000 slaves. The volume would presumably have been larger had not the planters developed by this time a strong preference for native slaves and an aversion toward the task of "breaking in'" fresh Africans.

South Carolina's repeal brought a wide repercussion of disapproval and an impatience to procure Federal prohibition. Jefferson in his annual message of 1806 congratulated Congress upon the approach of the time when it might constitutionally "withdraw the citizens of the United States from all further participation in those violations of human rights which have been so long continued on the unoffending inhabitants of Africa, and the best interests of our country have long been eager to proscribe." A bill, at once introduced, passed the Senate in January, 1807, providing a death penalty for the importation of slaves after the close of that year and prohibiting all interstate coasting trade in slaves. In the House a bill of lesser severity brought expression in debate of a general accord in essential purpose but a regional divergence as to practical details. Most of the Northern members wanted the death penalty for offenders, but opposed any confiscation of smuggled slaves as implying a sanction to the concept of property in human flesh. Josiah Quincy, Timothy Pitkin, and some other Northern realists endorsed the Southern contention that juries would balk at verdicts of guilt if penalties of death were in prospect or if the seized slaves were to be given freedom in the vicinage. When sundry members insisted upon such provisions, Peter Early, from Georgia, repudiating an earlier assertion of his that slavery was "an evil regretted by every man in the country," now said: "A large majority of the people in the Southern States do not consider slavery as a crime. . . . Some gentlemen appear to legislate for the sake of appearances. . . . I should like to know what honor you will derive from a law that will be broken every day of your lives." [16]

Eventually the bill took shape with a penalty of imprisonment between five and ten years, with the fate of illegally imported Negroes to be determined by the states wherein their cases were handled, and with a prohibition of maritime interstate conveyance in vessels of less than forty tons burthen. Despite a vehement objection by John Randolph to this last provision as impairing property rights and wrecking the Constitution, the bill in this form was passed by both houses and approved by the President. Enough Northern members had yielded to the Southern insistence upon mimimum severity for the sake of maximum effectiveness.

When in the next decade smuggling became notorious at Amelia Island on the Georgia-Florida coast and at Barataria Bay south of New Orleans, it was checked under a supplementary statute which increased the rewards to informers. Further legislation, by 1820,

[16] *Annals of Congress*, 9th Cong., 2nd sess. (1806–1807), 238, 239.

A QUESTION OF ETHICS

pronounced trans-Atlantic slave trading to be piracy, provided a police of African and American waters, and facilitated returns of captured slaves to Africa. Parallel contemporary legislation by the British Parliament made these policies international; and smugglings were so diminished as to have no longer a social or economic effect. All of this was a notable achievement; and it might have had a still happier sequel if a great and prosperous counter-flow had been instituted of civilized Negroes from America to the shores of Africa.

* * *

The free Negroes were not a mere stumbling block in the discussion of slavery. Unable to find a comfortable niche in the white man's world, their high ratio of pauperism and criminality made them a special nuisance in the cities of the North, while their very presence in the South, unobtrusive as it might be, gave irksome anxiety to the guardians of the public safety. To provide a channel for their exit was desirable in reducing a present incubus; it was imperative if by general consent a multitude of slaves were to be freed in future. To colonize them somewhere, anywhere, had been recommended now and then, with mention of the Western wilderness and the West Indies as asylums. But why not the shores of Africa, where the civilization and Christianity possessed by some of them might irradiate their ancestral continent and where the British benevolent enterprise of Sierra Leone gave a precedent? When a lull in the pressure of other affairs gave opportunity for active discussion of this, the American Colonization Society was organized in the winter of 1816–1817 under the patronage of a throng of distinguished men; and erelong its agents procured from African chiefs permission to plant "Liberia," the land of the free.

For a time there was prospect of large achievement. With initial impulse mainly from the middle zone, branches of the Society were spread throughout the Union, and contributions of money came from church congregations, Masonic lodges, individuals, and the Maryland and Virginia legislatures. But Congress, the one possible source of subventions great enough to permit wholesale operations, persistently refused to loosen the national purse. Furthermore the Liberian coast proved malarious in distressing degree; the neighboring tribes turned hostile; and the ill-assorted colonists were inert except when sometimes fractious. But the chief thwarting came from sectional reactions within the United States. As early as 1819 the

Society sought to placate hostile sentiment on both flanks by proclaiming its purpose to be neither "to rivet the chains of servitude" nor "to invade the rights of property secured by the constitution and laws of the several states." The design, as repeatedly stated, was to finance and induce emigration of those already free, and to facilitate private and voluntary manumission.

To abolitionists this was a dodging of the proper issue; to pro-slavery zealots it was the thin edge of a wedge intended to topple their institution. The Society, trying to tread its middle path in pure philanthropy, giving always mild answers, turned away some little wrath but wrought no miracles at home or abroad. Its languid colony did not illuminate Africa nor palpably mitigate the problem in America. The net result was an agency functioning on occasion as its petty resources might permit, and hoping that some turn of public affairs might bring a great enlargement of its plans and performance. Practically colonization seems to have appealed only to the squeamish among the whites and to the desperate or the specially persuaded among the blacks.

A revealing item among the copious records is a letter of 1835 by one Samuel O. Moon, a semi-literate Southerner, to the chief agent of the Society. Moon says that, while a spendthrift, godless youth, he had inherited and sold a slave boy named Moses. Becoming a church convert afterward, he felt such qualms at this episode that he resolved to save money, buy Moses back, and send him to Liberia. When several years of thrift had supplied the needed money, Moon broached his purpose. Moses demurred at emigration, but afterward consented; and the purchase was made. But "he was then Quite a Prayerless Wicked Man," and Moon decided to "keep him a year or two and try by the assistance of the Lord to be Instrumental in his Salvation." This had now been accomplished, and Moses was apparently "traveling that Road that Leads to the fair Climes of Immortal Joys." Accordingly, though distressed at the thought of parting with his protégé, Moon asked instructions for setting him on the way to cross the sea.[17]

Whether Moses throve or languished in Africa we cannot say. The chances for improvement were none too good. But such enlightened men as John McDonogh of New Orleans continued to send their freedmen thither, believing it the best recourse in an otherwise insoluble dilemma. On the other hand the throng of

[17] Early L. Fox, *The American Colonization Society* (Baltimore, 1919), pp. 38, 39.

politicians who had lent their names at the Society's inception had long since turned away. The sequel of a set of resolutions adopted in 1824 by the legislature of Ohio was discouraging. These asked Congress to provide, with the consent of the states, for the gradual emancipation of all slaves and to use proceeds of the public lands to colonize the Negroes as freed. The legislatures of South Carolina, Georgia, and Missouri protested, the Georgia resolutions attributing the "wild, fanatical and destructive" project to the Colonization Society itself and appealing for a united South to resist at every cost so ruinous an interference with its property under the cloak of a "hypocritical benevolence."[18] The hysteria here evinced was of course due not to the Society's harmless transactions but to events in which it had no hand.

* * *

The strident phase of the slavery question is commonly said to have begun with Garrison's launching of the *Liberator* in 1831. But the congressional crisis on the Missouri question, a dozen years before, was a more palpable beginning. Such acrid remarks were made in the debate and so sharp a sectional alignment appeared in the voting that, although the specific issues were adjusted within two years, the repercussions did not die.

What produced the crisis was the formation of a great Northern bloc to trench upon the South's expansion. In occurrence this had a suddenness warranting Jefferson's phrase of "a fire-bell in the night." But conditions made it fairly logical. The mechanism of the federal Constitution which counted slaves in apportioning representation afforded ground for a Northern grudge; the Louisiana Purchase, the admission of the state of Louisiana, and the pending purchase of Florida were tokens of enlargement in Southern power; the continuing "Virginia dynasty" of Presidents and the collapse of the Federalist party were to similar effect; the panic of 1819 brought chagrin to unemployed whites when seeing slaves assured of work and food; and Southern objections to the further heightening of tariff protection to Northern industries increased the tension. Thus when a commonplace bill was introduced into the House of Representatives authorizing the people of Missouri to frame a constitution with a view to statehood, it met by no means a routine experience. Mr. Tallmadge of New York offered an amendment prohibiting any

[18] H. V. Ames, *State Documents*, pp. 203-213.

further influx of slaves into the contemplated state and requiring that all children of slaves born therein become free upon attaining twenty-five years. A furious debate followed in both houses, involving the ethics of slavery, the sovereignty of the states, the federal ratio, the sectional equilibrium, the nature of republican government, the history of man, and the will of God.

Livermore of New Hampshire said: "How will the desire of wealth render us blind to the sin of holding both the bodies and souls of our fellow-men in chains! . . . In the present slaveholding states let slavery continue, for our boasted constitution connives at it; but do not, for the sake of cotton and tobacco, let it be told to future ages that, while pretending to love liberty, we have purchased an extensive country to disgrace it with the foulest reproach of nations." Colston of Virginia retorted that Livermore deserved to be hanged for inciting servile war. When the ballots were taken in the House a majority almost wholly Northern carried the Tallmadge proposals against a minority almost as entirely Southern.[19] The Senate, however, struck out the restrictive clauses; the House refused to concur; and the close of the session, in March of 1819, left the question open for debate everywhere.

When the next Congress resumed the discussion at the beginning of 1820, the desks were piled with memorials for and against the restriction. One from the Pennsylvania legislature, for example, denounced the Southern endeavor "to spread the crimes and cruelties of slavery from the banks of the Mississippi to the shores of the Pacific" and "open a new and steady market for the lawless venders of human flesh." [20] The Southern resolutions in reply were not much less vigorous.

The House had adopted a bill for admitting Maine as a state; and the Senate attached to it the former Missouri bill without restriction as to slavery. The hope of avoiding asperities by this maneuver was vain. Rufus King, a principal whip on the Northern side in the preceding year, had now been "vindicated" by election to a new term in the Senate, and was armed with fresh invective. J. Q. Adams jotted in his diary, "the great slave-holders in the House gnawed their lips and clenched their fists as they heard him"; and an Alabama Senator, while still writhing under King's words,

---

[19] Stimulated by the success, a Northern effort was made to apply the same provisions to the territory of Arkansas; but by a small margin this was defeated in the House.
[20] Ames, *State Documents*, pp. 197–199.

described them as an astonishing avowal of doctrine challenging the validity of slavery everywhere and unhinging the Union at a stroke. He said that the stenographer had not taken the speech and that King would not dare to publish it "in the naked ugliness of its original deformity." [21] In fact it was not printed; but it was answered in great elaboration by William Pinkney of Maryland and more tersely by several others.

The persistence of efforts to create and maintain a solid North was now giving grave alarm to devotees of the Union. Meigs of New York said in the lower house, where the Tallmadge amendment had been revived, that for no less than twenty years he had noted an increasing spirit of sectional dislike. "A continued series of sarcasms upon each other's circumstances, modes of living, and manners, so foolishly persevered in, has produced at length that keen controversy which now enlists us in masses against each other on the opposite sides of the line of latitude." [22] Mr. Hardin of Kentucky said: "On our side of the House, . . . we are contending not for victory, but struggling for our political existence. . . . Behold! and see how the nation is divided: eleven states against eleven; a small majority in this House in favor of the amendment; a small one in the Senate against it. . . ." [23] To stop the prospect of rending the Union he suggested that Missouri be admitted without the restriction and that a line be drawn through the remainder of the Western region limiting the extension of slavery. In pursuance of this idea Senator Thomas of Illinois offered an amendment fixing the demarcation at 36° 30'. When this was accepted by both houses and the amended bill enacted, the Missouri question seemed to be settled.

But the people of Missouri, resentful at efforts to infringe their prospective sovereignty, had a disturbing word to say. The delegates they chose to frame their constitution were of strong Southern attitude. Their convention saved labor by borrowing the Kentucky constitution and, having some energy to spare, added a clause requiring the legislature to debar free Negroes. When this was presented to Congress, a debate arose as bitter as before. A Virginia Senator wrote: "I fear an alarming crisis will ere long come on. The seeds of discord are sown in the negro question—and a degree

[21] Letter of John W. Walker, Feb. 11, 1820, to Charles Tait. (Manuscript in the Alabama Department of Archives and History.)
[22] *Annals of Congress*, 16th Cong., 1st sess. (1819–1820), I, 943.
[23] *Ibid.*, 1070, 1090.

of patriotism, of moderation and of wisdom is necessary to settle it. The designers of the North have resorted to it with a view to power. The South feels indignant at their hypocrisy and arrogance, and the chasm is, I fear, likely to increase." [24]

But Henry Clay found a solving, or at least a face-saving formula, by which Congress, while admitting the state, required a pledge of the legislature against any future enactment infringing the immunities of any citizens of other states. The legislature when making a technical compliance remarked that it had no power to bind succeeding assemblies. In fact the legislature in after years enacted laws contravening the pledge; and Congress, unwilling to do battle again over this detail, ignored the defiance.

John Taylor, happening as usual to be writing a book, included the Missouri question among its themes, and of course found in it an omen. Federal partialities to bankers, manufacturers, and pensioners, he said, had stimulated capitalists and other grafters to build a machine, becloud the public mind, and embrace all possible means to divert notice from their malefactions. Since they mostly dwelt in the North, where lay the major voting strength, an excitement upon some question of slavery would produce a sectional consolidation useful for their greedy purposes. Hence the campaign against Missouri, with an objective neither wise, just, nor constitutional. Eastern people, he said, were ignorant of Southwestern conditions, and their interference with race relations through congressional enactment might bring a frightful consequence. Congress, furthermore, was without authority to determine the question of slavery within a state. The most plausible ground of contention to the contrary was the most dangerous of all, *viz.*, the Constitution's guarantee to every state a republican form of government. Of the current argument from that clause he said that if slavery is not destructive of republican government the contention fails of application; but if that antipathy is valid, the clause vests in Congress a power to liberate all the slaves in the Union. A congressional prohibition of Missouri slavery, therefore, he would consider an earnest of an attempt at general abolition. In the face of such a crisis as this

[24] Letter of James Barbour, Jan. 7, 1821, to Charles Tait. (Manuscript in the Alabama Department of Archives and History.) Of himself Barbour said: "I look on as a calm spectator, with no other feeling than that of a disinterested spectator, for it has pleased the author of my nature not to have poisoned my cup with the dregs of an unequal or aspiring ambition."

A QUESTION OF ETHICS

would produce, the South must be thrown upon fundamental resources:

> There remains a right, anterior to every political power whatsoever, and alone sufficient to put the subject of slavery at rest; the natural right of self-defence. Under this right, societies . . . are justified, if they see danger at a distance, to anticipate it by precautions. It is allowed on all hands, that danger to the slave-holding states lurks in their existing situation, however it has been produced; and it must be admitted, that the right of self-defence applies to that situation, of the necessity for which the parties exposed to the danger are the natural judges.[25] [He concluded:] I leave to the reader the application of these observations.

Taylor's readers, never a multitude, would not in that day follow the logic which led to tragedy. When the specific issues relating to Missouri were compromised, Congress and the country relaxed in great relief. But if or when the slavery question, as one of ethics real or pretended, should come to be pressed with vigor, the community most concerned would not lack an answer.

[25] John Taylor, *Construction Construed, and Constitutions Vindicated* (Richmond, 1820), p. 314.

CHAPTER V

AN ANSWER OF RACE

In all pro-slavery discussion in the nineteenth century San Domingo was a name to conjure with because of what had there befallen in consequence of *liberté, égalité, fraternité*.[1]

This had been the greatest of the French possessions in the tropics. Its 200,000 slaves in 1789 were an index of its prosperity and an embodiment of its wealth. Some of their owners dwelt at Paris; most of them were among the 30,000 white inhabitants of the colony; but a good many, mostly mulattoes, were among the 25,000 free people of color. Conditions had been fairly placid so long as control was firm; but the human materials were known to be as inflammable as a ripe sugar-cane field. No sooner did revolutionary stirrings occur in France than planters began to give warning that if doctrines of inherent liberty were spread in the plantation colonies internecine war was inevitable and utter destruction probable. At Paris, on the other hand, the society of *les Amis des Noirs,* inspired by Thomas Clarkson's gospel from across the Channel, had committed Mirabeau, Robespierre, and many others to the purpose of extending to Negroes the full schedule of human rights. Their blithe plan was in clear harmony with the Declaration of the Rights of Man and with the program of the Jacobins concerning the world at large.

When in the face of proceedings at Paris the whites in San Domingo tried to maintain order as of old, the mulattoes and the blacks, rising in separate rebellions with diverse objectives, drove all surviving whites into seaport refuges. Pleas to the motherland for succor brought Jacobin commissioners, who, disagreeing among themselves, made confusion still worse confounded. By 1793 white authority was totally destroyed, and in two years more the mulattoes were subordinated to the blacks under Toussaint L'Ouverture.

---

[1] The French colony comprised the western third of the island. T. Lothrop Stoddard, in *The French Revolution in San Domingo* (Boston, 1914), gives a full narrative of the disorders which are here sketched.

AN ANSWER OF RACE

In France excess now produced reaction, but in San Domingo terror was unending. Spain and Great Britain, at war with France, tried to conquer the revolted colony for themselves, but were thwarted by Toussaint and yellow fever.

In 1801 Toussaint proclaimed an independent republic of Haiti with himself as dictatorial president. An intermission in European war now permitted Bonaparte to send an army of conquest which restored a semblance of control only to be decimated by fever and to surrender to British blockaders upon the resumption of international hostilities. Toussaint, seized in bad faith, died in an Alpine dungeon. His black lieutenant Dessalines proclaimed himself emperor as Jean Jacques I and exterminated or expelled the remnants of both whites and mulattoes before he was assassinated in 1806.

The powers of Europe now sought no more to subjugate these blacks. Republican forms were more or less maintained until the middle of the century when Soulouque, as Faustin I, established for a decade another fantastic monarchy. Whether under the style of republic or empire, barbarous irresponsibility was constant and revolution recurrent.

In the Southern United States the sardonic reports of current Haitian travesties did not weaken the grim recollection of the San Domingan cataclysm as a product of black and mulatto revolt against white rule. Citizens accepted it as permanent, irrefragable proof that whites dwelling in the midst of black masses must maintain a complete control or be destroyed. In times of peaceful routine the hand of iron might properly wear a velvet glove; but all disturbing propaganda must be prevented, and any conspiracy crushed in impressively drastic manner.

* * *

Slave revolts and plots very seldom occurred in the United States; and prior to the Missouri wrangle there was little Southern fear of external interference. But angry debates and the voting of most of the Northern congressmen in a solid bloc now made guardians of the South specially alert against menaces from without and within. The next major episode was by chance the revelation of a Negro plot in Charleston in the summer of 1822.

This was formidable in strength and specific in plan for a midnight seizure of the guard-house and arsenal and a sweeping of town and country with fire and sword. The leader was Denmark

Vesey, a talented native of Africa who had bought his freedom in consequence of a lottery prize. Among his diverse lieutenants Monday Gell, a literate slave harness-maker, professed to be in correspondence with auxiliaries in Haiti and Africa; and Gullah Jack, with Angola conjuring art, stood ready to make all participants invulnerable.

A special court, which published its full proceedings,[2] tried these and more than a hundred others, condemned thirty-five to death, ordered the deportation of about as many more, and acquitted the rest. This work of detection and repression was completed within three months; but a fear of recurrence and a zeal for prevention persisted. A memorial from the city to the state asked for a stiffening of police restraints and an expulsion of the free persons of color.[3] An association was launched, with Robert J. Turnbull as its secretary, to supplement public with private vigilance[4]; and sundry citizens put their individual views into print.

Thomas Pinckney, veteran of the Revolution, thought that the preponderance of Negroes in the city's population ought to be cured by driving most of the slaves to the plantations and encouraging immigrant whites to replace them.[5] Another pamphleteer exclaimed on his eighty-sixth page: "Let it never be forgotten that our NEGROES are truly the *Jacobins* of the country; that they are the *anarchists* and the *domestic enemy,* the *common enemy of civilized society,* and the barbarians who would, IF THEY COULD, become the DESTROYERS *of our race.*" He thought the free blacks ought to be expelled but the free mulattoes retained, for he said that many of these mulattoes were slave-holders themselves and watchful of slave-holding interests. Ranging farther afield, he discoursed upon malignant Northern hostility to slavery, and upon the Missouri debate in Congress as proving a Northern will to dominate and a need of the South to take a stand which would assure "beyond the possibility of all future cavilling, the full and uncontrolled enjoyment of our rights." He deprecated in particular the spreading

---

[2] *An Official Report of the Trials of Sundry Negroes Charged with an Attempt to Raise an Insurrection in the State of South Carolina* (Charleston, 1822).

[3] *Memorial of the Citizens of Charleston to the Senate and House of Representatives of the State of South Carolina* (Charleston, 1822).

[4] *Rules of the South-Carolina Association, adopted in the City of Charleston, on the Fourth Thursday in July, being the 25th Day, A. D. 1823* (Charleston, 1823).

[5] *Reflections Occasioned by the Late Disturbances in Charleston. By Achates* [Thomas Pinckney] (Charleston, 1822).

AN ANSWER OF RACE

of discontent and sedition among the slaves by Northern missionaries; and he cited Scripture to show their anti-slavery zeal to be misguided.[6]

Whither the laity led, the clergy soon followed. With a mandate from the Baptist convention of South Carolina, the Reverend Richard Furman of Charleston published an argument, with biblical citations, that slave-holding was consistent with Christian uprightness; that a general emancipation under existing circumstances would injure both blacks and whites; that the maintenance of a moderate but firm control was a proper function of masters and of public officials; and that religion ought to be steadily promoted among the Negroes for the sake of their temporal contentment as well as their immortal bliss.[7]

Dr. Frederick Dalcho, assistant rector of St. Michael's, promptly supplied further citations which Furman had overlooked, and argued on his own score that Negroes ought not to be permitted "to run after unknown itinerants" or "hold meetings of their own under teachers of their own colour," but ought to be guided by settled white pastors or discreetly given lessons from the Psalms, the Proverbs and the historical books of the Bible through manuals prepared with their particular needs and status in view. In a footnote he praised the purpose of the vigilantes to debar Negroes from Fourth of July celebrations where, from oratorical acclaim of liberty, they might "imbibe false notions of their personal rights and give reality in their minds to what has no real existence." [8]

In sympathy with this ado an act had been passed in 1822 requiring sheriffs to jail free Negro seamen during the stay of their ships in port. As a device of moral quarantine this was criticized in Charleston on the ground that the seamen when in jail would have more leisure and as much audience as if on the wharves; and the statute seems to have been applied only when local zealots prodded

---

[6] [Edwin C. Holland], *A Refutation of the Calumnies circulated against the Southern and Western States, respecting the Institution and Existence of Slavery among them* (Charleston, 1822). In the *Dictionary of American Biography*, VI, 94, following *The South in the Building of the Nation*, XI, 317, this is wrongly attributed to Benjamin Elliot.

[7] *Rev. Dr. Richard Furman's Exposition of the Views of the Baptists relative to the Coloured Population of the United States, in a Communication to the Governor of South Carolina* (Charleston, 1823; 2d ed., Charleston, 1833).

[8] *Practical Considerations founded on the Scriptures relative to the Slave Population of South-Carolina. By a South-Carolinian* [Rev. Frederick Dalcho] (Charleston, 1823).

the sheriff's memory. But in spite of, or perhaps because of, protests from the governments of Great Britain and Massachusetts, the law was not repealed.

When a year had passed without further alarm of conspiracies, the flood of pamphlets fell away. In the remainder of the 'twenties Whitemarsh B. Seabrook, a plantation youth of political ambition, pointed with alarm to the Colonization Society's petition for Federal funds; and R. J. Turnbull, the hottest of Hotspurs, having spent most of his *Crisis* essays in anathemas against the tariff, gave echo to Seabrook's warning. McDuffie had said that there were not twenty men in Congress who would vote for this proposal. Twenty such men, or even five, were in Turnbull's mind a menace. Forty years ago, said he, the members of the British Parliament advocating abolition in the West Indies were negligible; but now those islands "are hastening, with a very quick step, towards complete ruin. . . . And so will South-Carolina assuredly be ruined, if at this day, there are twenty men in Congress, who are for emancipation, sudden or gradual, and the right of Congress to take *even a vote*, is not RESISTED as an ACT OF WAR by South-Carolina." [9]

Turnbull made mention of Lundy's weekly *Genius of Universal Emancipation* among the grounds of his alarm; and he had no proposal for silencing such. Edward Brown, whose philosophical pamphlet on the general question leaves his own career obscure, likewise resented the conduct of abolitionists in playing up "insulated facts, at which humanity shudders, to represent the general treatment of slaves," and their false charges that slave-holders in the large were malicious, implacable, oppressive, and godless. Disproof had failed and would fail again to cure the wilful ignorance or silence the aspersions of these fanatics; but an exhibit of slavery's place in the social order might improve understanding among temperate men. Hence his essay to show that in the pattern of civilization everywhere a social stratification prevails, essential for morals and manners; that in any densely populated country the poor automatically compete for employment at low wages, thereby maintaining cultured classes; but in a new country, thinly peopled, an uncouth equality can be prevented only by some device like slavery. The slaves on hand, he said further, formed a racial caste with which the whites everywhere were determined not to mingle. If

[9] *The Crisis: or Essays on the Usurpations of the Federal Government. By Brutus* [R. J. Turnbull] (Charleston, 1827), p. 132.

emancipated they would in some degree be merged with the mass of the poor, and yet would be kept apart, friendless victims to prejudice and preys to vice.[10]

In 1829 the venerable Charles Cotesworth Pinckney repeated the burden of these clerical and lay pamphlets, adding little of his own; but Stephen D. Miller, in a message as governor of South Carolina, went so far as to say, under irritation of the sectional strain: "Slavery is not a national evil; on the contrary, it is a national benefit." [11] This was a novel assertion which Calhoun and others were to buttress as they might in later decades.

* * *

Affairs in Virginia now came to warrant for once Thomas Ritchie's refrain in his Richmond *Enquirer*, "The eyes of the world are upon us."

In sandy, placid Southampton County dwelt Nat Turner, a slave who read the Bible, saw visions and portents, heard unearthly voices, and felt an impulse to set his people free. Without plans or preparations, as afterward appeared, he told half a dozen followers on a Sunday night in August of 1831 that the time had come. They murdered the sleeping household of Nat's master, and began a zigzag roaming of the countryside, killing such whites as they found, recruiting such Negroes as they could persuade, seizing weapons and horses, and stiffening their courage with the product of an occasional brandy still. Through Monday and Monday night they continued the raid upon lonely homesteads, increasing their motley force to some fifty Negroes, and raising the tally of slain white men, women, and children to more than sixty.

Some of the slaves they met refused to join this amazing enterprise; and some of these ran to tell white people what was afoot. Some of their hearers met the news with a disbelief which quickly made them victims of oncoming slaughter. But by Tuesday morning armed citizens clustered to form a point of resistance; and at their first volley the rebels fled in all directions. While the woods were being searched for the now fugitive insurgents, a courier was killing horses on the road to Richmond and spreading panic as he went. The governor despatched arms, and called out the militia of

[10] [Edward Brown], *Notes on the Origin and Necessity of Slavery* (Charleston, 1826).
[11] Charleston *Courier*, Nov. 28, 1829.

all nearby counties. In Southampton quiet was gradually restored; and in due time, among fifty-three prisoners arraigned in court, seventeen slaves and three free Negroes were hanged, twelve transported, and the rest released.[12]

For several months afterward, if anyone saw a bush rustle he might imagine an uprising. Rumors of revolt started in a dozen places from North Carolina to Maryland; and the heads of some innocent Negroes were broken. The citizens could not be sure whether Nat and his fellows had run amuck of their own stupid impulse, or whether they were part of a widespread conspiracy. Two years before this a Negro, David Walker, had printed a pamphlet in Boston urging the blacks to throw off their oppressions; and now Garrison in his *Liberator* was excelling all predecessors in vituperating slave-holders. If such propaganda was reaching the black multitude, huge disaster might come at any moment. Some vocal citizens thought the menace could be removed only by deporting the Negroes *en masse*, others by discharging them from slavery, still others by stiffening the police restraints; while some there were, who, seeing that affairs on the whole had run smoothly for a long time past, found no cause for grave disquiet at a planless local disturbance, and opposed any drastic change.

When the legislature met in December, and the governor's message, a pile of petitions, and an editorial bombardment urged action, the members had had time in large degree to resume the normal channels of thought, which in Virginia politics had a sectional impress. The people of the Shenandoah valley and the region beyond, which now comprises West Virginia, had been seeking to heighten the taxation of slaves and to procure large appropriations to cheapen the movement of their own produce to market. Baffled in this, their spokesmen enjoyed making themselves a nuisance at Richmond by playing up the decline of eastward prosperity and by censuring the system of slavery. They now found enough allies among squeamish easterners to permit a full airing of their views. Through two weeks of January the House of Delegates rang with eloquence upon economic evils of slavery, projects of gradual emancipation, and the virtues of such a sturdy white democracy as blessed the westerly zone. Eastern defenders made little reply; but when the flood of speech subsided they readily mustered votes enough to defeat unwelcome resolutions. When this faint menace to slavery was

[12] W. S. Drewry, *Slave Insurrections in Virginia* (Washington, 1900).

AN ANSWER OF RACE

out of the way, the House adopted a project looking to the removal of the free Negroes; but this was defeated in the Senate.

* * *

The debate was given full report in the Richmond press,[13] and vigorously commented upon in every quarter of the country. From the southward came, as with one voice, a censure of the blazing indiscretion; and sundry Virginians undertook to dissuade the commonwealth from any repetition.[14]

By far the most important of these writings was an elaborate essay by Thomas R. Dew, professor of history, metaphysics, and political law in William and Mary College. What are nowadays called economics and sociology were also within his official purview.

The Virginia debate, he said, was a reckless indulgence in oratory by young speakers not wise enough to know that old adjustments may not be safely discarded at a stroke. Slavery had prevailed in many lands; and in its taming of savage men it was as valuable as the domestication of animals. The slaves in America were of a race and a condition requiring extreme caution for any safe readjustment. Mere abstract principles must yield to the lessons of the past and the concrete facts of the present.

In the debate, he continued, it was agreed that if the blacks were freed they must be removed. But the Virginia slaves, numbering nearly half a million, and constituting nearly one third of the gross wealth of the state, formed a mass utterly beyond the capacity of the commonwealth to purchase or to colonize. The buying and shipment of the mere annual increase, of some six thousand souls, as had been proposed by some, would strain the public revenue without bringing any solution. "We are to send out thousands of these, taken from a state of slavery and ignorance, . . . with dangerous notions of liberty and idleness, to elevate them at once to the condition of freemen, and invest them with the power of governing an empire, which will require more wisdom, more prudence,

[13] It is summarized in C. H. Ambler, *Sectionalism in Virginia* (Chicago, 1910), pp. 185–202; T. M. Whitfield, *Slavery Agitation in Virginia, 1829–1832* (Baltimore, 1930), pp. 65–118. Eight or ten of the speeches were printed as contemporary pamphlets.

[14] For example Benjamin W. Leigh, who told his whole tale in his title: *The Letter of Appomattox to the People of Virginia: Exhibiting a Connected View of the Recent Proceedings in the House of Delegates, on the Subject of Slavery; and a Succinct Account of the Doctrines broached by the Friends of Abolition, in Debate: also the Mischievous Tendency of those Proceedings and Doctrines* (Richmond, 1832), reprinted from the Richmond *Enquirer*, Feb. 4 and 28, 1832.

and at the same time more firmness than ever government required before." As the vicissitudes of Sierra Leone and Liberia had shown, it would be little short of a general condemnation to death. And this would bring no betterment in Virginia; for the great number of blacks remaining would continue to deter a white influx and a remodeling of social economy to fit a Northern or Western pattern.

A law to free the children born after a fixed date, upon their attaining adult age, Dew disapproved on the grounds that it would violate property rights, give grievance to those born before the date specified, and bring eventually the same insoluble problem of handling the freedmen.

He thought that emancipation without deportation was the more probable, and would prove the more pernicious. "Declare the negroes of the South free to-morrow, . . . and you depress, instead of elevating. The law would, in every point of view, be one of the most cruel and inhumane which could possibly be passed"; for it would convert slaves who were in a double sense cared for by their masters into forlorn victims of prejudice, indolence, and vice. It would wreck the livelihoods of planters and merchants, destroy land values, bring famine and grave disorder. But if these prognostications were unsound, the fact remained that race relations were too delicate a matter for a distant community, such as western Virginia, to deal with in ignorance of the complications. He repeated in conclusion: "Let us reflect on these things, and learn wisdom from experience; and know that the relations of society, generated by the *lapse of ages,* cannot be altered in a *day*." [15]

Dew's essay became at once a standard of Southern orthodoxy. The contribution of a qualified scholar to the clarification of social politics, its thoroughness of inquiry, its prudence of tone, its firmness of conclusion convinced all who wanted to be convinced that no proposal thus far made, radical or moderate, could eliminate Negro slavery without bringing more harm than good. Saying little that was new but much that was cogent, it reinforced a reaction of public opinion against projects of social change.

In the Virginia capitol, silence upon evils of slavery was hence-

[15] T. R. Dew, *Review of the Debate in the Virginia Legislature of 1831 and 1832* (Richmond, 1832). This was expanded from anonymous articles in the *American Quarterly Review* for October and December, 1832. Duff Green reprinted it as the whole content of his *Political Register* for Oct. 16, 1833, and stereotyped this issue for quantity sale at six dollars per hundred. The essay is most conveniently used, however, in *The Pro-slavery Argument; as maintained by the most distinguished Authors of the Southern States* (Charleston, 1852), pp. 287–490.

AN ANSWER OF RACE

forward golden. James McDowell of the Valley, a leading contemner in the debate of 1832, became a defender instead, and in due course was rewarded with the governorship. In North Carolina a deprecatory speech of Judge William Gaston at Chapel Hill had no political echo; but instead, when the constitution was revised in 1835, the free Negroes, who to that time had been eligible to the suffrage, were excluded from the voting element.

In Tennessee for fifteen years after Elihu Embree had begun an agitation in 1819 many petitions were sent to the legislature and then to the constitutional convention of 1834, asking emancipation of all after-born children.[16] The legislature having taken no favorable action, the convention resolved by a large majority not to deal with the matter. In explanation it adopted a committee's elaborate report which, while admitting slavery to be a great evil, argued much along Dew's lines against premature projects. As a special ground of deterrence it said that any emancipatory action "would have thrown a firebrand into the community and kindled strife that would not be extinguished for years to come"; and any news of its impending would have caused a stampede among slaveholders to put their property beyond the Tennessee boundaries. The report concluded with a pious hope that "under the approving smile of Heaven" slavery might "yet be extinguished in a way that will work no evil to the white man," and a wish that outside abolitionists would cease their ill-judged and obstructive interference.[17]

In Kentucky, thanks to Cassius M. Clay, an agitation for gradual emancipation continued to flicker; but when in 1849 an election of delegates to a constitutional convention was ordered and a specific anti-slavery campaign was made, hardly one of its candidates attained a seat. When the subject of slavery nevertheless came up for incidental discussion, a delegate, who said that he and his kindred had no slaves, made some keynote remarks:

The state of Kentucky has for all time to come to be either a frontier slavery, or a frontier non slavery state, and the great question which her

[16] Elihu Embree's first petition was sent to the Assembly in 1817, although he had joined the newly-formed Manumission Society of Tennessee the preceding year. The period of his most active agitation began in 1819 with the founding of his newspaper, the *Manumission Intelligencer*. See E. E. Hoss, "Elihu Embree, Abolitionist," in *Publications of the Vanderbilt Southern History Society* (Nashville, 1897), no. 2.

[17] Manuscripts in the Tennessee State Archives. Many of the petitions are on printed forms of identical phrasing, which shows them to be the fruit of systematic endeavor. A considerable number of the signers designated themselves as being slave-holders.

citizens have to determine is, whether she will separate from her old connections, her associates, those who are bone of her bone and flesh of her flesh, those who have been brought up with the same institutions, the same customs—whether she will forsake all these and unite herself with men who are foreign to us in interest, in purposes, and in all the associations of life. Kentucky, sir, will be ready for emancipation when she is ready to cut loose all her feelings for the South . . . . then will she be ready to unite with our northern friends, and not till then.[18]

Meanwhile the Southern anti-slavery societies, which numbered perhaps a hundred at their maximum in the 'twenties, were decimated year by year; and the middle of the century found few surviving units. Their temperate gospel of gradual emancipation had put them between the batteries of the root-and-branch abolitionists and the pro-slavery conservatives. The gradualists, in short, met the same fate as their allied colonizationists. The argument was increasingly to the vociferous.

* * *

Of course the main irritation producing the resolve to keep things as they were did not come at any time from within the South. The first source was Great Britain, whose agitators, though chiefly concerned with the West Indies, contributed most of the ideas and some of the money utilized in the United States. Before Garrison's day Wilberforce, for example, denounced slavery as "the full measure of pure, unsophisticated wickedness, . . . without a rival in the secure, undisputed possession of its detestable preeminence"; O'Connell had said "Of all men living, an American slaveholder is the most despicable"; and Elizabeth Heyrick said in a pamphlet which was reprinted several times in America: "But this *Gradual Abolition* has been the grand marplot of human virtue and happiness;—the very masterpiece of satanic policy." The devil, she continued, "the prince of slaveholders," has known that if he could persuade Christians "to *acquiesce* for but one year, or for one month, in the slavery of our African brother, . . . and degrading him to a level with the brutes; that then they could imperceptibly be brought to acquiesce in all this for an unlimited duration. . . . He knew that strong excitement was necessary to strong effort." And again: "The spirit of accommodation and conciliation has been a

[18] Speech of Elijah F. Nuttall of Henry County in the *Debates and Proceedings of the Convention for the Revision of the Constitution of the State of Kentucky, 1849* (Frankfort, 1849), p. 78.

spirit of delusion.... The Great interests of truth and justice are betrayed, rather than supported, by all softening, qualifying concessions." She said that even if any compensation were to accompany abolition it ought to be paid not to the masters but to the slaves.[19]

But the American eclipse of gradualism and compensation did not greatly simplify the controversy, for abolitionists were so diverse among themselves that an answer to one did not reply to another. "Anti-Slavery has no Platform" and no rules of order, said a protagonist. "No matter is extraneous . . . that Humanity in any of its forms feels cause to introduce. . . . Anti-Slavery fears no disturbance or confusion. It bravely takes its chance on the waves of freedom—preferring liability to hurricanes and tempests to the constrained and subject calms." [20] Some said the Bible gave the chief grounds for indicting slavery; others that the Bible ought to be rejected as sanctioning it. Some endorsed the federal Constitution and the Union; others repudiated both. Some sought power through politics; others urged abstention from the polls. Some used church apparatus; others would persuade all whom they could to "come out" from every congregation. Some damned slave-holders for cruelty; some, emphasizing sinfulness, contended that a kindly master was worse than a harsh one because his kindliness cloaked the sin. A few sought concrete knowledge of conditions; others fabricated horrors at will. Abolition, in short, was not so much a campaign as a clamor, an endless iteration of what came to each participant as the thing for him individually to shout.

* * *

Such few Southerners as endorsed outright abolition were likely to remove to a more congenial clime. The first were the Grimké sisters of Charleston. Sarah, sojourning by chance in Philadelphia toward the end of her morbid youth, became a convert to Quakerism, and adopted in full the scruples of that sect concerning slavery. Her much younger and more positive sister, Angelina, having found her own way from Episcopal to Presbyterian church connection, yielded to Sarah's persuasions, made rags of her laces, tore up her set of Scott's novels, forsook all other vanities, and followed her

[19] [Elizabeth Heyrick], *Immediate, not Gradual Abolition* (London, 1824; New York, 1825; Philadelphia, 1837; Boston, 1838). Assertions in all of these tenors were copiously repeated by the Garrisonians.
[20] N. P. Rogers, *Miscellaneous Writings* (2d. ed., Boston, 1849), p. 293.

sister to Philadelphia in 1829, intending to become a Quaker preacher. Their brother Thomas was ardent for prohibition, peace, and educational reform, though he did not add abolition to his enthusiasms. But Angelina, listening to the British agitator George Thompson, was converted in 1835 to root-and-branch abolition; and Sarah followed. The Southern origin of these women made them specially welcome recruits among the Garrisonians, who put platforms and printer's ink at their service. In a year-long speaking tour of New York and New England the sisters became almost convinced that the wrongs of women were more important to redress than those of the slaves; and they were not deaf to the calls of perfectionism and anarchy. But Theodore D. Weld, the chief manipulator of organized abolition, married Angelina, taking also Sarah to live in his house. The sisters were saved to the cause as an indispensable exhibit, giving testimony of having forsaken their ancestral home "to escape the sound of the driver's lash and the shrieks of his tortured victims." [21]

James G. Birney, born of a Kentucky slave-holding family, moved to northern Alabama as a lawyer, planter, and politician and served usefully in the legislature of that budding commonwealth. Impoverished by gambling, he sold his plantation and slaves. Then a religious conversion exalted a previous disrelish of slavery, and he became a vigorous agent of the Colonization Society. When his strictures upon slavery grew too strong for the local press to publish, he returned to Kentucky with a purpose of persuading the border state to provide for gradual emancipation, and thus whittle away the slave-holding area. But Kentucky proving obdurate, he moved to Ohio, struck hands with Weld, and toured the North repeatedly to promote a strangling of slavery by political action. A dullness of habit on the platform made him a poor campaigner, however. It was as a recruit from the South, not as a man of special quality, that he was given the Liberty party's nomination in two presidential campaigns.[22]

Moncure D. Conway, born of a Virginia Methodist family, was a

[21] Catherine H Birney, *Sarah and Angelina Grimké, the First American Women Advocates of Abolition and Woman's Rights* (Boston, 1855). Gilbert H. Barnes and Dwight L. Dumond edited in 1934 for the Beveridge Fund *The Letters of Theodore Dwight Weld, Angelina Weld and Sarah Grimké* (2 vols., D. Appleton–Century Company.) Ed.

[22] William Birney, *James G. Birney and His Times* (New York, 1890). In 1938 Dwight L. Dumond edited for the Beveridge Fund the *Letters of James Gillespie Birney, 1831–1857* (2 vols., D. Appleton–Century Company.) Ed.

Methodist preacher before he was out of his teens; but, seeking more light, he went to the Harvard Theological Seminary, became a Unitarian, an Emersonian transcendentalist, and an abolitionist, though to the end of his life he said that he had never seen a slave treated more severely than white children commonly were when being disciplined by their parents.

Several others of lesser note were like these four in reaching abolitionism through religious excitation and an abstract philosophy which ignored the racial factor. Another group, following the lead of the Westerners in the Virginia debate, and stimulated from the North, attained a trenchant anti-slavery position through more or less concrete study. Daniel R. Goodloe, a North Carolinian who moved to Washington, argued with a forcible moderation that slavery was an economic blight.[23] Henry Ruffner, with more vehemence, urged his fellow-citizens of western Virginia to repel this curse from their yeoman vales.[24] Hinton R. Helper, adventuring from North Carolina to California in the rush for gold and then finding a home at the North, assumed an extreme championship of the non-slaveholding Southern whites.

Angelina Grimké had said: "My Dictionary is the Bible; my standard authors, prophets and apostles." Helper depended instead upon the Federal census of 1850 and his own talent of alliterative objurgation. In his *Impending Crisis* he piled "figures of rhetoric" upon "figures of arithmetic" to "demonstrate the great moral triumph of Liberty over Slavery," and to flay the "lords of the lash." Exhibiting, for example, the relative sectional outputs of wheat, oats, rye, Indian corn, and Irish potatoes, he said at once: "What an obvious comparison between the vigor of Liberty and the impotence of Slavery." Adding to this a comparison of live-stock statistics, he asked:

Can it be possible that the slavocracy will ever have the hardihood to open their mouths again on the subject of terra-culture in the South? Dare they ever think of cotton again? Ought they not, as a befitting confession of their crimes and misdemeanors, and as a reasonable expiation for the countless evils which they have inflicted on society, to clothe them-

[23] *Inquiry into the Causes which have Retarded the Accumulation of Wealth and Increase of Population in the Southern States. By a Carolinian* [D. R. Goodloe], (Washington, 1846).
[24] Henry Ruffner, *Address to the People of west Virginia; shewing that Slavery is Injurious to the Public Welfare; and that it may be Gradually Abolished without Detriment to the Rights and Interests of Slaveholders* (Lexington [Va.], 1847; Louisville, Ky., 1847).

selves in sackcloth, and, after a suitable season of contrition and severe penance, follow the example of one Judas Iscariot, and go and hang themselves? [25]

Cotton, rice, tobacco, sugar, and sweet potatoes figured little in his reckonings, for they would have set his case askew. Climate and soil were ignored in an attribution of all disadvantages to slavery. Matters of race he likewise neglected until after slavery had been abolished. Then in another book, under the strange title of *Nojoque*,[26] he called for a merciless expulsion of all Negroes and mulattoes, as "black and bi-colored caitiffs," from the whole of the white man's world.

* * *

Such ecstasy, whether in religion or economics, did not greatly spread in any quarter. Many of the Northern clergy took pains to discourage it with tongue and pen; politicians with almost one accord, at least until the Kansas furor, avoided it as they would the plague; mobs here and there demonstrated their disapproval; and the great bulk of the people was either hostile or indifferent. It was only by linking their cause to the right of petition or to some adventitious question of the day that abolitionists could hope to procure a formidable array of Northern power in their behalf. Realizing this, they utilized their network of societies to bombard Congress with petitions against slavery in the District of Columbia and against the interstate slave trade; they organized an "underground railroad" to facilitate flight by fugitive slaves; and they promoted "personal liberty" legislation by the Northern states, while continuing always to berate slaveholders and prod them into counter-attacks. There were schisms among the societies, and schisms within the schisms, promoted by zealous diversity in the details of doctrine or policy; but nothing abated the clamor.

From the Southern point of view, the whole agitation had been answered at the beginning of its radical phase. But the replies merely brought more intense vituperation, which put the defenders into dilemma. If they conceded that slavery was an incubus which ought to be removed when safe plans could be laid, they were damned for a self-confessed procrastination which might easily prove endless. If

---

[25] H. R. Helper, *The Impending Crisis of the South: How to meet it* (New York, 1857), p. 73. Thanks to its endorsement by the Republican party, a hundred thousand copies of this book were printed before 1861, as well as innumerable copies of a *Compendium*.
[26] New York, 1867.

AN ANSWER OF RACE

they said that slavery was indispensable, whether admitting or denying that some of its features ought to be reformed, they were doubly damned as incorrigible despots. In the face of such a situation many counseled silence until the storm should spend its force. Others, in mild remonstrance, chided the critics of slavery for their harshness of epithets, argued that the circulation of "incendiary propaganda" was merely forcing the South to prohibit the teaching of Negroes to read, or as a diversion invited Northern and British attention to political and industrial abuses at home. But some sought to buttress their institution more thoroughly than ever by new searchings of Scripture, fresh analysis of the Constitution, and an exploitation of any social, economic, or ethnological doctrine which came to hand.

Hardly less than a thousand put their views into newspapers, and a hundred into magazines. Certainly scores printed pamphlets and dozens books, in the general endeavor to concert an attitude and consolidate a position. Some essayed fiction, especially when prodded by the prodigious effect of *Uncle Tom's Cabin*. William J. Grayson, postmaster of Charleston, resorted to verse in *The Hireling and the Slave*,[27] appending footnotes to strengthen his argument and explain his allusions.

With a somewhat epic sweep, though not at quite epic length, Grayson sketched the poverty, filth, and ignorance of English hirelings and the famine stress of Irish peasants, as "homebred misery" which might well absorb the British zeal in relief and reform. Yet, he said:

> Vainly the starving white, at every door,
> Craves help or pity for the hireling poor;
> But that the distant black may softlier fare,
> Eat, sleep, and play, exempt from toil and care,
> All England's meek philanthropists unite
> With frantic eagerness, harangue and write.

These blacks were victims brought in British ships for British gain,

> Forced on her subjects in dependent lands,
> By cruel hearts and avaricious hands.
> . . . . .
> But Providence, by his o'erruling will,
> Transmutes to lasting good the transient ill.
> . . . . .

---

[27] [W. J. Grayson], *The Hireling and the Slave* (Charleston, 1854); W. J. Grayson, *The Hireling and the Slave, Chicora and Other Poems* (Charleston, 1856).

> In this new home, whate'er the negro's fate—
> More bless'd his life than in his native state!
> No mummeries dupe, no Fetich charms affright,
> Nor rites obscene diffuse their moral blight.
> . . . . .
> Celestial light: religion undefiled
> Dawns in the heart of Congo's simple child.

With Christianity he learns also the ways of civilized industry, and contributes essential goods for the world's welfare:

> Instructed thus, and in the only school
> Barbarians ever know—a master's rule,
> The Negro learns each civilizing art
> That softens and subdues the savage heart,
> Assumes the tone of those with whom he lives,
> Acquires the habit that refinement gives,
> And slowly learns, but surely, while a slave,
> The lessons that his country never gave.

Prophets of Bible times had seen the like without revilement; but Clarkson and Brougham, Gerrit Smith and Garrison, Hale and Giddings, Sumner and Seward, Stowe "with prostituted pen," Chase, Parker, and Beecher "damn the master and for freedom rave." But the slaves have livelihood, security, patronage, and pleasures which abolition would destroy. At the North, freed, but a pariah, in

> human sties,
> In foul excesses sunk, the Negro lies;
> A moral pestilence to taint and stain,
> His life a curse, his death a social gain.
> . . . . .
> Why peril, then, the Negro's humble joys,
> Why make him free, if freedom but destroys?

Instead, let the present wholesome life and elevating discipline prevail, until in the fullness of time

> To Africa, their fatherland, they go,
> Law, industry, instruction to bestow;
> To pour, from Western skies, religious light,
> Drive from each hill or vale its pagan rite,
> Teach brutal hordes a nobler life to plan,
> And change, at last, the savage to the man.
> . . . . .

AN ANSWER OF RACE

> Let, then, the master still his course pursue,
> "With heart and hope" perform his mission too;
> . . . . .
>
> Justly, "as in the great Taskmaster's eye,"
> His task perform—the Negro's wants supply,
> The Negro's hand to useful arts incline,
> His mind enlarge, his moral sense refine,
> . . . . .
>
> Scorn the grave cant, the supercilious sneer,
> The mawkish sentiment and maudlin tear,
> Assured that God all human power bestows,
> Controls its uses, and its purpose knows,
> And that each lot on earth to mortals given,
> Its duties duly done, is blessed of Heaven.

* * *

The doctrine which Grayson reflected, that slavery was a positive good, worthy of perpetual cherishing, had originated as a defense reaction when milder contentions proved of no silencing avail. We have seen intimations of it shortly before 1830. In a message of 1835 as governor of South Carolina, George McDuffie said that by clear divine ordinance the African race had been consigned to the status of slavery "as more conducive to their happiness than any other. . . . Until 'the Ethiopian can change his skin' it will be vain to attempt by any human power to make freemen of those whom God has doomed to be slaves, by all their attributes." [28] Next year the Reverend James Smylie of Mississippi reinforced this with an assemblage of biblical citations which he had long been collecting. In a stream of other publications which ran to the same effect the book of John Fletcher of Louisiana, entitled *Studies on Slavery, in Easy Lessons*,[29] excelled all others in bulk and erudition, though not in ease or cogency. It replied in detail to Barnes, Wayland, Channing, and other anti-slavery clerics; it cited most of the books of the Bible and many of the Latin church fathers; it retold the primal transgression, the curse of Cain, and its inheritance by Ham; it gave evidence that Ham's descendants were black, and endorsed the wisdom of God in putting deteriorated races under the control of the more virtuous. Its last hundred pages are the hardest, wherein, with great display of Greek and Hebrew philology, it is argued that the words translated "servant" in the King

[28] Reprinted in *American History Leaflets*, no. 10.
[29] Natchez, 1852.

James version of the Scriptures have a true meaning nothing short of slave.

No less than 4,000 copies of this work were printed, and presumably sold. It is not easy to believe that it found so many actual readers. It served, at least, as a source of data for less pedantic writers, such as George S. Sawyer and Albert T. Bledsoe; but these we hardly need follow, since they can hardly have accomplished more than to convince those who sought conviction.

* * *

Certain men who migrated in either direction sought to mediate between the sections, mainly by pleas for Northern quiescence. One was William Drayton, who departed from Charleston when his unavailing resistance to nullification had wrecked his pleasant relationships there. A book [30] which he published after a few years in Philadelphia showed both his Unionism and his loyalty to the South. The free Negro at the North, he said with a good deal of truth,

is bowed down by the consciousness of inequality, and haunted by the fear of the prison. Incertitude and anxiety are with him each hour of his life; and when sickness or age steals upon him, it often finds him without resources or hope. Thus is he dogged through life by poverty, fear, humiliation and oppression. . . . The [slave] labourer of the South knows none of these evils. He is scarcely acquainted with the meaning of the word care. He never suffers from inordinate labour—he never sickens from unwholesome food . . . ; and in sickness or age he knows that he has a protector and a friend able and willing to shield him from suffering. His pleasures are such as his nature enjoys, and are unrestricted. He enjoys all the privileges which his simple heart craves, and which are wholesome for him.

Slave conditions would be still better, he said, were it not for necessary precautions against incitement to disorder. The abolitionists "cry peace, peace, but pursue a course which is designed to end and must end . . . in a servile war" unless a preventive is applied. "The South, on this point, is as *one man*—its attitude is one of self-defense—its voice one of warning. If the wrong be continued, it will act, *it must act*, not in revenge, not in anger, but in the performance of a holy duty—in defending its firesides from murder—its valleys from desolation." It must and will establish its national independence unless the

---

[30] [William Drayton], *The South Vindicated from the Treason and Fanaticism of the Northern Abolitionists* (Philadelphia, 1836).

North abstains from political aggression and suppresses hostile agitation.

To much the same effect, though in a more persuasive tone, was the contribution of the Reverend Rufus W. Bailey,[31] born in Maine but a Presbyterian minister for a decade in South Carolina. In that decade, ending with 1836, he had observed on the one hand as a common phenomenon a cordial attachment between masters and slaves, but on the other hand a sharp reaction against Northern propaganda. In consequence a few men were now declaring slavery to be a political and social blessing. Others thought it permanently necessary and justifiable. Still more, while holding slaves with easy conscience under existing circumstances, were "anxiously looking for some practicable scheme of emancipation, in which the real good of the slave, and the safety of the country, should be consulted and sustained." But, "there is the most perfect unanimity . . . on the *issue now made by the abolitionists.*" The South says to them, "you have forfeited the privilege of a further hearing . . . you shall not speak on this side of the Potomac, nor find a cover for your incendiary publications."

Bailey begged the Northerners to leave the matter in the hands of liberals in the South who sought a reform and an ultimate extirpation. This, he thought, had good prospect of success:

We speak the truth, unmixed with those errors into which on this subject you are constantly, though unconsciously betrayed. We shape our argument intelligently to the facts in the case. There is, therefore, no misapprehension of our words, motives, or true action. Hence, we are permitted to speak when you cannot. Our words are like oil on troubled waters, while yours are like borean blasts, which lash the troubled waters into rage.

What Bailey dreaded most was that the abolitionists, having "already united the South," would succeed in their disastrous purpose of uniting the North.

THIS IS THE ISSUE. It is inevitable. When the North shall say to the South, "we do not claim a constitutional right to interfere with your institutions, but you *must* and *shall* abandon your slavery, for it is wrong"—then this union is at an end. . . . "We are proceeding rapidly," said an eminent abolitionist, "to gain the North. Let us succeed in uniting the North and we will take care of the South." The last labor will be spared them. The South will then, be assured, take care of herself.

[31] Rufus W. Bailey, *The Issue, presented in a Series of Letters on Slavery* (New York, 1837).

Joseph Clay Stiles was a migrant in unusual degree. Born at Savannah, he went to Andover and Yale for study, worked as a Presbyterian evangelist in several Southern states, then held pastorates at New York and New Haven, and at length returned South. Greatly troubled at the growth of sectional tension, he made, after passing his sixtieth year, two efforts to relieve it. The plan of the first was to "examine and refute extreme Anti-Slavery views—set back liberty and slavery to their just and proper bounds in the public mind—and press the grounds of conciliatory appeal."

Abolitionism as an "epidemic mania," typical of "modern reform," he characterized in detail as arrogant, malignant, belligerent, impracticable, and destructive, exhibiting "too much nature and too little grace, too much glitter and too little gold, too much fury and too little force." The Northern conscience as to slavery he praised, but its uncharitable violence he deplored as defeating the needful purpose of leading the South "on the way toward Christian perfection on this subject." A kindliness of the North toward the South he considered essential whether for improvement in race relations or for safeguard against great national peril, for it was a Northern assault upon a Southern institution which had produced and was maintaining the Southern spirit of intransigeance. With a "fraternal exhortation" he concluded: "In humble *suggestion,* because fallible; in *honest* effort, because under duty, I put forth this word. If it is a right word, the Lord in faithfulness impower it. If it is a wrong word, God in mercy bury the work and forgive the workman."[32]

Though the response cannot have been highly stimulating, Stiles made another appeal to the hearts of his Northern countrymen when the Union was already splitting asunder. In this he labored the themes of legal obligation and practical comity. The fathers of the Constitution, he said, were in the main opposed in moderate degree to slavery; but in pursuance of a concrete purpose which could not otherwise be attained they gave it a definite sanction which nothing but a constitutional change could alter. This sanction, interpreted in good faith, can only mean that "the South is entitled to *all such toleration and countenance on the subject of slavery, both in language and in conduct, as shall afford her a reasonable opportunity of securing the profits of the institution, without being scandalized for its practice.*" This guarantee does not restrict free speech in tempered

[32] Joseph C. Stiles, *Modern Reform Examined; or the Union of North and South on the Subject of Slavery* (Philadelphia, 1857).

AN ANSWER OF RACE

criticism, but it does forbid all defamatory language, belligerent agitation, incendiary propaganda, interference with fugitive rendition, and exclusion from the territories. These things which are now done or countenanced by multitudes at the North cannot be justified by profession of new light of conscience, for they involve a breach of faith which no good conscience can approve. If the North does not wish to gain a free hand by dissolving the Union, she should give over "her wild attempt to inaugurate, in behalf of the man of color, a liberty-triumph, which he has no present culture to appreciate, and discard from her soul that feverish apprehension of the political power of the South, which has led her to plan the eternal confinement of the slave in his geographical prison." She should credit the South for what has been done in elevating and christianizing these imported Africans, and join her in a pact of sincere good-will for the Negroes' further social elevation. By no other means, he said, can the Union, "so long the pride of the North American, and the glory of the world," escape its doom, or "the *North* and the *South* . . . *feel* —that the *work of righteousness is—peace.*" [33]

* * *

Certain stay-at-home Southerners felt in the 'fifties that if yet a new gloss were put upon things as they were, the clouded future might be cleared. Two of them seized at the same time upon a blend of socialism with sociology as the newest of doctrines and sciences.

Henry Hughes of Mississippi published in 1854 a *Treatise on Sociology, Theoretical and Practical*, wherein theory is even more heavily cloaked with technical jargon than in sociologies of later times. This leads to the practical section, which compared Southern slavery with the system of social economy prevailing in the rest of the white man's world. In freely competitive society, he said, employment and livelihood are precarious, and wages have, inequitably, no relation to the number of an employee's dependents. But in so-called slavery the conditions are much more nearly ideal. Wages, in effect, run in sickness as in health, and always in accordance with the recipient's need. "The children do not cry because they lack. The cruse of oil is never empty, the meal never shows the bottom of the barrel."

The name of slavery he repudiated, because it implied that the bondman labored for his master's benefit alone, whereas in fact his

[33] J. C. Stiles, *The National Controversy; or, the Voice of the Fathers upon the State of the Country* (New York, 1861).

work was beneficial to the state, his master, and himself, and the state and his master had reciprocal duties to him. "The societary organization of the United States South is Warranteeism. . . . It is not forbidden by right . . . ; it is bidden by duty. . . . It is an organization whose essentials every society just to itself, must incorporate." His general scheme of labor and livelihood, anticipating Russian bolshevism under Lenin, he recommended for all the world; and he said that its existing and beneficial application to Negroes in America was accidental. He concluded with a rhapsodic forecast of the universal spread of plantation warranteeism, with plenitude and equity in its train: "Then shall this Federation and the World praise the power, wisdom and goodness of a system which may well be deemed divine; then shall Experience aid Philosophy and *vindicate the ways of God to man.*" Later in the decade Hughes endeavored through the Southern "commercial convention" at Vicksburg to propagate his doctrine and to foster a project of bringing more Negroes from Africa as "plantation apprentices." In fruit of these efforts, he got little more than leave to print.

George Fitzhugh, of Caroline County, Virginia, was more steadily vociferous. Following *Sociology for the South, or the Failure of Free Society* (1854) with *Cannibals All! or Slaves without Masters* (1857), he became reputed as "the boldest and ablest writer who has assumed the offensive in the slavery discussion"; and he then used the pages of *De Bow's Review* as a continuous forum. Endorsing the doctrines of Owen, Blanc, and Fourier, and praising Carlyle's *Latter Day Pamphlets,* he said labor everywhere is exploited, and so-called free labor more than slave. "We are all, North and South, engaged in the White Slave Trade, and he who succeeds best is esteemed most respectable. It is far more cruel than the Black Slave Trade, because it exacts more of its slaves, and neither protects nor governs them." "Capital, irresponsible capital" in free society rules and ruins. It "pursues the hireling from the hovel to the poor-house, the prison and the grave"; but where it owns a slave, as in the South, it supports and protects him.

As for liberty, Fitzhugh said at large, it "is unattainable; and if attainable, not desirable"; all the world was too little governed, not too much. In the existing, unregulated world, he said, Negroes were kept enslaved only because they were mere grown-up children, incapable of self-direction. "No one would have the labor and trouble of management, if his negroes would pay in hires and rents one-half what free tenants pay in rent in Europe." If set adrift by general emancipation, the Negro "would be welcome nowhere; meet with thousands of enemies and no friends. If he went North, the white laborers would kick him and cuff him, and drive him out of employment. If he went to Africa, the savages would cook him and eat him." The very weakness of the slave is a strength to him, for it invites and procures tolerance, benevolence, and affection, which competition and rivalry destroy. "The aversion to negroes, the antipathy of race, is much greater at the North than at the South; and it is very probable that this antipathy to the person of the negro is confounded with or generates hatred of the institution with which he is usually connected. Hatred to slavery is very generally little more than hatred of negroes."

* * *

The socialistic acrobatics of Hughes and Fitzhugh failing to meet the concrete occasion, the demand for cogent pro-slavery formulation became the more urgent as the sectional crisis grew more obvious. *The Southern Literary Messenger,* long non-partisan, made itself an organ in 1854; *De Bow's Review* multiplied its articles on slavery; *Russell's Magazine* was launched at Charleston in 1857 with the cherishing of "Southern civilization" a main purpose; and in the spring of 1860 J. A. Turner began to publish at Eatonton, Georgia, *The Plantation* as a quarterly devoted to the "defence of Negro Slavery—total, unqualified, unreserved" and to rousing the South "to maintain its just rights under the Constitution, and as sovereign States, in the teeth of all opposition, at all hazards and to the last extremity."

The copious books and essays proving in the main hackneyed and commonplace, De Bow called for another Dew to produce a definitive work suited to the later day: "It is scarcely to be expected that the question of slavery will ever be better understood than it is at this time. All that is now wanted is some master mind to systematize, to arrange, to digest and analyze the facts now known, and enunciate them in easy, familiar and perspicuous style." [34] But at the era's end the notable contributions came not in a massive Southern volume but in two pamphlets from Northern men.

Thomas Ewbank, of English birth, was a scientist living most of his life at New York. Turning for a time from technical pursuits, he published in 1860 *Inorganic Forces ordained to supersede Human Slavery*. Granting that races are diverse in capacity, that Caucasians are

[34] *De Bow's Review,* XXVII, 490 (October, 1859).

properly supreme and Negroes inferior for the purposes of the temperate zone, he thought that a just subordination would fall far short of slavery. But as moral suasion and penal statutes had failed to stop the trade in ardent liquors, they would fail to destroy Negro slavery. "Neither it nor its worst features can be suppressed till other agents of labor are ready to take its place." These he believed to be in assured prospect; for he took the development of steam engines to be a mere earnest of what was to come in inventions of new motors, to be driven either by electricity or by "explosive compounds." The progress of invention "shows us that we have the power and the means of doing the world's work without oppressing our own species or the tribes below us, since the demands for industrial labor, however great, are to be met in all coming times not by quivering flesh and fibre but by . . . peat, turf, coal, wood and other fuels." Mechanical power has already spread "from the factory into the highways; and, at the present writing, attempts are making to take it into the prairies— to make it a general field-laborer—to plow and sow, as well as thresh and bolt and grind. It already gins cotton, besides spinning and weaving it; nor is there any insuperable obstacle to its planting and hoeing and picking it, or something equivalent to picking it. It expresses the juice from the sugar-cane; why not cultivate and reap it? . . . Nothing is wanting but a proper combination of mechanical skill; and when that is realized, slavery dies, and dies amid the hosannas of both pro and anti-slavery men." He suggested that friends of the Negro divert their societies to the promotion of mechanical devices for raising and reaping tropical and semi-tropical crops, and otherwise possess their souls in patience.

In the same year came Negro slavery's best epitaph in a pamphlet by Sidney G. Fisher, who was a Philadelphia lawyer and at the same time an owner of plantations in Maryland. What is called the slavery question, he said, is actually the Negro question. Unless the factor of race is understood, the great anomaly must remain incomprehensible that in this free, Christian land four millions of men are held in a bondage which subjects them without protection "to the callousness of cupidity, the recklessness of passion, the brutality of lust. . . . Why do we do this thing? The answer is, because we cannot do otherwise. We have brought the negro to our shores, and therefore slavery with him." [35]

[35] [S. G. Fisher], *The Laws of Race, as connected with Slavery* (Philadelphia, 1860).

AN ANSWER OF RACE

The white Americans, Fisher continued, are transplanted Englishmen, essentially Teutonic and controlled by their own distinctive nature. They are lovers of liberty, truth, and justice, and quite as cogently lovers of power. They are colonizers and beneficent rulers. Churches, charities, order, industry, wealth, arts, and letters follow their footsteps. The Saxon as typified in America "hates slavery unless he is the master, and he is not by choice a master," for he prefers to gain his ends by other means.

In the North, the aboriginees having withered and vanished before him, because they would neither submit to him nor be civilized by him, the Saxon finds no race inferior to his own . . . so numerous as to require any laws to insure his superiority. . . . Moreover, the vast majority of the whites are themselves laboring men; they cannot therefore own slaves. Ruling as they do the lawmaking power, they would not permit the rich to own slaves—for this toiling and governing class, will endure no competition in industry by the negro. Neither do the rich desire to have him for a slave, because the free, intelligent industry of their own race is far more productive and profitable, and brings with it to the employer, no responsibility, no duties and no danger.

But though the negro in the North is not a slave, he is made an outcast and a pariah. . . . He may not lay a finger on one of those three wonderful boxes, the ballot box, the jury box and the cartridge box, . . . by which freemen defend their rights. . . . The spirit of caste drives the negro out of the churches, theatres, hotels, rail-cars, steamboats, or assigns to him, in them, a place apart. It drives him into the cellars, dens and alleys of towns, into hovels in the country; and it does all this without laws, without concert or design, without unkindness or cruelty, but unconsciously, simply because it cannot help doing it, obeying thus instinctive impulse, and the immutable, eternal laws by which the races of men are kept apart.

The Negroes, wherever they dwell, are improvident, weak of will, acquiescent, and fit for servitude. In the South, where they are a multitude, a definite legal subordination is indispensable and beneficent. Slavery not only provides industrial guidance but it performs the functions of magistrates, police, prisons, poor-houses, and hospitals for the Negroes without public expense and far more efficiently than government agencies could perform them. It maintains the security and prosperity of the whites and also the physical well-being of the blacks.

The Saxon residing in the South with the negro, has chosen this system for his government. He claims the right to choose it or any other, and he claims this right by prerogative of race, by the decree of nature, which made him superior to the negro, in force of mind and character, and therefore his ruler. He will not relinquish this claim. He cannot if he would. . . . He will resist whilst he can, any power that shall attempt to interfere with that right or dictate to him how he shall use it.

In public affairs throughout the land the Negroes themselves are inarticulate and impotent. Yet, "by means of their weakness they control our politics; they conquer us by abject submission; they overwhelm us by mere prolific growth." The North and South have come to a clash as to the control of a vast western space.

True to his instincts of conqueror, colonizer, founder, the Saxon of the North claims this land for himself; he claims that he, and not the negro, shall occupy and till it, live on it and by it. Moved by the same inherent spirit, the Saxon of the South makes a similar demand. He will possess this region of promise, he says, and take with him his subject race, his serfs and vassals, to work it not for themselves, but for him; and to give plausibility to his claim, he calls them not citizens, not people, not even men, but property. Why may not he, as well as the northern man, go to the new territories with his property? To this the northern Saxon replies, that these negroes are not property, but men, and bring with them human influences, not of the highest order; but whether property or not, they will occupy the land and consume its produce, both and all of which he wants for his own race.

This affords one of several instances in which, after evolving an interpretation all my own, further delving in the records has brought forth a document expressing my novel views decades before I was born. In such cases emotions are mixed: satisfaction at the corroboration, with chagrin at having been anticipated. But, after all, historical discoveries are very likely to be rediscoveries; and they may not be less in point for that. It is well to be humble in esteem of our own exploits.

Having philosophized upon race relations at large in a manner comporting thoroughly with Southern thought, Fisher cast his own advocacy on the territorial question to the side of the North. But he hoped that a Southern acquiescence in this might come from an assurance that Northern will, abiding by the clear implications of the Constitution, and enlightened by true knowledge of racial necessities, would not endanger the "Saxon" control of Negroes in the Southern states.

* * *

When the dread clash of arms had come and gone, when slavery was abolished and radical "reconstruction" in full sway, Edward A.

Pollard, a historian of the Confederacy who had mingled endorsement of its objective with censure of its program, found ground for hope and set it forth in *The Lost Cause Regained*.[36] Analyzing the past and present, he saw the crux of Southern purpose in the maintenance of white supremacy as a safeguard of civilization and orderly government. In its social phase, as a barrier against interracial equality and conflict, he thought slavery had had so great a value that its economic phase ought to have been made merely incidental in public discussion. He therefore scolded the Southern spokesmen for having subordinated the major phase to the minor and for having indulged overmuch in futile emphasis upon constitutional sanctions. He cited the refusal in 1866 and 1867 of sundry Northern states to extend their suffrage to the Negroes as evidence that even in sequel to the war the rehabilitation of white control in the South, with Northern acquiescence, was not hopeless. How much better would it have been, he therefore argued, if the crucial question had been cogently set forth and never beclouded by technicalities and false issues.

In this long chapter we have seen that more than a few Southerners had endeavored with zeal to do what Pollard thought ought to have been done. To see how their clear purpose was complicated we turn again to politics.

[36] New York, 1868. This book, though much less known, is quite as important as Pollard's *Lost Cause* (New York and Baltimore, 1867). His *Southern Spy* (New York, 1859), also published under the title *Black Diamonds*, shows that the racial phase of slavery was of active concern in his earlier thought.

CHAPTER VI

THE FIRE-EATERS

The more one explores the records, the more elusive are the beginnings of any doctrine and the more complex the progress of any policy. The standard historians, in blissful ignorance of many matters, have simplified the programs in and for the Old South till the participants if they should now come to life would hardly recognize the result. A crowd of monographic writers in our century have brought to light so many details of long-forgotten lore that students are now taken aback by the new knowledge of currents, crosscurrents, and counter-currents, of pushes and pauses, of personal ambitions and thwartings, accords, antipathies, and contrarieties, to the effect that a new simplification is now demanded even though it involves, as always, a risk of error. Perhaps it will help us to remark that men of that time lived in a welter of conditions which they sought to grasp, of doctrines and policies which they tried to appraise and choose among, of uncertainties as to just how any of these would work and of what in general the future was to bring. Even as we are, so were they; and as they are so shall we be, *mutatis mutandis,* in the judgment of posterity.

Quoting the *Century Dictionary,* fire-eater means (1) "a juggler who pretends to eat fire"; (2) colloquially, "a person of recklessly defiant disposition, especially a persistent duellist; specifically in the United States before the Civil War, a violent and bitter Southern partisan." While this may facilitate identifications, our concern will not be with violence and bitterness as earmarks but with persistent advocacy of Southern independence. Let us examine the grounds and the hamperings of that advocacy, while not ignoring its method or its tone.

The main ground, of course, was the conviction, false or true, that an overpowering North was going to use federal authority sooner or later to impose Northern will for the promotion of Northern advantage and the indulgence of Northern impulse, mulcting the South financially and destroying the Southern industrial and

THE FIRE-EATERS

social order quite regardless of local consequences. Anyone so convinced was impelled thereby to seek an exit for his community from the Union. Mere honesty and belief in his own intelligence made him zealous for disunion. His personal traits and his diagnosis of the temper of his neighbors would influence his choice of method as between quiet persuasion and fervid exhorting.

The main breeding ground of the fire-eaters lay in South Carolina, and more specifically in the coastal plantation district on either flank of Charleston. The city itself was a forum rather than a focus. Like all Southern cities, it had a minority of Negroes in its population, so small as to constitute no serious menace even if they were freed. Furthermore, its commerce in goods and ideas was with all the world, including the less apprehensive upland communities. Therefore, while individual Charlestonians were at any time likely to view prospects with great alarm and indulge a vehemence of expression, the citizens when going to the polls tended to show majorities in favor of temperate and somewhat cautious policy.

But in the plantation parishes, where the Negroes outnumbered the whites several fold, and where a planter's family typically dwelt amid a horde of blacks, complete and chaotic ruin was envisaged as a result of upheaval or overthrow. These lowland planters, numbered by hundreds rather than by thousands, were far too few to contemplate a separate political destiny for themselves; and South Carolina was too small to make of herself an independent republic unless in dire emergency and in prospect of prompt adhesion by neighboring commonwealths. No confines but those of the great and greater South limited the plans of regional indoctrination and the hopes of separate integration.

Without seeking an Adam for this genus, we may find a stem for the fire-eaters' family tree in Robert J. Turnbull, who gave coastal Carolina clamant voice in the 'twenties and early 'thirties. In the Northern bloc in Congress on the Missouri question, in the Northern increase of tariff spoliations, in the abolition agitation and in other phenomena he saw ruin impending for the South, and he demanded intrepid resistance to the Northern "conspiracy" whether within or without the Union.

In an elaborate pamphlet of 1827 he harangued South Carolina:

> Let her only WILL that she will *not submit* to the tariff, and to impertinent interferences of Congress, with her policy, and the business is three-fourths finished.—There will, perhaps, be no necessity for calling out the

militia— There will, probably, be no civil war. . . . Let South-Carolina act for herself, and the other [neighboring] States for themselves. It is time enough to enter into league when war shall be declared. Should we even be subjugated, what then? We shall have the proud consolation of not having submitted without a struggle. . . . There is not an atom of disgrace in being vanquished. But there is meanness in submission. [He concluded:] I have written for the Planters of South-Carolina, and for the Merchants, Mechanics and other freemen of our State, who live amongst us and who are to *sink* or *swim* with the Southern Country; and not for those men who in every dispute between the North and the South, . . . *look* to Boston for their *instructions*. . . . Least of all do I care, whether I please those busy politicians, who are moving heaven and earth for JACKSON or for ADAMS, and who are alarmed at any sentiment, which can divert the public mind, from a subject, in which they themselves may have a strong interest, and the people of South-Carolina little or none, compared to the subject of these numbers.[1]

Turnbull here identified a factor which was to clog the program of the fire-eaters for many years. The supporters of Adams and of Jackson in 1827 were the Whigs and the Democrats of the next decade and the next; and even a Calhoun man, in the sense of a supporter of him for the Presidency, knew that good-will must be won in the far quarters as well as in the great middle zone of the United States.

The Democratic and Whig parties originated in a linking of local factions within sundry states to constitute country-wide organizations. In this process local purposes, while not wholly laid aside, were subordinated more or less consciously to federal or national programs, whatever they might be. The name Democrat implied enlargement of the franchise, increase of activity by the mass of the people, that the will of the millions be made to control the law and the public policy. The name Whig, borrowed from English history, implied a restraint of autocracy, an emphasis upon legislative deliberation as against executive power and in particular against the furious whims of Andrew Jackson in the White House.

Thanks to the tariff compromise of 1833, the protectionists and the nullifiers were able to lock their shields in joint phalanx to protect the good and the rich, the conservative and intelligent, with constitutional safeguards against irresponsible impulses of the common, untrained, short-sighted masses—to cherish, as they would say, "justice, forbearance, generosity, moderation and magnanimity" as

---

[1] *The Crisis: or Essays on the Usurpations of the Federal Government. By Brutus* [Robert J. Turnbull], pp. 163, 165.

traits of policy. Andrew Jackson was himself a slave-holding planter, as also James K. Polk, Jefferson Davis, and many another Democratic partisan, while on the other hand thousands of Southern Whigs had no slaves nor lively hopes of acquiring large property of any sort. Likewise at the North it was a mere tendency, by no means complete, for the well-to-do to become Whigs, the ill-to-do to vote as Democrats. The rich could not afford to stress this cleavage, for the poor were in majority always and everywhere; and the poor were often averse to proclaiming it, for their poverty was a bit of a disgrace in their own eyes.

The degree of social cleavage between the parties is, however, not of much present moment, nor the details of Democratic and Whig programs. Suffice it here to say that each party had a clientele distributed in every state and county of the land, and each was concerned with retaining every part and person of its constituency. In particular the machine politicians, Whig or Democratic, were at all times assiduous in keeping open the road to office and the spoils of power. County, city, and state "rewards for service" were not ignored, but power at Washington was the highest goal. And apart from spoils, repute of presidents and great senators was so high that state functionaries were satellites of these luminaries, and federal action was of such large scope that state problems and programs were comparatively trivial in esteem. A Virginian wrote from the Hall of Delegates at Richmond in 1841: "We are doing but little in the Legislature. The only questions which excite much interest are of a Federal character, and except when some such topic is under discussion everything is calm and uninteresting. But let any reference be made to party interests and the fever is up forthwith, and a prolonged session and much excitement is the result."[2] The like might have been said in all other chambers most of the time.

The South had no President, no Congress, no capital, no principal focus of any sort. Men who were zealous for some regional policy might use the halls of the federal Congress if and when they could, or a state assembly, a rustic rostrum, an urban soap-box, a local newspaper, or a pamphlet press. Southern advocates made use of all of these, except maybe the soap-box; but the few fire-eaters who went to Congress found party restraints there so cogent as to baffle their purposes. Whigs and Democrats at large, and as such, did not wish to hear sectional grievances and regional threats. They wanted

[2] Manuscript in private possession.

to keep their own parties united and the country peaceful for the sake, among other things, of party prosperity. Northern politicians were not averse to scoring off the South, and *vice versa,* now and then. Thus David Wilmot introduced his famous Proviso to prove to his Pennsylvania constituents that a recent vote of his for tariff reduction did not imply a sale of himself to the South. But Northern and Eastern, Western and Southern party men were under party pressure to collaborate with fellows from every region, to placate irritations and to repress disrupting movements. Thus Turnbull was correct in appraising party devotees and men of high political ambition as actual or potential opponents of any sharply sectional program.

Turnbull died in 1833, and his mantle fell upon Robert Barnwell Rhett, who had been born in 1800 and bred in the southernmost corner of South Carolina, where slave plantations filled all the cleared landscape and completely determined the mental climate. Turnbull had said in '27 that the South ought to court and hasten a decision because every passing year was lessening its relative strength and diminishing its prospect of success in case of a clash of arms. Rhett in the next year exhorted his fellow-citizens:

The day of open opposition to the pretended powers of the Constitution cannot be far off; and it is that it may not go down in blood that we now call upon you to resist. . . . If you love life better than honor,—prefer ease to perilous glory, awake not! stir not! . . . Live in smiling peace with your insatiable oppressors, and die with the noble consolation that your submissive patience will survive triumphant your beggary and despair.

The flamboyant rhetoric of this was very soon discarded. Whatever may have been his traits in youth, in manhood Rhett was a firm religionist, a total abstainer from liquors, a contemner of duelling, and in spite of excitable temper, a man of austere habit. His earnestness undiminished, he had no camaraderie with which to give it a charm. His appeal was to reason, amid a people who loved emotion. Devoid of personal magnetism, his career must needs have been somewhat lonely. Though his thought continued violent, and was often bitter, his phrase was explicit, seldom fervid. By 1833 he had settled into his tone as well as into his course. He then said in the convention of South Carolina:

I ask the gentlemen upon this floor whether they can lay their hands upon their hearts, and say, that they are "ardently attached to the Union of these States." . . . Sir, if a Confederacy of the Southern States could now be obtained, should we not deem it a happy termination—happy beyond expectation, of our long struggle for our rights against oppression? . . . A people owning slaves are mad, or worse than mad, who do not hold their destinies in their own hands.[3]

This was too strong for even his fellow nullifiers to stomach, and Rhett resigned his public appointment. After a few years, however, he was elected to Congress, and there offered a resolution in 1838:

> The constitution of the United States having proved inadequate to protect the Southern States in the peaceful enjoyment of their rights and property, it is expedient that the said constitution should be amended or the Union of the States dissolved.
> Resolved—that a Committee of two members from each State in the Union be appointed, to report upon the expediency and practicability of amending the Constitution, or the best means of peaceably dissolving the Union.

This of course failing of adoption, Rhett contented himself with the gesture, and labored to promote Calhoun's election to the Presidency. When this failed in 1844, and meanwhile the tariff had been heightened again and a treaty for Texan annexation thwarted and the House rule against anti-slavery petitions undermined, Rhett, impatient at Calhoun's quietism, preached at Bluffton and elsewhere in his district a crusade to nullify the tariff afresh and to prepare the South for independence: "I proclaim to you that if you value your rights you must resist; submit not, discharge your duties faithfully to yourselves, your children, your country and your God, and we will ensure a glorious triumph." The "Bluffton movement" evoked endorsement from the veterans Langdon Cheves and George McDuffie; but Calhoun quashed it, and Rhett went back to Congress to be mollified by Texan annexation in '45, tariff reduction in '46, and prospects of Calhoun's election to succeed Polk.

Rhett did not shun honors and emoluments of office. He was quite willing to serve as congressman and then senator of the United States, and willing to believe, from time to time, that his party (Whig until 1839, Democratic afterward) might so shape the temper and policy of the Union as to make the prospect of the South tolerable therein. Pity the poor fire-eater. Upon the stage he swallows flame; but in private life he needs more solid sustenance, three times a day. Rhett had a wife and a dozen children, and then another wife. His plantation proceeds were uncertain, and his interest in

[3] Laura A. White, *Robert Barnwell Rhett, Father of Secession* (New York, 1932), pp. 26, 27.

the Charleston *Mercury* brought more deficits than dividends. He therefore compromised once in a while; he was mad in an utter intransigeance only when a threatening wind blew from the North. While austere, he was human. More than this, he knew that as a leader of his people he could head the column only when and whither they were willing to march. Meanwhile as a public servant he took honest part in such routine as occasion required.

In a final friendly breach with Calhoun, Rhett opposed the project of a Southern convention in 1849 and '50, preferring separate state action, which he thought might be more or less concerted in advance and which he hoped would be followed by coalition in independence. Southern independence by separate secessions was the watchword whenever he was officer of the day.

Thanks to the searching biography just published by Miss Laura White, Rhett's career may be seen in detail. The lives of the rest of the fire-eaters can be known as yet only in outline, and their views gathered from out-of-the-way sources.

William Lowndes Yancey, the premium orator of secession, was a South Carolina planter who was bankrupted by the poisoning of his corps of slaves. Migrating to Alabama, he found a new career in law, politics, and agitation. Serving briefly in Congress during the middle 'forties, he soon became convinced that the South could have no effective voice nor he any useful function in those halls. He still hoped, however, that the Democratic party might be made an agent for Southern security; and from 1848 to '60 he made himself somewhat a nuisance as the leader of Alabama delegates to the Democratic national conventions, presenting intransigent platform demands concerning slavery in the territories. Between times he used every propitious occasion to exhort and organize the South for independence. Yancey kept always in friendly, collaborative touch with Rhett.

James D. B. De Bow, though very lean of purse, had a vision of great prosperity for the South to be promoted by his editing of a monthly commercial review. To launch this in 1846 he migrated from South Carolina to New Orleans. His initial zeal was in behalf of railroads, manufactures, and improvements of plantation method. His urging was to *"action!* ACTION!! ACTION!!!—not in the rhetoric of Congress, but in the busy hum of mechanism, and in the thrifty operations of the hammer and the anvil." The crisis of 1850 prompted him, in his issue for July, to declaim against Northern

THE FIRE-EATERS

aggressions, lament the Nashville convention's abortiveness, and appeal for Southern resistance. Such a flood of remonstrance poured in from subscribers that in October he humbly promised no more political fulminations. From the middle of the decade onward, however, he gave space increasingly to direct and indirect exhortations to Southern self-esteem and solidarity; and by 1860 he was a leading advocate of independence.

Another son of South Carolina, more explicitly fire-eating, was Louis T. Wigfall, who found his career in Texas. Not long after his migration he described his attitude in a letter of 1849 to Calhoun:

> Texas would probably not take the lead in opposition to the application of the Proviso to the Territories of New Mexico and California; but would follow willingly and almost unanimously the lead of any other State. I see from the papers that South Carolina is thinking about "United Southern action." I trust that 'tis not all she thinks of. The South I have hitherto thought could not be united for a blow, but when the blow is struck would unite for defense and stand as one man. There must be a Wat Tiler to knock down the excise man. I shall be disappointed if South Carolina does not on this occasion strike the blow.[4]

Edmund Ruffin caught the spark when making an agricultural survey of South Carolina, nourished it after his return home; and when Virginia declined to secede in the first months of '61 he "expatriated" himself to the Confederate States as then constituted, where, as a special mark of honor, he, though an aged civilian, was permitted to fire the first gun against Fort Sumter. Four years afterward, when Lee had surrendered, Ruffin wrapped himself in a Confederate flag and put a bullet through his brain. With the South conquered, life was to him intolerable.

Touch with South Carolina, nevertheless, was not essential as a source of the fire-eating impulse. Beverly Tucker in Virginia, George M. Troup, Wilson Lumpkin, and Henry L. Benning in Georgia, David Yulee in Florida, Mirabeau B. Lamar, a Georgia migrant to Texas, and a considerable sprinkling of others here and there found provocations in their own communities or their own minds. John A. Quitman, born and bred in the state of New York, moved in early manhood to Natchez for the practice of law. There he married a widow with a plantation, and whether from his wife or his neighbors he caught a fire-eating zeal. As governor of Mississippi in

[4] C. S. Boucher and R. P. Brooks, eds., "Correspondence Addressed to John C. Calhoun, 1837–1849," in the *Annual Reports of the American Historical Association for the Year 1929* (Washington, 1930), p. 494.

1850–51 he strove mightily to produce a secession then and there in concert with South Carolina. When the convention of Mississippi took action to the contrary, he was greatly chagrined but undaunted. Only death, before the decade's end, stopped his labors for independence.

Benning of Georgia, mentioned a moment ago, was one of many who contributed original notions, useful or fruitless as events might prove. He wrote in 1849:

I think . . . , that the only safety of the South from abolition universal is to be found in an *early* dissolution of the Union. . . . I think that as a remedy for the South, dissolution is not enough, and a Southern Confederacy not enough. The latter would not stop the process by which some states, Virginia for example, are becoming free, viz. by ridding themselves of their slaves; and therefore we should in time with a confederacy again have a North and a South. The only thing that will do when tried every way is a *consolidated* republic formed of the Southern states. That will put slavery *under the control of those most interested* in it, and nothing else will; and until that is done nothing is done.[5]

This advocacy of a unitary republic was without echo, for the stress of nearly all of the zealots upon the sovereignty of the several states as a rightful thing to be cherished carried an overwhelming implication after as well as before secession.

C. A. Price, quite unknown to fame, edited at Camden, South Carolina, in 1851 a weekly sheet entitled the "Southern Republic, a family newspaper devoted to literature, religion, science, arts, and Southern Rights." In his issue for July 5 he printed an editorial which is little short of marvelous as a piece of prophecy, though a decade instead of a year as he expected was required for its fulfilment. The rationale was equally pertinent in both periods:

We will secede! We lay this down as a fixed proposition, for we cannot believe in the accusation of our State's disgrace, in other words, that she will submit, until it becomes history. . . . The first assault will be made upon us by the Federal Government by the act of retaining the Forts about Charleston. *This will be war.* We entered the Confederacy [i.e. the Union] by delegating certain powers to the Federal Government as our *agent*—for certain purposes. With those *powers* we delegated or gave the Government certain portions of land in the neighborhood of Charleston for the purpose of the defence of our port. The *powers*, because *abused*, we *resume*. We take the defence of our ports in our own hands, and there-

[5] U. B. Phillips, ed., *The Correspondence of Robert Toombs, Alexander H. Stephens, and Howell Cobb*, being Volume II of the *Annual Report of the American Historical Association for the Year 1911* (Washington, 1913), p. 171.

THE FIRE-EATERS

fore the cause for the possession of those places by the Government having ceased, . . . by matter of right they revert to us. . . . Should the General Government then retain possession of them— It would be war, . . . not of our seeking, but that of the Government.

An anonymous Charlestonian in the same year was one of many to deny the charge of hastiness. When the convention then about to be elected secedes, he said, its action will be far from precipitate. For more than twenty years our people have argued, remonstrated, and threatened in the face of federal aggressions, and have waited in hope of a returning sense of justice in the North and sensible foresight in the South.

In '48 they called upon the Southern States to come up and do battle for Southern Rights, expressing repeatedly the willingness and desire of the State [South Carolina] to follow any leader in this momentous cause. One by one, States giving at first some indications of preparedness, have come short of effective resistance, and Carolina now stands in advance of her sister States, the only one ready for action. [Advocacy of prompt secession is not rash.] It is the shape which the slowly-formed conviction of years of observation have given to Resistance.[6]

This challenges comparison with a statement by J. F. Rhodes in his *History of the United States*[7] that although South Carolinians in 1860 were fond of analogies between their status and that of Boston, and often appealed to the spirit of 1776, the likeness was merely superficial "between that early protest accompanied by deliberate action against unjust taxation and this precipitate movement to break the bonds with States whose offence lay in the declaration that slavery was wrong and should not be extended." Nearly ten years in further deliberation intervened between our fire-eater's disavowal of precipitateness and the stroke which Rhodes thinks was precipitate when eventually made. Certainly the fire-eaters thought in 1851 that already their labors had been long enough.

We have now given these men enough of a hearing. Their Southern contemporaries read and heard them at much greater length, if not always with patience or conviction. A flood of pamphlets, editorials, and contributed articles poured from the presses at the mid-century, the Southern writers agreeing that the prevailing social order should be cherished, but much at odds in all things else. Wil-

[6] Letter signed "Action," in the Charleston *Mercury*, Feb. 11, 1851.
[7] III, 117.

liam J. Grayson of Charleston, for example, was firm for the maintenance of slavery, but equally firm for the preservation of the Union, praising it as maintaining internal peace, affording free trade and social intercourse throughout a broad country, conferring unexampled prosperity, and not really menacing Southern home rule. While United Italy and Germany were daydreams of patriots in those lands, he hoped that Americans, with their sense of the benefit of union deadened by long familiarity, would not test its value by its destruction. He thought that no states east of South Carolina or west of Mississippi would join a Southern confederacy, and that if such were formed it would be paralyzed by strife between the people of the mountains and those of the coast, and the chain of states would be but a rope of sand. Some, indeed, went so far as to say that the maintenance of the Union was the one sure means of perpetuating slavery. These men, who were not South Carolinians, argued that the North was not then and would not become abolitionist; but an attempt to split the Union would arouse hostility, precipitate a war, and thereby put all things at hazard, including particularly Negro slavery as the basic occasion for the conflict.

Still others took a middle ground, expressing a full sense of Southern grievance and apprehension, but contending that any stroke for independence would be folly without simultaneous action by several if not all of the Southern states. These coöperationists denied that they were submissionists or Unionists of any sort, but they firmly opposed separate state action and any decisive action unless and until interstate pledges were procured. William Capers, Protestant Episcopal bishop of South Carolina, was especially cogent against a separate stroke. After a journey to Tennessee and Louisiana, getting an impression that some three fourths of the citizens of those states, and of Georgia, Alabama, and Mississippi likewise, were opposed to disunion, he proclaimed upon return to Charleston in early '51: "There is no battle to be fought for glory by secession, but a fearful struggle with poverty, high taxes and hard times, without hope of improvement, and great and sore humiliation. And may God grant us deliverance."

Deliverance, or more truly postponement, was already in fair prospect, because the immediate secessionists acquiesced in a trial of coöperation, though they had no faith in that experiment. Calhoun had procured in 1849 a call from the Mississippi legislature

THE FIRE-EATERS

for a general convention of the Southern states, to meet at Nashville in June, 1850, with a view to deliberation and concert. Party politicians tended to look askance at any sectional project which might break habituated alignments, and they were busy enough with proceedings in Congress at this excited time. Some of them, however, procured their own election as delegates in order to keep the convention from drastic action. Sundry legislatures refrained from providing for the choice of delegates, and from such states unofficial delegates were seated. The convention was thus paralyzed in advance for anything beyond mere hortatory resolutions. After such were adopted the convention adjourned to await the decision of Congress upon a complex of pending bills; and in a second session, held after Congress had enacted the Compromise measures, no more than a rump attended. The distraughtness of this gathering, from first to last, proved that a Southern convention, at least under the conditions of that day, was a futile device. The fire-eaters had foretold this; and they remembered it afterward.

Meanwhile the Mississippi, Georgia, and South Carolina legislatures had provided for conventions of their own states, authorized to exercise sovereign power at discretion. The delegates in each case were elected after the congressional enactment of the Compromise of 1850; those of South Carolina purposely last of all in order that some other state might have prior opportunity to secede. But the Georgia convention endorsed the Compromise as a basis of preserving the Union, though it warned the North that this action would be reconsidered if Georgian hopes of inter-sectional justice and obligation proved false. The Mississippi convention was captured by thoroughgoing Unionists who caused it to declare by majority resolution, not only that Mississippi would not then secede, but no state had authority to secede.

When at last the South Carolina convention met, in April of 1852, its opportunity had flown in all esteem but that of the most thorough fire-eaters, who found themselves in a minority. That thorough Unionists numbered not a dozen delegates was no great solace. The convention having rejected many diverse proposals, adopted, by majority of 136 to 19, a manifesto:

> That the frequent violations of the constitution of the United States by the Federal government, and its encroachments upon the reserved rights of the sovereign states of this Union, especially in relation to slavery, amply justify this state, so far as any duty or obligation to her confederates

is involved, in dissolving at once all political connection with her co-states; and that she forbears the exercise of this manifest right of self-government from considerations of expediency only.

Thus thwarted in hopes of neighborly concert, and by delay till complete isolation would be the prospect if secession were adopted, South Carolina resolved to bide her time and to risk an imputation of mere gasconade. Rhett, willy-nilly, must acquiesce in the biding. But he was outraged at the convention's refusal to take measures of retaliation against the North or of preparedness for future conflict. He promptly wrote to the governor: "Sir,— In consequence of the proceedings of the Convention which has just adjourned, I deem myself no longer a proper representative of the position and policy of the people of South Carolina with respect [to] aggressions of the General Government. I therefore resign into the hands of your excellency the office I now hold as Senator in the Congress of the United States from the State of South Carolina." The governor, himself a secessionist, asked him to reconsider; but Rhett insisted upon retiring into private life until further notice. Thus ended the fire-eating ado of that period.

* * *

It seems to be the nature of men, women, and children to consider as right what possessions, privileges, and immunities they have and a good many that they desire. Some of these are so much a matter of course in an enlightened land that when established they cease to be discussed. The right of children to be schooled at public expense, though procured not many decades ago, is now not debatable. Woman suffrage, though not relished by all men, is accepted as irrevocable. Politics were bad before; they are worse now; but nothing can be done about it. Private property seemed quite as impregnable until Russia went communist. A steady job at a living wage for honest work seemed a right until for millions the present panic made it an aspiration instead.

Even wrongdoers, doubtless even the Chicago gangsters, manage to give their crime a color of right in their own eyes. By a process nowadays called rationalization, that is by framing a plausible justification, they more or less deceive themselves by seizing upon false premises or pursuing false logic. Many substantial citizens, lawyers, corporation executives, ministers of the gospel, perhaps even you and I, do something like this unaware. Certainly politicians indulge and actually cherish the proclivity.

The champions of any program or interest under public discussion are under pressure to magnify small matters and minimize large ones, to emphasize a particular phase, to channel the thought of the people, to simplify and again simplify an issue that it may be grasped by the meanest intelligence and therefore by the multitude, to seize a symbol and exalt it that men may be made ardent in their persuasion.

A Southern philosopher, so long forgotten that it is barely worth naming him as Albert T. Bledsoe, said of the churches: "The Christian rule, 'first cast the beam out of thine own eye,' is utterly despised and neglected by the Christian sects. If any sect has an absurd dogma in its creed, that is sure to be its 'burning article.' " [8] But Bledsoe himself was a very warm champion of Southern rights, and in that capacity was blissfully unaware that he was doing just what he charged upon the churches.

More directly concerned with Southern rights; with a minimum of meretricious rationalization, was an anonymous article in *Russell's Magazine*, published at Charleston, May, 1857.

> The existence of slavery at the South, and its connection with the Union, [said its writer] has placed us in a peculiar position. Our whole fabric of society is based upon slave institutions, and yet our conventional language is drawn from scenes totally at variance with those which lie about us. Our books come from England and the North, and they appear *prima fâcie* to be our teachers. For some time we have been content to compromise with our supposed teachers, that is, to adhere rigorously to the facts but complacently adopt the cant, (for on our lips it is no better,) of a free society. The rude manner in which we have been assailed has opened our eyes to our real condition, and in the spirit of truthfulness some of us have dared to look boldly upon it, and are daily employed in giving utterance to thoughts in strict accordance with the facts presented. And the more truthful the language we have used, the more virulent the denunciations with which our society has been assailed. . . . We of the South were formerly taught to believe that slavery is a social, moral and political evil. . . . We are now condemned for changing our views on this subject. It is an omen for good that we have changed them. . . . We assert, not that slavery is a good thing, but that it is not an evil thing . . . which . . . must be abated. . . . Slavery and poverty are alike disagreeable conditions to look forward to; but in the economy of nature they appear alike indispensable. . . . So long as we regarded slavery as an

[8] *Southern Review*, VIII, 428 (Oct., 1870).

evil, it was a prohibited subject. . . . Things have changed. There are few persons in the South who have not read Uncle Tom's Cabin. . . . We may well rejoice at the result. We can now respect ourselves. The truth is rapidly emancipating us from the bondage of fear. [After discussing the sectional tension, he said:] We . . . conclude that the Union of these States, under any circumstances, is a serious obstacle to our fair development. The philosophy of a people must concentrate itself in their metropolis, . . . and all that portion of the people which is not represented there must be regarded as provincials. Circumstances have placed the metropolis of this Union beyond the direct influence of the slaveholding power. . . . Our place in the Union is provincial, and as such our peculiarities will have to be defended, excused, ridiculed, pardoned. We can take no pride in our national character, because we must feel that from our peculiar position we do not contribute to its formation. . . . In the Union we can never enjoy that repose which is necessary to a healthy development of our character. . . . As London was to our fathers, so are New York and Boston to ourselves. We can never be other than dependants and inferiors so long as we continue to live with them on a footing of political alliance. . . . The philosophy of the North is a dead letter to us. . . . Our philosophy has yet to be developed. We can not live honestly in the Union, because we are perpetually aiming to square the maxims of an impracticable philosophy with the practice which nature and circumstances force upon us. We can not do ourselves justice so long as the drag of provincialism is forever clinging to our wheels.

If this was too philosophical for the multitude, there were plenty of zealots to simplify the message. Preston Brooks, after his assault upon Sumner and his resignation from the House, exhorted his constituents in South Carolina in 1856:

We have the issue upon us now; and how are we to meet it? I tell you, fellow citizens, from the bottom of my heart, that the only mode which I think available for meeting it, *is just to tear the Constitution of the United States, trample it under foot, and form a Southern Confederacy, every State of which will be a slaveholding State.* [Loud and prolonged cheers.] I believe it, as I stand in the face of my maker; I believe it on my responsibility to you as your honored representative, that *the only hope of the South is in the South, and that the only available means of making that hope effective is to cut asunder the bonds that tie us together, and take our separate position in the family of nations.* These are my opinions. They have always been my opinions. *I have been a disunionist from the time I could think.*[9]

A humble and illiterate response to such harangues appears in the prayer of a plantation overseer, which I transcribed from his

[9] Loring Moody, *The Destruction of Republicanism the Object of the Rebellion* (2d ed., Boston, 1863), p. 11.

journal on a sugar estate forty miles down-river from New Orleans. It is highly individual in spelling, and altogether innocent of punctuation:

Thursday 13 June 1861
This Day is set a part By presedent Jefferson Davis for fasting and praying owing to the Deplorable condition ower southern country is In My Prayer Sincerely to God is that every Black Republican in the Hole combined whorl either man woman o chile that is opposed to negro slavery as it existed in the Southern confederacy shal be trubled with pestilents and calamitys of all Kinds and Drag out the Balance of there existance in Misray and Degradation with scarsely food and rayment enughf to keep sole and Body to gather and o God I pray the to Direct a bullet or a bayonet to pirce The Hart of every northern soldier that invades southern soile and after the Body has rendered up its traterish sole gave it a trators reward a Birth In the Lake of Fires and Brimstone my honest convicksion is that every man wome and chile that has gave aide to the abolitionist are fit subjects for Hell I all so ask the to aide the southern Confederacy in maintaining ower rites and establishing the confederate Government Believing this case the prares from the wicked will prevaileth much Amen.[10]

These expressions, whether calm or frenzied—and a hundred others might be quoted—have a representative quality not the product of a season but of a span of time long enough for a multitude to become indoctrinated and grow strong in its faith. The span, as we have seen, was more than a decade. Jefferson Davis, who was not a fire-eater in the consistent sense, had said in the Senate, early in 1850:

A large part of the non-slaveholding States have declared war against the institution of slavery. They have announced that it shall not be extended, and with that annunciation have coupled the declaration that it is a stain upon the Republic—that it is a moral blot which should be obliterated. Now, sir, can anyone believe, does anyone hope, that the southern States in this Confederacy will continue, as time goes by, to support the Union, to bear its burdens in peace and war, . . . if that very Government is to be arrayed in hostility against an institution so interwoven with its interests, its domestic peace, and all its social relations, that it cannot be disturbed without their overthrow?

Again in the same year he said that the Northern movement was "no longer the clamor of a noisy fanaticism, but the steady advance of a self-sustaining power to the goal of unlimited supremacy." In persuasion against this he made earnest appeal:

[10] See page 153. [Repetition there made necessary by the context. ED.]

Then, Senators, countrymen, brethren—by these and by other appellations, if there be others more endearing and impressive than these,—I call upon you to pause in the course which, pressed by an intemperate zeal, you are pursuing, and warn you, lest blinded by the lust for sectional dominion, you plunge into an abyss in which will lie buried forever the glorious memories of the past, the equally glorious hopes for the future, and the present immeasurable happiness of our common country. It is not as one who threatens, nor as one who prepares for collision with his enemies, but as one who has a right to invoke your fraternal feelings and guard you against an error which will bear equally on us both; . . . it is as an American citizen that I speak to an American Senate—it is in this character that I have ventured to warn you; it is with this feeling that I make this solemn appeal.

If this oratory was a bit unctuous, the sincerity can hardly be questioned. Throughout the 'fifties Davis denied that any conflict between the sections was irrepressible. Like Calhoun, part of whose mantle fell upon him, he hoped to become President of the United States; and I think he would have served in that office with much better effect than he did as chief executive of the Confederacy.

When Senator, Secretary of War, and Senator again, Jefferson Davis was chief spokesman of the United States Army, advocating its improvement and enlargement, while the Free-soilers and Republicans, wanting river and harbor appropriations and other local benefits from the federal treasury, resisted measures of military preparedness. In our wisdom after the event it seems incredible that the man who was to become an arch-rebel should labor to prepare the means of his own destruction, while those who were destined to use that machine in the 'sixties opposed its improvement. But he and they were ignorant of this destiny. More than that, they denied the prospect when some fire-eaters and others foretold it. In the thought of Davis and of many others the rights of the South were so clear and essential that all rational men must admit and endorse them. If these rights were expounded clearly and in firm but friendly tone, ultimate denial by the North was incredible.

Thomas Jefferson had long ago shuddered at the consequences "of the coincidence of a moral principle and a geographical line." But John Quincy Adams had said, when celebrating the semicentennial of the Constitution in 1839: "If the day should ever come (may Heaven avert it) when the affections of the people of these states shall be alienated from each other, . . . far better will it be for the people of the disunited states to part in friendship from each other, than to be held together by constraint. Then will be the time . . . to form again a more perfect union, by dissolving that which could no longer bind, and to leave the separated parts to be reunited by the law of political gravitation to the centre." And Webster, on the celebrated seventh of March, said that, convinced that slavery was excluded from the Mexican acquisitions by physical geography, considering that "both California and New Mexico are destined to be free, . . . I would not take pains to reaffirm an ordinance of nature, nor to reënact the will of God. And I would put in no Wilmot proviso, for the purpose of a taunt or a 'reproach.' " [11]

The doctrine of Southern rights was in essence that the community must possess and be assured of possessing control of its own domestic régime; that the South must be and remain a white man's country not menaced with the turmoil sure to come from an incautious, extraneous elevation of the millions of Negroes out of their necessary subordination. This was the crux, the test in which "true" Southerners were adamant. Additional, and in some Southern opinion superfluous, were demands intended to test the Northern purpose, most important of these the demand for congressional sanction of slavery's territorial expansion. To use Bledsoe's phrase again, it was a questionable dogma made into a burning article.

This demand had arisen from the mathematics of the Constitution. It had been effective though compromised in the Missouri struggle, and again in the Wilmot crisis. In 1850 the conditions changed. Congress, while admitting California as a free state and thereby destroying the sectional equilibrium in the Senate, had organized Utah and New Mexico as territories without excluding slavery from them. On the one hand the Northern predominance in Congress was made complete; on the other hand a technical territorial demand of the South had prevailed. Sundry other vexed questions were settled in so far as Congress could settle them; and, as we have seen, the bulk of the community was calmed enough to quash the fire-eaters' projects. But the doctrine of Southern rights had been completely formulated, and its devotees put upon permanent *qui vive*.

The lull in sectional clamor was not long. Abolitionists railed at the fugitive slave act of 1850, riots obstructed its enforcement, and the Northern states began to paralyze it by their own "personal liberty laws." *Uncle Tom's Cabin* made an unprecedented sensation

[11] *Congressional Globe*, 31st Cong., 1st sess. (1849–1850), vol. 21, pt. 1, 480, 481.

on both sides of the Atlantic. In England it was reported that 150,000 people were employed in printing and binding copies to meet the British demand. In America millions were put to sobbing over the noble victim's fate. A Southerner said that Uncle Tom was more Christlike than anyone short of Christ himself, and if slavery produced him it was an accolade for that abused institution. But Southerners at large were aware that the world and the North were not accepting the "terrible book" in that sense. The Whig party began to break up, depriving the Union of an important cement. Yet except for a new Western imbroglio the prospect was not ominous.

Douglas had sought for years to promote a railroad to the Pacific in the latitude of Chicago, and, as a facilitation of this as well as for general Western purposes, to open the Nebraska region to settlement by organizing a territory there. But again and again Eastern and Southern members in the Senate or the House had combined to defeat his bills. Douglas as a Western spokesman accepted the doctrine of "popular sovereignty"; and as 1853 drew to its end he applied it as a device to draw Southern votes to Northwestern advantage. Thus was begun the project which took form in '54 as a bill to organize the territories of Kansas and Nebraska with a repeal of the Missouri Compromise prohibition of slavery in that region. Most of the Southerners took this as a gesture of generosity from the North; they rallied to support it; and the bill was enacted with speed. This act's implications were opposite to those of the Wilmot Proviso; but its repercussions were similar and far more serious. If Southerners rejoiced in this unexpected if slender opportunity, Northerners by mounting thousands condemned it as a breach of established controls, as treason to liberty's cause, as a calamity which must be conquered.

A contest of speed in colonizing voters in Kansas ensued, fraud in elections there, fisticuffs and shooting affrays between Border Ruffians and Jayhawkers, and John Brown's murders on Pottawatomie Creek. In Congress came an almost equal hurly-burly, and at the polls a new party, styled Republican, committed to the complete exclusion of slavery from the territories and laboring to solidify the North in a phalanx.

The South was greatly chagrined and alarmed. Her spokesmen refurbished their armor of Southern rights, proclaiming that under the Constitution slavery could not be excluded from any territory whether by Congress or the local population. The Supreme Court

THE FIRE-EATERS

endorsed this in the Dred Scott case, only to embitter the question instead of settling it. Union-savers, mainly dwelling in the middle zone of the country, had a fresh task of pacifying the two extremes. The people of Virginia, whose rôle had long been placative and mediatory, were profoundly stirred by John Brown's onslaught at Harper's Ferry and by Northern sympathy for that fanatic's fate.

Meanwhile in the decade's middle and later years, appeals were cogent for the South to consolidate its own strength and seize firmer control of its own destiny. A series of annual gatherings, instituted initially to discuss business questions and styled commercial conventions, was caught up for politico-sectional purposes. In their agenda the promotion of railroads and steamship lines was mingled with advocacy that Southern youths be sent only to Southern colleges, free from infection by Northern social heresies; that textbooks of Southern tone be prepared and published for the same sectionally patriotic purpose; that the South patronize Southern manufactures and watering-places, to diminish Northern profits and increase home resources and solidarity; that Cuba be annexed and the African slave trade reopened; and that the Southern forts be strengthened.

Though more or less endorsed by press and politicians, these projects mostly came to naught. As to textbooks, the single response which has come to my knowledge is *Elements of Algebra*, by D. H. Hill, then a professor in a North Carolina college and afterward a Confederate officer of high rank. Among its problems is this: "A Yankee mixes a certain number of wooden nutmegs, which cost him $\frac{1}{4}$ cent apiece, with a quantity of real nutmegs, worth 4 cents apiece, and sells the whole assortment for $44; and gains $3.75 by the fraud. How many wooden nutmegs were there?" And this: The Buena Vista battlefield is $6\frac{1}{2}$ miles from Saltillo. "Two Indiana volunteers ran away from the battle at the same time; one ran half a mile faster than the other, and reached Saltillo 5 minutes and $54\frac{6}{11}$ seconds sooner than the other. Required, their respective rates of travel." The answer, if you care to know it, is $5\frac{1}{2}$ and 6 miles per hour, which are but moderate speeds for Indiana volunteers in flight.

A combing of the book yields only nine other problems having implications derogatory to the North or hortatory to the South. Hill's spirit was willing, but his performance was weak. Others may have put more propaganda into textbooks, but presumably they did not get them into print, for the Southern demand was not large enough to warrant a publisher's expenditure as against competing claims of books which would not be debarred from Northern use.

Likewise the demand for a reopening of the African slave trade was a forlorn hope at best. The main bulk of the Southerners who discussed it expressed opposition on cogent economic and social grounds; and the Federal Congress was certain never to repeal its prohibitory laws. The question had no value except a possibly provocative one, to suggest to the people that here was a thing which if they should perchance want they could not get so long as the South continued under the control of the North. Yancey, with some other fire-eaters, fell in with the project as a mere means of agitation. But the so-called commercial conventions became in some degree discredited as meetings of cranks, condemned by their own futility. In a measure they contributed to keep the South alert; but it was in the halls and lobbies of Congress and the state legislatures, in the press, on the hustings, and in leisurely summer conversation between drinks at White Sulphur Springs that the most weighty views were expressed and actions planned.

It was fittingly in the Senate at Washington that Robert Toombs of Georgia, long a watch-dog of the federal Treasury and a tribune of the Southern people, answered his own question, "What do these rebels demand?" They demanded that slave property be nowhere prohibited by Congress, and by no authority in any territory, but be protected like other sorts of property everywhere except in such states as forbade it by their own laws; that abductors of slaves who might flee from one state to another be delivered up in the same way as persons committing crimes against other property, to be tried under the laws of the state where the crime had been committed; that fugitive slaves be surrendered as provided by act of Congress, without obstruction of laws in any state into which they might flee; and that Congress legislate efficiently to punish persons in any state who should abet invasion or insurrection in any other state.

> We demand these five propositions. . . . Take them in detail, and show that they are not warranted by the Constitution, by the safety of our people, by the principles of eternal justice. We will pause and consider them; but, mark me, we will not let you decide the question for us. [This was Toombs's farewell speech to the Senate. He concluded:] Restore us these rights as we had them, as your court adjudges them to be; . . . re-

dress these flagrant wrongs, . . . and it will restore fraternity, and peace, and unity, to all of us. Refuse them, and what then? We shall then ask you, "Let us depart in peace." Refuse that, and you present us war. We accept it; and . . . will trust to the blood of the brave and the God of battles for security and tranquillity.[12]

But even Toombs declared at home that he stood ready to drink all the blood that was going to be shed in this crisis. He could not believe that the North would put an imperious military veto upon a program so much in keeping with American precedent and the gospel of self-government, so legitimated by state sovereignty, so long considered, and now supported by such a multitude of conservative citizens as that for Southern independence.

[12] *Congressional Globe,* 36th Cong., 2nd sess. (1860–1861), pt. 1, 269, 271.

[Professor Phillips wrote the following article some years before the preceding six chapters; but as it contains the germs of important points later developed in "The Course of the South to Secession," it has been republished here as helping to complete the unity of this volume.]

THE CENTRAL THEME OF SOUTHERN HISTORY [1]

An Ohio River ferryman has a stock remark when approaching the right bank: "We are nearing the American shore." A thousand times has he said it with a gratifying repercussion from among his passengers; for its implications are a little startling. The northern shore is American without question; the southern is American with a difference. Kentucky had by slender pretense a star in the Confederate flag; for a time she was officially neutral; for all time her citizens have been self-consciously Kentuckians, a distinctive people. They are Southerners in main sentiment, and so are Marylanders and Missourians.

Southernism did not arise from any selectiveness of migration, for the sort of people who went to Virginia, Maryland, or Carolina were not as a group different from those who went to Pennsylvania or the West Indies. It does not lie in religion or language. It was not created by one-crop tillage, nor did agriculture in the large tend to produce a Southern scheme of life and thought. The Mohawk valley was for decades as rural as that of the Roanoke; wheat is as dominant in Dakota as cotton has ever been in Alabama; tobacco is as much a staple along the Ontario shore of Lake Erie as in the Kentucky pennyroyal; and the growing of rice and cotton in California has not prevented Los Angeles from being in a sense the capital of Iowa. On the other hand the rise of mill towns in the Carolina Piedmont and the growth of manufacturing at Richmond and Birmingham have not made these communities Northern. It may be admitted, however, that Miami, Palm Beach, and Coral Gables are Southern only in latitude. They were vacant wastes until Flagler, Fifth Avenue, and the realtors discovered and subdivided them.

The South has never had a focus. New York has plied as much of its trade as Baltimore or New Orleans; and White Sulphur Springs did not quite eclipse all other mountain and coast resorts for vacation patronage. The lack of a metropolis was lamented in 1857 by

[1] This article formed the basis of a discussion at the meeting of the American Historical Association at Indianapolis, in 1928.

an advocate of Southern independence,[2] as lack of an essential for shaping and radiating a coherent philosophy to fit the prevailing conditions of life. But without a consolidating press or pulpit or other definite apparatus the South has maintained a considerable solidarity through thick and thin, through peace and war and peace again. What is its essence? Not state rights—Calhoun himself was for years a nationalist, and some advocates of independence hoped for a complete merging of the several states into a unitary Southern republic; not free trade—sugar and hemp growers have ever been protectionists; not slavery—in the eighteenth century this was of continental legality, and in the twentieth it is legal nowhere; not Democracy—there were many Federalists in Washington's day and many Whigs in Clay's; not party predominance by any name, for Virginia, Georgia, and Mississippi were "doubtful states" from Jackson's time to Buchanan's. It is not the land of cotton alone or of plantations alone; and it has not always been the land of "Dixie," for before its ecstatic adoption in 1861 that spine-tingling tune was a mere "walk-around" of Christie's minstrels. Yet it is a land with a unity despite its diversity, with a people having common joys and common sorrows, and, above all, as to the white folk a people with a common resolve indomitably maintained—that it shall be and remain a white man's country. The consciousness of a function in these premises, whether expressed with the frenzy of a demagogue or maintained with a patrician's quietude, is the cardinal test of a Southerner and the central theme of Southern history.

It arose as soon as the Negroes became numerous enough to create a problem of race control in the interest of orderly government and the maintenance of Caucasian civilization. Slavery was instituted not merely to provide control of labor but also as a system of racial adjustment and social order. And when in the course of time slavery was attacked, it was defended not only as a vested interest, but with vigor and vehemence as a guarantee of white supremacy and civilization. Its defenders did not always take pains to say that this was what they chiefly meant, but it may nearly always be read between their lines, and their hearers and readers understood it without overt expression.[3] Otherwise it would be impossible to ac-

---

[2] *Russell's Magazine* (Charleston), I, 106.

[3] Many expressions were explicit, for example, the remarks of Mr. Standard at Richmond in 1829: "The property we seek to protect . . . is not mere brute matter . . . but it consists of intelligent, sentient, responsible beings, that have passions to be inflamed, hearts to feel, understandings to be enlightened, and who

CENTRAL THEME OF SOUTHERN HISTORY 153

count for the fervid secessionism of many non-slave-holders and the eager service of thousands in the Confederate army.

The non-slave-holders of course were diverse in their conditions and sentiments. Those in the mountains and the deep pine woods were insulated to such a degree that public opinion hardly existed, and they chose between alternatives only when issues created in other quarters were forced upon them. Those in the black belts, on the other hand, led lives conditioned by the presence of the Negroes; and they had apparatus of court days, militia musters, and political barbecues as well as neighborhood conversation to keep them abreast of affairs. A mechanic of Iuka, Mississippi, wrote in the summer of 1861: "I am a Georgian Raised I am Forty years Old A tinner By Trade I Raised the First Confederate Flag that I Ever Heard Of that was in 1851 in the Town of Macon Miss. Notwithstanding the Many Radicules I Encounter'd I Told the Citizens that they would All Be Glad to Rally under Such a Flag Some Day which is at present true." [4] This personal tale was told to prove his title to a voice in Confederate policy. His main theme was a demand that the permanent Confederate constitution exclude Negroes from all employment except agricultural labor and domestic service in order that the handicrafts be reserved for white artisans like himself.

The overseer of a sugar estate forty miles below New Orleans inscribed a prayer on the plantation journal:

Thursday 13 June 1861
This Day is set a part By presedent Jefferson Davis for fasting and praying owing to the Deplorable condition ower southern country is In My Prayer Sincerely to God is that every Black Republican in the Hole combined whorl either man woman o chile that is opposed to negro slavery as it existed in the Southern confederacy shal be trubled with pestilents and calamitys of all Kinds and Drag out the Balance of there existance in Misray and Degradation with scarsely food and rayment enughf to keep sole and Body to gather and o God I pray to Direct a bullet or a bayonet to pirce The Hart of every northern soldier that invades southern soile and after the Body has rendered up its traterish sole gave it a trators reward a Birth In the Lake of Fires and Brimstone my honest convicksion

---

are capable of catching the flame of enthusiasm from the eloquent effusions of agitators . . . ; and who may not only be lost to their masters as property, but may change conditions and become masters themselves, so far at least as the ravages of a servile war shall have [error for *leave*] any subject to be ruled over." *Proceedings and Debates of the Virginia State Convention of 1829–30* (Richmond, 1830), p. 306.
[4] Manuscript letter in private possession.

is that every man wome and chile that has gave aide to the abolishionist are fit subjects for Hell I all so ask the to aide the southern Confederacy in maintaining ower rites and establishing the confederate Government Believing this case the prares from the wicked will prevaileth much Amen [5]

This overseer's penciled prayer is the most rampant fire-eating expression which I have encountered in any quarter. He and the tinner had an economic interest in the maintenance of slavery, the one to assure the presence of laborers for him to boss, the other to restrain competition in his trade. But both of them, and a million of their non-slave-holding like, had a still stronger social prompting: the white men's ways must prevail; the Negroes must be kept innocuous.

In the 'forties when most of the planters were Whig, some of the Democratic politicians thought it strange that their own party should be the more energetic in defense of slavery; and in 1860 they were perhaps puzzled again that the Bell and Everett Constitutional Union ticket drew its main support from among the slave-holders. The reason for this apparent anomaly lay doubtless in two facts: Men of wealth had more to lose in any cataclysm, and masters had less antipathy to Negroes than non-slave-holders did. In daily contact with blacks from birth, and often on a friendly basis of patron and retainer, the planters were in a sort of partnership with their slaves, reckoning upon their good-will or at least possessing a sense of security as a fruit of long habituation to fairly serene conditions. But the white toilers lived outside this partnership and suffered somewhat from its competition. H. R. Helper in his *Impending Crisis* (1857) urged them to wreck the system by destroying slavery; and when this had been accomplished without their aid he vented in his fantastic *Nojoque* (1867) a spleen against the Negroes, advocating their expulsion from the United States as a preliminary to their universal extermination. Thus he called for class war upon a double front, to humble the "lords of the lash" and then to destroy the "black and bi-colored caitiffs" who cumbered the white man's world. By his alliterative rhetoric and shrewdly selected statistics Helper captured some Northern propagandists and the historians whom they begat, but if he made any converts among Southern yeomen they are not of record. His notions had come to

---

[5] When I made this transcript twenty years ago the manuscript journal was on Magnolia plantation in Plaquemines Parish, Louisiana. The item is in the handwriting of J. A. Randall, overseer.

him during residence in California and the North; they were therefore to be taken skeptically. His programs repudiated humane tradition, disregarded vital actualities, and evoked Northern aid to make over the South in its own image. These things, and perhaps the last especially, were not to be sanctioned. In fact, for reasons common in the world at large, the Southern whites were not to be divided into sharply antagonistic classes. Robert J. Walker said quite soundly in 1856:

> In all the slave States there is a large majority of voters who are nonslaveholders; but they are devoted to the institutions of the South—they would defend them with their lives—and on this question the South are [sic] a united people. The class, composed of many small farmers, of merchants, professional men, mechanics, overseers, and other industrial classes, constitute mainly the patrol of the South, and cheerfully unite in carrying out those laws essential to preserve the institution. Against a powerful minority and constant agitation slavery could not exist in any State.[6]

Walker wrote this to explain the poor prospect of slavery in Kansas; he might have used the same phrasing to explain its persistence in Delaware or Missouri. Habitat grouping, it is clear, had a cementing force great enough to overcome the cleaving tendency of economic stratification. So strong was it, indeed, that sundry free Negroes gave warm endorsement to the project of Southern independence.[7]

It is perhaps less fruitful to seek the social classes at large which were warm and those which were cool toward independence than to inquire why the citizens of certain areas were prevailingly ardent while those in another zone were indifferent or opposed, why for example the whole tier from South Carolina to Texas seceded spontaneously but no other states joined them until after Lincoln's call for troops. The reason lay in preceding history as well as in current conditions. The economic factor of the cotton belt's interest in free trade and its recurrent chagrin at protective tariff enactments is by no means negligible. The rancor produced by nullification and the "force bill" had been revived in South Carolina by the repeal of the compromise tariff in 1842, and it did not then die. The quarrels of Georgia with the federal authorities over Indian lands, with Alabama and Mississippi looking on in interested sym-

[6] *De Bow's Review*, XXI, 591–592.
[7] U. B. Phillips, *American Negro Slavery* (New York, 1918), p. 436; R. H. Williams, *With the Border Ruffians* (London, 1908), p. 441.

pathy, were contributing episodes to make the lower South alert; and the heavy Negro proportions in their black belts, together with immaturity in the social order, made their people more sensitive than those of Virginia to the menace of disturbance from outside.

Slavery questions, which had never been quite negligible since the framing of the Constitution, gained a febrile activity from the abolition agitation; and the study of congressional mathematics focused the main attention upon the rivalry of the sections in territorial enlargement. The North had control of the lower house, as recurrent votes on the Wilmot Proviso showed; and California's admission upset the sectional equilibrium in the Senate. For Yancey, Rhett, and Quitman and for the pamphleteers Longstreet, Bryan, and Trescot, this was enough. The North now had the strength of a giant; the South should strike for independence before that strength should grow yet greater and be consolidated for crushing purposes. But the gestures of Cass, Webster, and Fillmore gave ground for hope that the giant would not use his power against Southern home rule, and the crisis was deferred. Southern friends and foes of the Compromise of 1850 were alert thenceforward for tokens of Northern will. Events through the ensuing decade, somewhat assisted by the fire-eaters and culminating in a Republican's election to the Presidency, converted a new multitude to the shibboleth: "The alternative: a separate nationality or the Africanization of the South." [8]

Walter Lippmann has analyzed political process in general as if he had our present study specifically in mind:

Since the general opinions of large numbers of persons are almost certain to be a vague and confusing medley, action cannot be taken until those opinions have been factored down, canalized, compressed and made uniform. The making of one general will out of a multitude of general wishes . . . consists essentially in the use of symbols which assemble emotions after they have been detached from their ideas. . . . The process, therefore, by which general opinions are brought to co-operation consists in an intensification of feeling and a degradation of significance.[9]

The tension of 1850 had brought much achievement in this direction. "Southern rights" had come to mean racial security, self-determination by the whites whether in or out of the Union, and all things ancillary to the assured possession of these. Furthermore

[8] The title of a pamphlet by William H. Holcombe, M.D. (New Orleans, 1860).
[9] *The Phantom Public* (New York, 1925), p. 47.

a program had been framed to utilize state sovereignty whether to safeguard the South as a minority within the Union or to legitimate its exit into national independence.

The resurgence of these notions and emotions after their abeyance in 1851 need not be traced in detail. Suffice it to say that legal sanction for the spread of slave-holding, regardless of geographical potentialities, became the touchstone of Southern rights; and the rapid rise of the Republican party which denied this sanction, equally regardless of geographical potentialities, tipped the balance in lower Southern policy. Many were primed in 1856 for a stroke in case Frémont should be elected that year; and though he fell short of an electoral majority, the strength shown by his ticket increased the zeal of South-savers through the next quadrennium. The so-called Southern commercial conventions became a forum and *De Bow's Review* an organ for the airing of projects, mad or sane, for annexing Cuba, promoting direct trade with Europe, boycotting Northern manufacturers and Northern colleges, procuring Southern textbooks for Southern schools, reopening the African slave trade— anything and everything which might agitate and perhaps consolidate the South in a sense of bafflement within the Union and a feeling of separate destiny. Many clergymen gave their aid, particularly by praising slavery as a biblical and benevolent institution.

Pierre Soulé tried in 1857, as Calhoun had done eight years before, to create a Southern party separate from the Democrats [10]; and next year Yancey launched his League of United Southerners. Ere long a rural editor blurted what many must have been thinking:

> That the North sectionalized will acquire possession of this Government at no distant day we look upon as no longer a matter of doubt. . . . It is inevitable. The South—the whole South even—cannot avert it. We may determine to fight the battle with our foes within the Union, . . . but we will fight only to be defeated. The Union of the South is indeed of great moment—not however for successful resistance in this Union, but for going out of it under circumstances the most favorable to the speedy formation of a separate and independent government.[11]

Various expressions in Northern papers, debates in Congress, and events in Kansas and elsewhere had fanned these flames when the stroke of John Brown fell upon Harper's Ferry. This event was

---
[10] New Orleans *Crescent*, June 17, 1857.
[11] The *Southron* (Orangeburg, S. C.), quoted in the *Southern Guardian* (Columbia, S. C.), May 20, 1859.

taken as a demonstration that abolitionists had lied in saying they were concerned with moral suasion only, and it stimulated suspicion that Republicans were abolitionists in disguise. In December the South Carolina legislature when expressing sympathy with Virginia intimated that she was ripe for secession and invited all Southern states to meet in convention at once to concert measures for united action. In February the Alabama legislature asserted that under no circumstances would the commonwealth submit to "the foul domination of a sectional Northern party," and it instructed the governor in the event of a Republican's election to the Presidency to order the election of delegates to a convention of the state to consider and do whatever in its judgment her rights, interests, and honor might require.

There was little to do in the interim but discuss principles and portents and to jockey the situation slightly to prepare for the crisis or try to prevent it according to what individuals might think best. In an editorial of January 9, 1860, on "The true position of the South: Not aggrandisement but safety," the New Orleans *Crescent*, which was long an advocate of moderation, said:

> The South does not claim the right of controlling the North in the choice of a President; she admits fully and explicitly that the Northern people possess the prerogative of voting as they please. But at the same time the South asserts that while the North holds the legal right of casting her voice as to her may seem best, she has no *moral* right to so cast it as to effect the ruin of the South; and if she does so cast it, in full view of its injurious effects upon us, . . . she, in effect, commits an act of covert hostility upon us that will render it impossible for us to live longer in intimate relations.

On April 15, the *Delta*, replying to a recent lecture at New Orleans by George D. Prentice of Louisville, denied that Clay and Webster, "those demiurgic heroes of his political faith," could have sufficed for the present occasion:

> The period of mere political formation is past, and the period for the solution of great social and industrial problems is at hand. Mere constitutional lore here can do nothing; mere skill in adjusting balances of political power can do nothing. Is it just to hold the negro in bondage? Is negro slavery inimical to the rights of white men? Is it best for both the white and black man—best for the interests of agriculture, best for the needs of commerce and useful arts, and best for social stability and civilization? These and kindred questions imperiously demand to be answered, and they are precisely the questions which the old school of statesmen strenu-

ously refused to look in the face. . . . The truth is, we are in the midst of facts having a philosophy of their own which we must master for ourselves, leaving dead men to take care of the dead past. The Sphinx which is now propounding its riddles to us the dead knew nothing about; consequently no voice from the grave can tell us how to get rid of the monster.

After the nominating conventions had put four tickets in the field the newspapers began a running debate upon the relative merits of Douglas, Breckinridge, and Bell for Southern purposes and the degree of menace in the Lincoln candidacy. The Natchez *Free Trader,* which until June 27 mastheaded the names of Albert G. Brown and Fernando Wood, accepted next day the Richmond nominations:

We hoist today the flag of the Union-saving National Democratic nominees, Breckinridge and Lane, *sans peur et sans reproche*. With records so fair that none can attack them, they will win the hearts of all the people of the land, be elected by a vote so flattering as to cause the hearts of the noblest and best to beat with honest exaltation and pride, and so administer the Government as to have the blessings of the people showered on them and elicit the unrestrained admiration of an enlightened world.

Such bombast as this might survive the summer; but when the October elections brought a virtual certainty of Lincoln's election the discussion took another phase. The friends of each minor ticket demanded that the other two be withdrawn or forsaken. Douglas and Bell men agreed at least that Breckinridge ought to be abandoned. The Nashville *Union and American,* in reply on October 16 to such a demand from the Nashville *Patriot,* said that Breckinridge might still be elected by Southern concentration upon him, "in as much as it will prove to the North that we are determined to have our rights." And as a last appeal, November 6, the New Orleans *Delta* said, urging votes for Breckinridge as against Bell or Douglas:

Is this the time to indorse the representatives of a half-way, compromising, submissive policy? When the whole North is sectional shall the South be national, when nationality can mean nothing but an acquiescence in the employment of national means to accomplish sectional purposes? Never before in the history of any free and brave people was so bold a challenge as that which the North now throws at us received in any other way than the stern and proud defiance of a united and determined community.

Among the Bell organs the New Orleans *Bee* gave a remarkably sound analysis in an editorial of July 27: "The restlessness of the South touching the agitation of the slavery question arises rather from the apprehension of what the aggressive policy of the North may hereafter effect, than from what it has already accomplished. For . . . we may safely affirm that thus far no practical injury has resulted." The Southern failure in colonizing Kansas, it continued, was not a grievance, for "prudent and far-seeing men predicted the utter impracticability of carrying the design into execution. . . . Slavery will go where it will pay. No slaveholder for the sake of an abstraction will amuse himself by earning five per cent in Kansas on the labor of his chattels, when with absolutely less toil it will give him fifteen per cent in the cotton or sugar fields of Louisiana." On its own score the *Bee* concluded: "We apprehend that the Black Republicans are dogs whose bark is more dangerous than their bite. The South is too precious to the North to be driven out of the Union." Its colleague the *Crescent* expressed a belief as late as October 20 that, if the Republican party should win the contest, its "unnatural and feverish vitality" would reach exhaustion within a year or two. In the United States thus far, the *Crescent* argued, parties had arisen and fallen in rapid succession.

But all of these parties were national. The principles they advocated were of common application to the whole country, and their members and adherents were found in every quarter and every State of the Union. If these parties were temporary and short-lived in their character and constitution, still more so must the Black Republican party be, sectional as it is in its organization and principles, and obnoxious to a deeper hatred and more bitter opposition than any other organization that has yet made its appearance in the political arena. It is impossible that such a party can long exist.

Just before election day George Fitzhugh of Virginia wrote to the Charleston *Mercury* a long letter concluding: "In the Union there is no hope for us. Let us gather courage from despair, and quit the Union." The editor when printing this, November 9, remarked: "Mr. Fitzhugh is a little excitable. We intend to 'quit the Union,' but without any 'despair' whatever. We'll quit it with a round hip! hip! hurrah!!"

But now that the partisans of Breckinridge, Bell, and Douglas had met a common defeat, their lines were broken with regard to the Southern recourse. Some of the Breckinridge men opposed

CENTRAL THEME OF SOUTHERN HISTORY 161

secession unless and until the Lincoln government should commit an "overt act" of injury, but many supporters of Bell and Douglas turned to the policy of prompt strokes.[12] The New Orleans *Crescent* and *Bee* are again clear exponents. On November 8 the *Crescent* said: "We read the result in the face of every citizen upon the street. There is an universal feeling that an insult has been deliberately tendered our people, which is responded to not by noisy threats or passionate objurgations, but a settled determination that the South shall never be oppressed under Mr. Lincoln's administration." But it cherished a shadowy hope that electors chosen on the Republican ticket might yet refrain from putting "a sectional President in the chair of Washington!" On December 17 the *Bee* admitted that it had yielded to the prodigious tide of public sentiment, and said in explanation: "It was evident indeed, that amid all the lip service professed for the Union there had dwelt in the hearts of Southerners a tacit determination to regard the election of Lincoln as proof of a settled and immutable policy of aggression by the North toward the South, and to refuse further political affiliation with those who by that act should declare themselves our enemies." On the following January 3 the *Crescent* said:

It is by secession alone that we [Louisiana] can be placed in close affinity with all of our sisters of the Gulf and South Atlantic seaboard, who have given guarantees . . . that they will be out of the Union long in advance of our action and ready to receive us in the Government that shall have been established.[13] South Carolina, Georgia, Mississippi, Florida, Alabama, Louisiana and Texas are knit by God and their own hearts indissolubly together. . . .

Believe not that any State has the right to expect another to await her action in an emergency like this. *We have as much right to complain of*

---

[12] Unionism among many of the Bell supporters had been conditioned from the first, almost explicitly, upon constitutionalism as interpreted in favor of Southern rights. For example the convention in Georgia which responded to the call for organizing the party and sent delegates to Baltimore adopted a platform asserting that slavery was established in the Constitution, that the territories were the property of the states jointly, that Congress and the territorial legislatures were alike incapable of impairing the right of slave property, and that it was the duty of Congress to protect the rights of slave-holders in the territories. *Southern Recorder* (Milledgeville, Ga.), May 8, 1860.

[13] These pledges had been conveyed by commissioners appointed by the governors of sundry commonwealths to convey to the governors, legislatures, and conventions of other states assurances of secession as soon as the procedure could be completed and invitations for union in a new nation or confederacy. A study of these commissioners as agents of coördination has been made by Mr. Dwight L. Dumond of the University of Michigan, but has not yet been published. [Subsequently it appeared in his *The Secession Movement, 1860–61* (New York, 1931). —Editor.]

the tardiness of the border States as they have of our haste. . . . A people who wait for others to aid them in vindicating their rights are already enslaved, for now, as in every other period of history—

> "In native swords and native ranks
> The only hope of freedom dwells."

The upper South had votaries of independence no less outspoken than those of the cotton belt, but they were too few to carry their states prior to a Northern "overt act." Arguments and eloquence by visiting commissioners might sway the minds and thrill the hearts of delegates, but none of these conventions took a decisive step until Lincoln's call for troops. Indeed there was a project of organizing the border states for a course of their own, even to the extreme of a central confederacy separate alike from the "Black Republican" North and the "hotspur" South. When this was pinched out, the sequel showed that the boundary of predominant Southern loyalty was not Mason and Dixon's line but a curving zone seldom touching that landmark.

Many Virginians, perhaps most of them, sanctioned the change of allegiance reluctantly; and some, chiefly in the Wheeling panhandle, revolted sharply against it. On the other hand the course of the federal government during the war and after its close alienated so many borderers that in a sense Kentucky joined the Confederacy after the war was over.

While the war dragged its disheartening length and the hopes of independence faded, queries were raised in some Southern quarters as to whether yielding might not be the wiser course. Lincoln in his plan of reconstruction had shown unexpected magnanimity; the Republican party, discarding that obnoxious name, had officially styled itself merely Unionist; and the Northern Democrats, although outvoted, were still a friendly force to be reckoned upon. Die-hard statesmen and loyal soldiers carried on till the collapse. The governors in the "late so-called Confederate States" were now ready with soft speeches, but the Federal soldiery clapped them into prison until Andrew Johnson relaxed from his brief punitive phase.

With Johnson then on Lincoln's path "back to normalcy," Southern hearts were lightened only to sink again when radicals in Congress, calling themselves Republicans once more, overslaughed the presidential program and set events in train which seemed to make "the Africanization of the South" inescapable. To most of the whites, doubtless, the prospect showed no gleam of hope.

But Edward A. Pollard, a Virginian critic of Davis, chronicler of the war, and bewailer of the "lost cause," took courage in 1868 to write his most significant book, *The Lost Cause Regained*. The folly of politicians, he said, had made the South defend slavery seemingly "as a property tenure, or as a peculiar institution of labour; when the true ground of defence was as of a barrier against a contention and war of races."[14] The pro-slavery claims on the basis of constitutional right he denounced in retrospect as flimsily technical and utterly futile in the face of a steadily encroaching moral sentiment; and the stroke for independence in the name of liberty he thought as fallacious as the later expectation of generosity which had brought the Confederate collapse.[15]

> It has been curiously reserved for the South to obtain *after* the war the actual experience of oppression, and of that measure of despotism which would have amply justified the commencement of hostilities. If it fought, in 1860, for principles too abstract, it has superabundant causes for rebellion now, which although they may not, and need not produce another war, yet have the effect to justify, in a remarkable way, the first appeal to arms.[16]

In elaboration of this Pollard wrote: "The black thread of the Negro has been spun throughout the scheme of Reconstruction. A design is betrayed to give to him the political control of the South, not so much as a benefit to him, . . . as to secure power to the Republican party."[17]

But in the defeats of proposals for Negro suffrage in seven states from Connecticut to Colorado, and particularly in the ovation with which the Philadelphia convention of 1866 had received a resolution urging the Southern whites not to submit to Negro rule, he saw promise of effective support and eventual success in undoing Reconstruction.[18] Therefore:

> Let us come back to the true hope of the South. It is to enter bravely with new allies and new auspices the contest for the supremacy of the white man, and with it the preservation of the dearest political traditions

[14] E. A. Pollard, *The Lost Cause Regained* (New York, 1868), p. 13.
[15] *Ibid.*, pp. 20, 50, 116.
[16] *Ibid.*, pp. 51–52.
[17] *Ibid.*, p. 129.
[18] *Ibid.*, pp. 133, 162.

of the country. "WHITE" is the winning word, says a North Carolina paper, and let us never be done repeating it. . . . It is the irresistible sympathy of races, which will not, cannot fail. . . . It is this instinct which the South will at last summon to her aid, when her extremity demands it.[19]

Before the farther bank of the slough of despond was fully attained, the question was raised as to the path beyond. In a remarkable address in 1875 Wiley P. Harris of Mississippi lamented the political exploitation of the Negroes: "The mass of them don't vote, but are literally voted. They are ridden and driven by a little nest of men who are alien to the state in feeling. . . . The result is a government at once imperious and contemptible, a tyranny at once loathesome and deadly." He bade the carpet-baggers farewell in advance of their going: "I assure these men that their last card has been played, and it has not won. This trumpery no longer deceives anybody, and it matters not which party prevails in 1876, no national administration will again incur the odium of propping them up." But with merely restoring white local domination he would not be content. Appealing specifically for a renewed and permanent union of Democrats with liberal Republicans throughout the country, he said:

To reconcile and nationalize the South, to lead it out of the cul de sac of sectionalism into the broad stream of national life, . . . to restore peace, good will and confidence between the members of this great family of States, will lay the solid and durable foundation of a party which will surely win and long retain the hearts of the American people. . . . For one, I long to see a government at Washington, and a government here, toward which I can feel a genuine sentiment of reverence and respect. It is a dreary life we lead here, with a national government ever suspicious and ever frowning, and a home government feeble, furtive, false and fraudulent. Under such influences the feeling of patriotism must die out amongst us, and this will accomplish the ruin of a noble population. . . . We are in a new world. We are moving on a new plane. It is better that we hang a millstone about our necks than cling to these old issues. To cling to them is to perpetuate sectional seclusion.[20]

Lamar's eulogy of Sumner and the speeches and editorials of Grady were much to the same effect, and likewise were the efforts of other broad-minded men. But a certain sense of bafflement and of defensive self-containment persists to our own day, because the Negro popula-

[19] *Ibid.*, p. 165.
[20] Speech of W. P. Harris at a Democratic campaign meeting, Jackson, Mississippi, Aug. 23, 1875. Lowry and McCardle, *History of Mississippi*, pp. 396–400.

tion remains as at least a symbolic potentiality. Virtually all respectable whites had entered the Democratic ranks in the later 'sixties to combat à outrance the Republican program of Negro incitement. A dozen years sufficed to restore white control, whereupon they began to differ among themselves upon various issues. Many joined the People's Party; and in some quarters a fusion was arranged of Populists and Republicans to carry elections. In the stress of campaigning this threatened to bring from within the South a stimulus to Negroes as political auxiliaries.

But by Southern hypothesis, exalted into a creed, Negroes in the mass were incompetent for any good political purpose and by reason of their inexperience and racial unwisdom were likely to prove subversive. To remove the temptation to white politicians to lead Negroes to the polls again, "white primaries" were instituted to control nominations, educational requirements for the suffrage were inserted in the state constitutions, and the Bryanizing of the Democratic party was accepted as a means of healing a white rift. Even these devices did not wholly lay the specter of "Negro domination"; for the Fifteenth Amendment stood in the Constitution, and the calendar of Congress was not yet free of "force bills." For every Lodge and Foraker there arose a Tillman and a Vardaman, with a Watson and a Blease to spare.

The sentiments and symbols have not been wholly divorced from reason. When California whites made extravagant demands in fear that her 3 per cent of Japanese might increase to 4 and capture the business of "The Coast," Congress responded as if it were an appendage of the state legislature. But white Southerners when facing problems real or fancied concerning the 10,000,000 Negroes in their midst can look to the federal authorities for no more at best than a tacit acquiescence in what their state governments may do. Acquiescence does not evoke enthusiasm; and until an issue shall arise predominant over the lingering one of race, political solidarity at the price of provincial status is maintained to keep assurance doubly, trebly sure that the South shall remain "a white man's country."

INDEX

A

Abolitionists, 114-115, 120; oppose American Colonization Society, 94; nature of campaign of, 110-111; examples of, 111-114
Acadians, 12
Adams, John, 15, 60, 66, 80
Adams, John Quincy, 132; on Missouri Compromise, 96; on disunion, 144-145
Adams, Samuel, 15
Address to the People of South Carolina (1794), 34
Alabama, 1, 38, 112; refuses to submit to Northern rule, 158
Alamance Creek, battle of, 14
Albany Congress, 7
Albemarle Sound, 12, 41, 42n
Alien and Sedition Acts, 68, 69
Altamaha River, 36
Amelia Island, 92
American Colonization Society, 112; organized, 93; efforts to colonize Negroes in Africa, 93-95
American Historical Association, 151n
"American System," 76
Amherst County, Va., 19
Andover Academy, 120
Ann Arundel County, Md., 54
Annapolis, Md., 27, 53
Appalachian Mountains, 73
"Appius," *see* Harper, Robert G.
Arator, 64
Arkansas, territory of, 96n
Articles of Confederation, 27, 47, 73
Athens, Ga., 38
Atlanta, Ga., made state capital, 38

B

Bacon, Nathaniel, 6
Bailey, Rufus W., defends slavery, 119
Baldwin, Abraham, 38
Baltimore, Lord, 6
Baltimore, Md., 53, 54
Baltimore County, Md., 54
Bannister, Thomas, 21-22
Barataria Bay, 92
Barbados, 2, 12
Barnes, Albert, 117
Barnwell, Robert, 30
Beecher, Henry W., 116
Bell, John, 159
Benezet, Anthony, on slavery, 86
Benning, Henry L., Georgia fire-eater, 135, 136
Benton, Samuel, 13, 13n
Benton, Thomas Hart, 13n
Berkeley, Sir William, 6
Beveridge, Albert J., 49n
Bible, in slavery dispute, 84, 103, 111, 117
Birney, James G., abolitionist, 112
Bishop of London, supports Virginia clergymen, 9
Blair, John, 47
Bland, Richard, supports Virginia "tuppenny act," 9, 10
Blease, Cole, 165
Bledsoe, Albert T., 118, 141
Bloodworth, Timothy, 41
Blount, William, 41; political career of, 43, 44, 44n
"Bluffton Movement," 133
Bonaparte, 73, 101
Boone, Thomas, 7
Boonesborough, Ky., 55
Border Ruffians, 146
Boston, Mass., 15, 72, 84
Boston tea party, 16
Botetourt County, Va., 43n
Breckinridge, John, introduces state rights resolutions in Kentucky legislature, 67; presidential candidate, 159
Brief and Candid Answer, A, 84-85
Bristol, merchants of, 7
Broad River, in South Carolina, 33
Brooks, Preston, advocates disunion, 142

INDEX

Brougham, Lord, 116
Brown, Albert G., 159
Brown, Edward, on slavery, 104
Brown, John, in Kansas, 146; at Harper's Ferry, 147, 157
Brown, Thomas, Revolutionary Tory, 23
Buena Vista, battle of, 147
Burr, Aaron, 32, 71, 74
Butler, Pierce, delegate to Federal Constitutional Convention, 28; becomes Southern partisan, 31
Byrd II, William, 85

C

Caldwell, David, 41
Calhoun, John C., 105, 133, 134, 152; on South Carolina's settlement of state representation question, 35-36; on crisis of 1850, 138-139
California, 73; admission of, into the Union, 145
Camden, S. C., 136
Campbell, Arthur, 43, 44
Canada, 11
Cannibals All or Slaves without Masters, 122
Cape Fear region, 12
Capers, William, on secession, 138
Carlyle, John, 122
Caroline County, Va., 122
Carroll, Charles, 32, 87
Carroll, Daniel, 54
Carroll, John, 15, 64
Carrolls, of Maryland, 53
Cass, Lewis, 156
Caswell, Richard, 15, 41, 42, 43, 44
Channing, William E., 117
Chapel Hill, N. C., 42n, 109
Charles City, Va., 4
Charleston, S. C., 14, 24, 59, 72, 101, 103, 111, 115, 118, 123; characterization of, 129
Charleston *Mercury*, 134, 160
Charlotte, N. C., 17
Chase, Samuel, characterized, 53, 54, 55, 64n
Cherokees, 37, 39, 43
Chestertown, Md., 53
Cheves, Langdon, 133
Chicago, Ill., 146

Chickasaws, 38
Chisholm *vs.* Georgia, 39
Choctaws, 38
Christie's minstrels, 152
Clark, George Rogers, 55
Clarkson, Thomas, 100, 116
Clay, Cassius M., opposes slavery, 109
Clay, Henry, 76, 158; in Missouri Compromise debate, 98
Cobbett, William, berates Jefferson, 70
Cohens *vs.* Virginia, 78, 79
College of New Jersey, 32
Colonial commerce, 2
Colston, Edward, in Missouri Compromise debate, 96
Columbia, S. C., made capital, 33; college set up at, 36
Commerce, colonial, 2
Confederacy, Southern, 127
Confiscation laws, 24
Connecticut, resolutions of, on War of 1812, 76
Constitution of United States, debated in Virginia ratifying convention, 47-53; interpretation of, 73-77
Constitutional Union party, 154
Constitutions, state, nature of, 19
Continental Congress, 16, 17, 27
Conway, M. D., abolitionist, 112-113
Coral Gables, Fla., 151
Cotton, cultivation of, 35, 151
Cotton gin, effect of, 91
Court day, 4-5
Creeks, 37, 39
Crisis, 104
Cuba, 157
Cumberland, Richard, 14
Cumberland River, 43
Curse, on Union, by Southerner, 143, 155

D

Dalcho, Frederick, on slavery, 103
Dartmouth College Case, 77
Davie, William R., 15, 41
Davis, Jefferson, 131; conservative sentiments of, 143-144
De Bow's Review, 123; states Southern program, 157
De Bow, J. D. B., 123; fire-eater, 134-135
Declaration of Independence, 12, 18-19

INDEX 169

Delaware, 6n; free Negroes in, 89; prohibits foreign slave trade, 91
Democratic Clubs, 72
Democratic party, 165; organization of, 67-71; origin of, 72; changing attitude of, on the Federal Constitution, 75-76; characterization of, 130-132
Desaussure, Henry W., 34-35
Dessalines, 101
Detroit, Mich., 56
Dew, Thomas R., 123; defends slavery, 107-108
Dickinson, John, 15
District of Columbia, 79, 114
"Dixie," 152
Douglas, Stephen A., 159; on Kansas-Nebraska bill, 146
Drayton, John, defends slavery, 89
Drayton, William Henry, 14, 15; seeks to annex Georgia to South Carolina, 36-37; defends slavery, 118-119
Dred Scott Case, 147
Dulaney, Daniel, 15
Dunmore, Lord, 7, 16n

E

Early, Peter, defends slavery, 92
East India Company, 16
Eatonton, Ga., 123
Edenton, N. C., 41
Education, in Maryland, 53-54
Election, of 1800, in South Carolina, 32; of 1860, 159-160
Elements of Algebra, 147
Eleventh Amendment, 40
Ellsworth, Oliver, 65, 66
Emancipation, of slaves, 57-58; discussed in South, 106-110
Embargo, 76
Embree, Elihu, favors emancipation, 109
England, 41, 101; attitude of American colonies toward, 12-13; Revolutionary activities in American colonies against, 15-21; engages in slave trade, 83; Parliament of, opposes foreign slave trade, 93; abolitionism in, 110; *Uncle Tom's Cabin* in, 146
Entail, abolished, 19
Ewbank, Thomas, on slavery, 123-124

F

Fairfax, estates of, 78
Fanning, David, Revolutionary Tory, 23
Faustin I, 101
Federal Constitutional Convention, 27-28
Federalist, The, 53, 63
Federalist party, 31; in Georgia, 40; in Maryland, 54, 55; attitude of, on Louisiana Purchase, 75
Fifteenth Amendment, 165
Fillmore, Millard, 156
Fire-eaters, 128-149
Fisher, Sidney G., on slavery, 124-126
Fitzhugh, George, defends slavery, 122-123; favors secession, 160
Fletcher, John, defends slavery, 117
Fletcher vs. Peck, 77
Florida, 1, 11, 12, 44n
Foraker, J. B., 165
Ford, Timothy, 34-35
Fort Sumter, 135
France, 48; aid of, to American colonists, 18; troubles of, in San Domingo, 100-101
Franklin, Benjamin, 15, 22
Franklin County, Ky., 68
Free Negroes, 89-90; efforts at colonization of, in Africa, 93-95; in North, 118, 125
Frémont, John C., 157
French Revolution, 72; effects of, on San Domingo, 100-101
French and Indian War, effect of, on America, 11-12
Fugitive Slave Law of 1850, 145-146
Furman, Richard, on slavery, 103

G

Gadsden, Christopher, 15, 22, 24; on slavery, 86
Gallatin, Albert, 72
Garrison, W. L., 95, 106, 110, 116
Gaston, William, on slavery, 109
Gell, Monday, 102
Genius of Universal Emancipation, 104
George II, 8
George III, 6, 8
Georgia, 1, 2; colonial government of, 6, 7; attitude toward English con-

INDEX

Georgia (continued)
 trol, 12; Revolutionary leaders in, 15; abolishes foreign slave trade, 28n; quarrel with South Carolina in colonial and Revolutionary times, 36-37; constitutional developments, 37-38; land speculations in, 38-39; aid of, in framing Federal Constitution, 39; quarrel with Federal Government, leading to Eleventh Amendment, 39-40; sells Western lands to United States, 39; introduces slavery, 86; prohibits foreign slave trade, 91; opposes freeing Negroes, 95; attitude on Compromise of 1850, 139; quarrel with United States over Indians, 156

Gibbons vs. Ogden, 78
Giddings, Joshua, 116
Giles, William B., 62
Gillon, Alexander, Revolutionary radical, 24, 25, 26, 28, 30, 31; defends foreign slave trade, 91
Glasgow, merchants of, 7
Goodloe, D. R., abolitionist, 113
Governor, colonial, in South, 6
Granville, Lord, 13
Granville County, N. C., 13
Grayson, William J., 48; defends slavery, 115, 117, 138
Great Britain, see England
Green, Duff, 108n
Green River, 55
Grimké, Angelina, abolitionist, 111-112, 113
Grimké, Sarah, abolitionist, 111-112
Grimké, Thomas, 112
Gullah Jack, 102

H

Habersham, James, 15; on slavery, 86
Haiti, 32, 35; slave uprising in, 72-73; beginnings of Republic of, 101
Hale, E. E., 116
Halifax, N. C., 41
Hall, Lyman, 15, 38
Hamilton, Alexander, 27, 31, 32, 45, 53, 62, 65, 74; political philosophy of, 60-61, 63
Hancock, John, 15
Hanover County, Va., 9
Harford County, Md., 54

Harper, Robert G., South Carolina political leader, 32, 34
Harris, W. P., on Negro political exploitation, 164
Harrison, Benjamin, 48
Harrod, James, 55
Hartford Convention, 77
Harvard Theological Seminary, 113
Havana, Cuba, 72
Helper, H. R., abolitionist, 113-114; opposed Negroes, 154-155
Henderson, Richard, 43; organized Transylvania, 55
Henry, Patrick, 15, 39n, 43, 46, 53, 55, 58, 59, 62, 64n; opposes "Parsons' Cause," 9-11; characterization of, 45; part in Virginia convention ratifying Federal Constitution, 46-53
Heyrick, Elizabeth, 110
Hill, D. H., author of textbook, 147
Hireling and the Slave, The, 115-117
History of the United States, by J. F. Rhodes, 137
Hooper, William, 41
Howards, of Maryland, 53
Hughes, Henry, defends slavery, 121-122, 123
Hunter, James, 14

I

Illinois, free Negroes in, 89
Impending Crisis, 113, 154
Indiana, 147; free Negroes in, 89
Indians, removal of from Georgia, 39
Inflation, in colonial times, 7-8
Innes, Harry, 57
Inorganic Forces Ordained to Supercede Human Slavery, 123-124
Insurrection, slave, in San Domingo, 88; Gabriel's, 88; Vesey's, 101-102; Nat Turner's, 105-106
Iredell, James, 15, 21; characterization of, 40-41, 42n
Izard, Ralph, 25-26, 31, 91

J

Jackson, Andrew, 130, 131
Jackson, James, opposes Yazoo sales, 38; on slavery, 88
Jacksonborough, S. C., 24
Jacobins, 72, 100

INDEX

Jamaica, 2, 8, 12
James City, Va., 4
Jay, John, 15; negotiations of, with Spain over navigation of Mississippi, 46-47
Jayhawkers, 146
Jean Jacques I, 101
Jefferson, Thomas, 15, 18, 32, 33, 41, 45n, 46, 48, 53, 58, 64, 73, 77, 81, 144; advises North Carolina to delay ratification of Federal Constitution, 42; characterization of, 45; political philosophy of, 60-63; letter of, supporting Union, 66-67; promotes Virginia and Kentucky Resolutions, 67-71; personal platform of, 71-72; defends Louisiana Purchase, 73-75; on the Constitution, 76; opposes slavery, 88; on Missouri Compromise, 95
Jenifer, Daniel of St. Thomas, 54
Johnson, Andrew, in Reconstruction, 162-163
Johnson, Samuel, remarks on English parties, 23
Johnston, Samuel, 41, 42n, 44
Jones, Willie, 41, 42
Jonesboro, Tenn., 44

K

Kansas, 73; "bleeding," 146
Kansas-Nebraska bill, 146
Kentucky, 58n, 112; delegates from, in Virginia convention ratifying Federal Constitution, 47, 50, 51, 51n; beginnings of, 55; efforts to secure statehood, 56, 57; Spanish intrigue in, 56, 57; passes state rights resolutions, 68, 70; attitude on Federal Constitution, 75-76; free Negroes in, 89; debates slavery, 110; nature of people of, 151; after the Civil War, 162
King, Rufus, 65, 66; in Missouri Compromise debate, 96, 97

L

Lamar, L. Q. C., 164
Lamar, M. B., 135
Land, speculation in, 38-39, 43, 44; system of disposal in Georgia, 39

Latter Day Pamphlets, 122
Laurens, Henry, opposes slavery, 86
Lay, Benjamin, on slavery, 85-86
Lee, Henry, 63
Lee, Richard Henry, 15, 49
Lees, of Virginia, 15
Lewis and Clark Expedition, 73
Liberator, 95, 106
Liberia, 93-95, 108
Liberty County, Ga., 12
Liberty party, 112
Lincoln, Abraham, 159, 162
Lippmann, Walter, on public opinion, 156
Livermore, Arthur, in Missouri Compromise debate, 96
Liverpool, merchants of, 7
Livingston, Robert R., 15
Locke, John, 6, 18
Lodge, H. C., 165
Logan, Benjamin, 55
London, 16; merchants of, 7
London Company, 6
Longstreet, A. B., 156
Lost Cause Regained, The, 127, 163
Louisa County, Va., 10
Louisiana, 1, 4n, 44, 44n, 56, 57, 154n; purchase of, 73-74
Louisville, Ga., made state capital, 38
Louisville, Ky., 56, 158
L'Ouverture, Toussaint, 73, 100, 101
Lowndes, Rawlins, 59, 91; opposes ratification of Federal Constitution, 28-29, 30
Lucas, Eliza, 27
Lumpkin, Wilson, Georgia fire-eater, 135
Lundy, Benjamin, 104

M

McCulloch *vs.* Maryland, 78
McDonogh, John, interest in colonizing free Negroes, 94
McDowell, James, on slavery, 109
McDuffie, George, 54, 133; on slavery, 104, 117
Maclaine, Alexander, 41
Macon, Nathaniel, 72
Madison, James, 39n, 46, 62, 72, 77, 81; characterization of, 45; part in Virginia convention ratifying Federal Constitution, 46-53; politi-

INDEX

Madison, James (*continued*)
  cal philosophy of, 63-64; writes state right resolutions for Virginia, 68
Madrid, 57
Maine, 2; admission of, into the Union, 96
Manigault, Gabriel, 31
Marbury vs. Madison, 77
Marine Anti-Britannic Society, 25
Marion, Francis, 21
Marshall, John, 39n, 62, 74, 75, 81; characterization of, 45; in Virginia convention ratifying Federal Constitution, 50-53; declares for supremacy of Federal judiciary, 70-71; promotes nationalism, 77-80
Maryland, 4, 57, 124; popular assembly in, 6; attitude toward English control, 12; Revolutionary leaders in, 15; first constitution of, 53; debates and adopts Federal Constitution, 54; slavery in, 87; free Negroes in, 89; prohibits foreign slave trade, 91
Martin vs. Hunter's Lessee, 77, 78, 81
Martin, Alexander, 41, 43
Martin, D., on Missouri Compromise debate, 97
Martin, Josiah, 7, 14
Martin, Luther, characterized, 53, 54, 55, 64n
Mason, George, 15, 18, 19, 39n; in Virginia convention ratifying Federal Constitution, 47-53
Massachusetts, 8, 12, 14; Revolutionary leaders in, 15; resolutions of, on War of 1812, 76
Mecklenburg County, N. C., 17
Mecklenburg Declaration of Independence, 17
Meigs, Henry, on Missouri Compromise debate, 97
Mercer, John F., 54
Miami, Fla., 151
Middleton, Arthur, 15
Milledgeville, Ga., made state capital, 38
Miller, S. D., on slavery, 105
Mirabeau, 100
Miro, 57
Mississippi, 1, 38; calls Nashville Convention in 1850, 138-139
Mississippi River, navigation of, discussed, 46-47, 57, 73; treaty with Spain on, 47n
Missouri, 73; free Negroes in, 89; debate on the admission of, into the Union, 95-99
Missouri Compromise, 81; debate on, 95-99
Mobile, Ala., 73
Molasses Act, 2
Monroe, James, 48, 52, 62, 77; position in history, 64
Montague, Charles, 7
Moon, Samuel O., interest of, in colonization of free Negroes, 94
Moses, free Negro, 94
Mount Vernon, 27, 48
Murray, William, opposes Kentucky state rights resolutions, 69
Muscle Shoals, land speculation at, 38

N

Napoleon, *see* Bonaparte
Nash, Abner, 41, 43
Nashville Convention of 1850, 138-139
Nashville *Union and American*, 159
Nat Turner's Rebellion, 105-106
Natchez, Miss., 57, 136
Natchez *Free Trader*, 159
Navarro, 57
Negroes, uprisings of, in San Domingo and Haiti, 100-101; in Southern consciousness, 151-165; *see also* Free Negroes, Slaves, Slavery, Slave insurrections
Nelson, Thomas, 15
New England, 2, 7, 8, 12; village system of, 3, 4; interest of, in Yazoo sales, 38; attitude of, on Louisiana Purchase, 74-75; attitude of, on War of 1812, 76-77
New England Confederation, 7
New Haven, Conn., 120
New Jersey, 4
New Orleans, 1, 56, 57, 72, 73
New Orleans *Bee*, 160, 161
New Orleans *Crescent*, 158, 160, 161
New Orleans *Delta*, 158, 159
New York, 2, 4; Revolutionary leaders in, 15
New York City, 71, 120, 123
Newbern, N. C., 41
Nicholas, Virginia brothers, 62

INDEX

Nojoque, 114, 154
Non-slave-holders, 153-155
Norfolk, Va., 72
North Carolina, 7, 8, 12, 67; popular assembly in, 6; colonial developments in, 12-14; Revolutionary leaders in, 15, 40-42; Mecklenburg Declaration of Independence in, 17; first constitution of, 41-42; in Federal Constitutional Convention, 42; refusal and later ratification of Federal Constitution, 42; Federalist party in, 42-43; Western lands of, 43-45; slavery in, 86-87; prohibits foreign slave trade, 91; debates slavery, 110; abolitionists in, 113
Notes on Virginia, 61
Nova Scotia, 12

O

O'Connell, Daniel, 110
Oglethorpe, James Edward, 7
Ohio, 112; free Negroes in, 89; asks Congress to free Negroes, 95
Ohio River, 55, 55n
Oregon, 73
Otis, James, 15

P

Paca, William, attitude on Federal Constitution, 54
Page, John, 15
Palm Beach, Fla., 151
Paper money, in colonial times, 7-8
Paris, 100
Parliament, declares American colonies in rebellion, 18
Pendleton, Edmund, 15, 91; in Virginia convention ratifying Federal Constitution, 48, 49
Pennsylvania, 2, 4; Revolutionary leaders in, 15; resolutions of, on slavery, 96
People's party, 165
Person, Thomas, 41
Philadelphia, Pa., 27, 112, 124
Phillips, U. B., 150; appreciation of, vii-ix
Pickens, Andrew, 21
Pinckney, Charles, South Carolina leader, 31, 32, 33

Pinckney, C. C., delegate to Federal Constitutional Convention, 27, 31; in election of 1800, 32; on slavery, 105
Pinckney, Thomas, 27, 31, 47n, 57; on slavery, 102
Pinckneys, of South Carolina, 15, 59, 75, 91
Pinkney, William, 87, 97
Pipkin, Timothy, 92
Plantation, The, 123
Polk, James K., 131, 133
Pollard, E. A., on slavery, 126-127; characterizes South in Reconstruction, 163
Popular sovereignty, 146
Populists, 165
Portugal, engages in slave trade, 83
Potomac River, 78
Prentice, George D., 158
Price, C. A., South Carolina editor, 136
Primogeniture, abolished, 19
Pringle, John J., 26, 30
Pro-slavery argument, 115-127
Puritans, character of, 3

Q

Quakers, oppose slavery, 83, 85, 86; petitions of, against slavery, 88
"Quarter races," 4n
Quebec, 12
Quincy, Josiah, 15, 92
Quit rents, 13
Quitman, John A., 156; Mississippi fire-eater, 135-136

R

Race, Negro, in Southern consciousness, 151-165
Ramsay, David, 26, 30, 91
Randall, J. A., overseer, 154n
Randolph, Edmund, in Virginia convention ratifying Federal Constitution, 47, 49, 51
Randolph, John, 53, 55, 62, 63, 64, 77, 78, 92
Randolphs, of Virginia, 15
Rappahannock River, 78
Reconstruction, after Civil War, 162-164
Regulators, 13-14

INDEX

Representative Reform Association, in South Carolina, 34
Republican party, of Jefferson, *see* Democratic party
Republican party, 114n, 164-165; origin of, 146; characterization of, 160; in Civil War, 162
Revolution, American, 2; parties in, 23-24
Rhett, Robert B., 156; fire-eater, 132-134; on Compromise of 1850, 140
Rhode Island, paper money in, 8
Rhodes, J. F., refuted on historical statement, 137
Rice, culture of, 26
Richmond, Va., 48, 53, 105
Richmond *Enquirer*, 78, 105
Ritchie, Thomas, 105
Roane, Spencer, 62; defends states' rights, 77-81
Roanoke River, 41
Robertson, James, 43
Robespierre, 100
Royal veto, 7, 12
Ruffin, Edmund, Virginia fire-eater, 135
Ruffner, Henry, abolitionist, 113
Russell's Magazine, 123, 141-142
Rutledge, Edward, favors adoption of Federal Constitution, 29
Rutledge, John, 15, 91; remarks on British excesses, 23; delegate to Federal Constitutional Convention, 27
Rutledges, of South Carolina, 59

S

Saffin, John, defends slavery, 85
St. John's College, 53-54
St. Marys River, 36
St. Michael's Church, Charleston, 103
Saluda River, 33
San Domingo, slave uprisings in, 100-101
Sandiford, Ralph, on slavery, 85
Savannah, Ga., 15, 72
Savannah River, 36, 37
Sawyer, George S., 118
Seabrook, W. B., on slavery, 104
Sebastian, Benjamin, 57
Secession, 1; agitated in South, 135-149; of South advocated, 161-162

Sectionalism, colonial, 2-3
Sedition Act, 60
Selling of Joseph, The, 84
Sewall, Samuel, opposes slavery, 84
Seward, William H., 116
Sharp, Granville, 88n
Shenandoah Valley, 47n, 106
Sierra Leone, 93, 108
Sims, George, 13
Slave insurrection, *see* Insurrection
Slave trade, foreign, 8; abolished, 28, 28n; promoted by Portuguese and British, 83-84; prohibited by states, 91; prohibited by Federal government, 91-92; reopening of, advocated, 148
Slavery, 62, 64, 72-73; Patrick Henry on, 51; early safety of, 59; in ancient times, 83; introduced to Europe by Portuguese, 83; introduced to America by British, 83; opposed by Sewall, 84; defended by Saffin, 84-85; opposed by Quakers, 85-86, 87; established in Georgia, 86, in early South Carolina, 86, in North Carolina, 86-87, in Virginia, 87, in Maryland, 87, in Delaware, 87; abolished in Massachusetts, 87, in New Jersey, 87, in Pennsylvania, 87; opposed by Jefferson, 87, 88; debated in Virginia legislature, 106-107, in North Carolina, 110, in Kentucky, 110; in Tennessee, 110; nature of, 152-153
Smith, Gerrit, 116
Smith, William, on slavery, 88
Smylie, James, defends slavery, 117
Society of Friends, *see* Quakers
Sociology for the South or the Failure of Free Society, 122
Soulé, Pierre, 157
Soulouque, 101
South, sectionalism of, 2, 4; local government in, 4; regard of, for religion, 4; sports in, 5; social order in, 5-6; colonial government in, 5-6; paper money in, during colonial times, 7-8; importation of slaves opposed in, 8; during the Revolution, 21; quarrels with Union, 155-156
South Carolina, 1, 7, 8, 12, 76; popular assembly in, 6; colonial disorders

INDEX

in, 14; Revolution in, 15, 24; developments after the Revolution, 25-27; in Federal Constitutional Convention, 27-28; abolishes foreign slave trade, 28n; debates and adopts Federal Constitution, 29-30; post-Revolutionary party developments, 31-33; contest between upcountry and lowlands over representation, 33-36; quarrels with Georgia, 36-37; slavery in, 86; prohibits foreign slave trade, 91; slave insurrections in, 101-102; passes law against free Negro seamen, 103-104; attitude on Compromise of 1850, 139-140; on nullification, 155; favors secession, 158
Southampton County, Va., 105, 106
Southern Commercial Convention, program of, 147, 148
Southern Literary Messenger, The, 123
Southern rights, 145-149, 156-157
Southern Republic, South Carolina newspaper, 136
Southerners, nature of, 151-152
Spaight, Richard Dobbs, 41
Spain, 11, 101; intrigues in West, 56-57
Speculation, in land, *see* Land
Sports, in colonial South, 5
Stamp Act, 10, 11, 15
Stamp Act Congress, 22
State of Franklin, 44
States Rights, 64-67
Stiles, Joseph C., defends slavery, 120-121
Stowe, Harriet Beecher, 116
Studies on Slavery, in Easy Lessons, 117-118
Sumner, Charles, 116, 164
Sumter, Thomas, 21
Supreme Court, of United States, 39, 77-80

T

Tallmadge, James, in Missouri Compromise debate, 95, 96
Tammany Hall, 71
Tariff, 60
Taylor, John, 62, 67, 77, 78; political philosophy of, 64-67; adopts designation "of Caroline," 64; introduces Virginia state rights resolutions, 68, 69; defends **Louisiana Purchase**, 74; sets forth political philosophy, 80-81; defends slavery, 89; on Missouri Compromise debate, 98-99
Tea tax, opposition to, 16
Tennessee, 57; beginnings of, 44; free Negroes in, 89; debates slavery, 110
Territories, slavery in, 145
Texas, 1, 73
Thomas, J. B., on Missouri Compromise debate, 97
Tilghmans, of Maryland, 53
Tillman, Benjamin, 165
Tobacco, 151; medium of exchange in Virginia, 8-9
Toombs, Robert, on Southern rights, 148-149
Tories, in Revolution, 23-24
Townshend Tariffs, 11, 15, 16
Transylvania, 55
Treatise on Sociology, Theoretical and Practical, 121
Trescot, W. H., 156
Treutlen, J. A., 37
Troup, George M., Georgia fire-eater, 135
Tryon, William, 13, 14
Tucker, Beverly, fire-eater, 135
Tucker, St. George, on slavery, 88
"Tuppenny act," in Virginia, 8-10
Turnbull, Robert J., 30; on slavery, 102, 104; fire-eater, 129-130, 132
Turner, J. A., 123
Turner, Nat, rebellion of, 105-106
Tuscaroras, 7

U

Uncle Tom's Cabin, 115; in England, 145-146
United States Bank, first, 60
United States Supreme Court, in Chisholm *vs.* Georgia case, 39
University of Georgia, founded, 38
University of Maryland, 54
University of North Carolina, founded, 42n

V

Vardaman, J. K., 165
Vermont, 69

INDEX

Vesey, Denmark, attempts slave insurrection, 101-102

Vicksburg, Miss., 122

Virginia, borough in, 4; House of Burgesses in, 6; uses tobacco to pay clergy, 8-9; "Parsons' Cause" in, 9-11, 12; Revolutionary leaders in, 15, 45; opposition to England in, 15-16; first constitution of, 45-46; convention for ratifying Federal Constitution, 46-53; attitude on admission of Kentucky, 56; passes states rights resolutions, 68-69; dynasty of, 60-82; slavery in, 87; debates slavery, 88-90; prohibits foreign slave trade, 91; slave insurrection in, 105-106; legislature of, debates slavery, 106-107

Virginia and Kentucky Resolutions, 67-71, 78

W

Walker, David, free Negro, 106

Walker, Robert J., on non-slaveholders, 155

Walker, Thomas, 43

Walkerton, Va., 7

War of 1812, 76-77

Washington, George, 15, 28, 46, 47, 48, 49, 53, 60, 61n, 62, 87; characterization of, 45

Washington College, in Maryland, 53-54

Watson, Thomas, 165

Wayland, Francis, 117

Webster, Daniel, defends states' rights, 77; on Compromise of 1850, 145, 156, 158

Weld, Theodore D., abolitionist, 112

West, 4; people of, 74-75

West Indies, 12

West Virginia, 106

Whig Club of Six Hundred, 25

Whig party, characterization of, 130-132

Whigs, in Revolution, 23-24

White, Laura, 134

Wigfall, Louis T., Texas fire-eater, 135

Wilberforce, William, 110

Wilkinson, James, intrigues with Spain, 56-57

William and Mary College, 88, 107

Williamsburg, Va., 10

Wilmington, N. C., 41

Wilmot, David, 132

Wilmot Proviso, 132, 145, 146, 156

Wilson, James, 15

Wood, Fernando, 159

Woolman, John, on slavery, 86

Wright, Sir James, 12

Wythe, George, 15; in Virginia convention ratifying Federal Constitution, 47; resolutions of, 52

Y

Yale University, 120

Yancey, W. L., 156, 157; Alabama fire-eater, 134

Yankee shrewdness, 3

Yazoo Fraud, 38-39

Yazoo River, 38

Yulee, David, Florida fire-eater, 135

AMERICAN CENTURY SERIES

WHEN ORDERING, please use the Standard Book Number consisting of the publisher's prefix, 8090-, plus the five digits following each title. (Note that the numbers given in this list are for paperback editions only. Many of the books are also available in cloth.)

The Hoosier School-Master by Edward Eggleston (0001-6)
The Magnificent Ambersons by Booth Tarkington (0002-4)
The Harbor by Ernest Poole (0003-2)
The Flush Times of Alabama and Mississippi by Joseph Baldwin (0005-9)
The Higher Learning in America by Thorstein Veblen (0007-5)
The Shame of the Cities by Lincoln Steffens (0008-3)
Company K by William March (0009-1)
The Influence of Seapower upon History by Alfred T. Mahan (0010-5)
A Daughter of the Middle Border by Hamlin Garland (0011-3)
How the Other Half Lives by Jacob Riis (0012-1)
His Fifty Years of Exile (Israel Potter) by Herman Melville (0013-X)
Barren Ground by Ellen Glasgow (0014-8)
Hospital Sketches by Louisa May Alcott (0015-6)
A Traveler from Altruria by William Dean Howells (0016-4)
The Devil's Dictionary by Ambrose Bierce (0017-2)
Moon-Calf by Floyd Dell (0018-2)
The Big Rock Candy Mountain by Wallace Stegner (0019-9)
The Octopus by Frank Norris (0020-2)
Life on the Mississippi by Mark Twain (0021-0)
Troubadour by Alfred Kreymborg (0022-9)
The Iron Heel by Jack London (0023-7)
Georgia Scenes by A. B. Longstreet (0024-5)
The Grandissimes by George W. Cable (0025-3)
The Autocrat of the Breakfast Table by Oliver Wendell Holmes (0026-1)
The Jeffersonian Tradition in American Democracy by Charles Wiltse (0028-8)
The Narrative of Arthur Gordon Pym by Edgar Allan Poe (0029-6)
A Connecticut Yankee in King Arthur's Court by Mark Twain (0030-X)
Theodore Roosevelt and the Progressive Movement by George E. Mowry (0031-8)
The Autobiography of an Ex-Coloured Man by James Weldon Johnson (0032-6)
Jack London: Short Stories (0033-4)
Jefferson by Albert Jay Nock (0034-2)
America Goes to War by Bruce Catton (0035-0)
Hemingway and His Critics ed. by Carlos Baker (0036-9)
Writers in Crisis by Maxwell Geismar (0038-5)
The Best of Simple by Langston Hughes (0039-3)
American Social Thought ed. by Ray Ginger (0040-7)
William Dean Howells ed. by Rudolf and Clara Marburg Kirk (0041-5)
Walt Whitman ed. by Floyd Stovall (0042-3)
Thomas Paine ed. by Harry Hayden Clark (0043-1)
American Moderns by Maxwell Geismar (0044-X)
The Last of the Provincials by Maxwell Geismar (0045-8)
Edgar Allan Poe ed. by Hardin Craig and Margaret Alterton (0046-6)
Jonathan Edwards ed. by C. H. Faust and T. H. Johnson (0047-4)
Benjamin Franklin ed. by F. Mott and C. E. Jorgenson (0048-2)
Indian Tales by Jaime de Angulo (0049-0)
A Time of Harvest ed. by Robert E. Spiller (0050-4)
The Limits of Language ed. by Walker Gibson (0051-2)
Sherwood Anderson: Short Stories ed. by Maxwell Geismar (0052-0)
The World of Lincoln Steffens ed. by Ella Winter and Herbert Shapiro (0053-9)
Mark Twain on the Damned Human Race ed. by Janet Smith (0054-7)
The Happy Critic and Other Essays by Mark Van Doren (0055-5)
Man Against Myth by Barrows Dunham (0056-3)
Something in Common and Other Stories by Langston Hughes (0057-1)
Writers in Transition: Seven Americans by H. Wayne Morgan (0058-1)
The Lincoln Nobody Knows by Richard N. Current (0059-8)
The Disinherited by Jack Conroy (0060-1)
Eisenhower As President ed. by Dean Albertson (0061-X)
Rebels and Ancestors by Maxwell Geismar (0062-8)
Mount Allegro by Jerre Mangione (0063-6)
Thoreau: People, Principles, and Politics ed. by Milton Meltzer (0064-4)
The Big Sea by Langston Hughes (0065-2)
The Golden Age of Homespun by Jared van Wagenen, Jr. (0066-0)
The Senate Establishment by Joseph S. Clark and Other Senators (0067-9)

I Wonder As I Wander by Langston Hughes (0068-7)
Science in Nineteenth-Century America ed. by Nathan Reingold (0069-5)
The Course of the South to Secession by Ulrich Bonnell Phillips (0070-9)
American Negro Poetry ed. by Arna Bontemps (0071-7)
Horace Greeley by Glyndon G. Van Deusen (0072-5)
David Walker's Appeal ed. by Charles M. Wiltse (0073-3)
The Sentimental Years by E. Douglas Branch (0074-1)
Henry James and the Jacobites by Maxwell Geismar (0075-X)
The Reins of Power by Bernard Schwartz (0076-8)
American Writers in Rebellion by H. Wayne Morgan (0077-6)
Policy and Power by Ruhl Bartlett (0078-4)
Wendell Phillips on Civil Rights and Freedom ed. by Louis Filler (0079-2)
American Negro Short Stories ed. by John Henrik Clarke (0080-6)
The Radical Novel in the United States: 1900–1954 by Walter B. Rideout (0081-4)
A History of Agriculture in the State of New York by Ulysses Prentiss Hedrick (0082-2)
Criticism and Fiction by William Dean Howells and *The Responsibilities of the Novelist* by Frank Norris (0083-0)
John F. Kennedy and the New Frontier ed. by Aïda DiPace Donald (0084-9)
Anyplace But Here by Arna Bontemps and Jack Conroy (0085-7)
Mark Van Doren: 100 Poems (0086-5)
Simple's Uncle Sam by Langston Hughes (0087-3)
Stranger at the Gates by Tracy Sugarman (0088-1)
Waiting for Nothing by Tom Kromer (0089-X)
31 New American Poets ed. by Ron Schreiber (0090-3)
From Plantation to Ghetto: An Interpretive History of American Negroes by August Meier and Elliott M. Rudwick (0091-1)
Documents of Upheaval ed. by Truman Nelson (0092-X)

THE MAKING OF AMERICA

Fabric of Freedom: 1763–1800 by Esmond Wright (0101-2)
The New Nation: 1800–1845 by Charles M. Wiltse (0102-0)
The Stakes of Power: 1845–1877 by Roy F. Nichols (0103-9)
The Search for Order: 1877–1920 by Robert H. Wiebe (0104-7)
The Urban Nation: 1920–1960 by George E. Mowry (0105-5)

AMERICAN PROFILES

Thomas Jefferson: A Profile ed. by Merrill D. Peterson (0200-0)
Franklin D. Roosevelt: A Profile ed. by William E. Leuchtenburg (0201-9)
Alexander Hamilton: A Profile ed. by Jacob E. Cooke (0202-7)
Mark Twain: A Profile ed. by Justin Kaplan (0203-5)
Theodore Roosevelt: A Profile ed. by Morton Keller (0204-3)
Woodrow Wilson: A Profile ed. by Arthur S. Link (0205-1)
John C. Calhoun: A Profile ed. by John L. Thomas (0206-X)